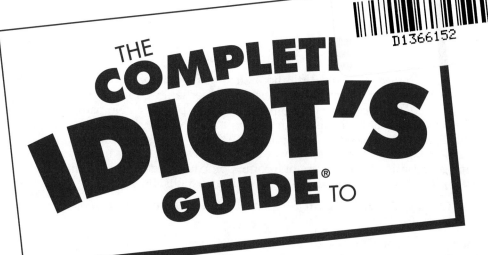

THE COMPLETE **IDIOT'S** GUIDE® TO

Family Games

by Amy Wall

ALPHA

A Pearson Education Company

I would like to dedicate this book to Dr. Robert E. Wall, my father and my best friend.

Produced by BookEnds, LLC.

Copyright © 2002 by BookEnds, LLC.

International Standard Book Number: 0-02-864008-X
Library of Congress Catalog Card Number: 2001092304

04   03   02   8   7   6   5   4   3   2   1

Interpretation of the printing code: The rightmost number of the first series of numbers is the year of the book's printing; the rightmost number of the second series of numbers is the number of the book's printing. For example, a printing code of 02-1 shows that the first printing occurred in 2002.

Printed in the United States of America

Note: This publication contains the opinions and ideas of its author. It is intended to provide helpful and informative material on the subject matter covered. It is sold with the understanding that the author and publisher are not engaged in rendering professional services in the book. If the reader requires personal assistance or advice, a competent professional should be consulted.

Publisher
Marie Butler-Knight

Product Manager
Phil Kitchel

Managing Editor
Jennifer Chisholm

Acquisitions Editor
Randy Ladenheim-Gil

Development Editor
Amy Gordon

Production Editor
Katherin Bidwell

Copy Editor
Brad Herriman

Illustrator
Jody Schaeffer

Cover Designers
Mike Freeland
Kevin Spear

Book Designers
Scott Cook and Amy Adams of DesignLab

Indexer
Brad Herriman

Layout/Proofreading
Svetlana Dominguez
John Etchison
Natashia Rardin
Stacey Richwine-DeRome
Kimberly Tucker

Contents at a Glance

Part 1: Family Fun   **1**

  1 A Family That Plays Together   3
      Finding the time for family games and choosing the right
      game for your family.

  2 The Importance of Rules   15
      Setting up the rules so everyone has a good time and tips
      on how to avoid squabbles and tantrums.

  3 From Start to Finish   23
      How to make family game night a success from beginning
      to end.

  4 The Name of the Game   33
      The types of games: from parlor games to road trips, card
      games to outdoor fun.

Part 2: Parlor Games   **41**

  5 Hands on the Table: Table Games   43
      Making the moves: Chess and Checkers.

  6 More Table Games   55
      Fun with Backgammon, Pick-Up Sticks, Tic-Tac-Toe, and
      Tiddlywinks!

  7 See Spot Run   65
      Just a roll of the dice: Yahtzee and Dominoes.

  8 Bull's-Eye!   75
      All you ever wanted to know about Darts and different
      Dart games.

  9 Rack 'Em Up   87
      What's the difference between Pool and Snooker? Find out
      here!

  10 Direct Hit!   101
      Tabletop scoring: Hockey games, Ping-Pong, and Foosball.

Part 3: House of Cards   **113**

  11 The Trumps Have It   115
      Card games for two or more players of all ages from easy
      to tricky.

  12 Classic Cards   127
      You'll remember these all-time favorite card games from
      your own childhood.

13 Fun for One: Games of Solitaire   141
    Trying to keep someone busy? Hand them a deck of cards
    for solitary fun.

14 Cards for the Kids   151
    Keep little ones laughing and learning with card games
    from Old Maid to War.

15 Casino Games   163
    All bets are on: gambling at home.

Part 4: Let's Make a Deal   **173**

16 Rummy Noses   175
    Rummy galore: from Basic to Rummy 500.

17 Building Bridges   185
    The basics of Bridge. Invite the neighbors over!

18 Poker Face   195
    Learn all about Poker hands and betting. Break out those
    pennies!

19 A Royal Marriage: Pinochle for Everyone   207
    Pinochle made simple.

Part 5: Everywhere Games   **219**

20 Road Trip: Car Games   221
    What to do in the car or waiting at the dentist? Look here!

21 They Say It's Your Birthday!   229
    Party games for everybody: from Simon Says to Red Rover.

22 Giggle Games   241
    Get the whole family laughing with these side-splitting
    favorites.

23 Say the Word: Word Games   247
    Break out the pen and paper and put your thinking
    caps on.

24 Let's Go Team!   255
    Here's your kids' chance to finally take sides.

Part 6: Outdoor Games   **265**

25 Take Me Out to the Ball Game   267
    Outdoor games from Touch Football to Croquet.

26 Fun in the Sun   277
    Badminton, Hopscotch, Marbles, and more.

27 Going on a Picnic: Picnic Games   289
Pack up the basics and jump in the car. Don't forget the Frisbee!

28 Water World   299
Wet and wild fun for everyone.

Appendixes

A Glossary   307

B Resources   313

Index   317

Contents

Part 1: Family Fun   **1**

1 A Family That Plays Together   **3**

Why Play Games? 4
A History of Games and Gaming 4
  Tag, You're It! 4
  Games, Games, Games 5
How Do We Start? 7
Finding Time for Family Fun..7
What Should We Play? 8
  The Treasure Chest..9
  Fun for Everyone 9
  Hello, Sunshine 10
  Go Team!...11
A Word on Ages 11
  The Early Bird 11
  Time to Categorize 12
  Older and Wiser...13
  Raising the Stakes 14

2 The Importance of Rules   **15**

Setting the Rules 16
Keeping the Peace 17
  Compromise: The Name of the Game 17
Dare to Play Fair 18
  Get Involved...18
  Cheat Sheet 18
  Be a Winner! 19
Settling Disputes 20
  Talk Amongst Yourselves 20

3 From Start to Finish   **23**

A Basis for Bonding 23
  Get 'Em Young...24
  Keen Kids...25
  Mixed Bag 25
  Take It Outside 26

Choosing Sides: Team Games 27
What Shall We Play? 28
Assigning Clean-Up 29
Shhhh! Quiet Time 30

4 The Name of the Game   33

Come into My Parlor ... Parlor Games 33
Set the Table 34
On a Roll 34
Ebony and Ivory 35
Bull's-Eye! 35
Rack 'Em Up 36
Table Games 36
Let's Make a Deal: Card Games 37
Everybody Outside! 38
Break Out the Equipment 38
Just Bring Your Sense of Fun 38
Everyone into the Pool! 39
Games Are Everywhere! 39

Part 2: Parlor Games   41

5 Hands on the Table: Table Games   43

Checkmate! 44
History of the Game 44
We Are the Champions 44
Piece by Piece 45
Setting Up 46
From Antiques to Computer Games 47
Basic Moves and Rules 48
Tournament Moves: Playing with the Pros 48
Check and Checkmate 49
Stalemate 49
Let's Get Going 50
Chess Notation 50
Checkers...51
The Board 52
Piece by Piece 52
Setting Up 52

Making the Moves 52
Capturing 52
Crowning 53
Huff or Blow 53
Don't Touch! 54
The Win 54

6 More Table Games **55**

Backgammon 55
Picking Up the Pieces 56
The Point of It All 56
Getting Started 57
Language of the Game...58
Scoring Points and Making Primes 59
Blots 59
Closed Board 59
Bearing Off 59
Doubling 60
Pick-Up Sticks...60
Tic-Tac-Toe 61
Tiddlywinks! 62
Piece by Piece 62
Let's Play 63
Potting Out 63

7 See Spot Run **65**

Dice Games 66
Let's Play Yahtzee! 66
How to Play 66
The Scorecard...67
Let 'Em Roll: Poker Dice and More 67
Other Dice Games 68
Dominoes..68
The Draw Game 70
Getting Started 71
The Plays 71
Let's Go Domino 71
The Block Game..72
How to Start 72
The Rules 72
The Domino Effect 73

8 Bull's-Eye!   75

Learning the Lingo 76
The Playing Area 79
  The Proper Surroundings....................................79
  Hanging the Board 80
  Marking the Throw Line 80
Understanding the Board 80
Let's Play Darts: The General Rules 80
x01 81
  The Object 82
  Scoring..82
  Getting Started 82
  Getting Out 83
Cricket 84

9 Rack 'Em Up   87

Cuing Up the Past 87
But What About Today? 89
Your Own Pool Hall...89
  The Truth About Tables 90
  Billiard Basics 90
Pocket Billiards Games 91
  Racking and Breaking......................................91
  Lagging for the Break 92
  The Play 92
Pool Game: Eight Ball 92
  The Rules..93
  Stripes or Solids? 94
  Making Contact 94
  Fouls and Ball-Jumping 94
  Illegal Pocketing...95
  Combination Shots...95
  Scoring..95
  Losing the Game 95
Pool Game: Nine Ball 95
  Racking the Balls 96
  Break Shot 96
  Push Out 96

Snooker 97
   Getting Started 97
   Opening Break 97
   Playing the Game 98

10 Direct Hit!   101

Air Hockey, Anyone? 102
   How to Play 102
   The Rules 103
   Footing 104
   The Puck 104
   The Board 105
   Score! 105
   The Shots 106
Are You Ready for Some Foosball? 106
   Tables 107
   Let's Play! 107
Ping-Pong Party 108
   The Setup 109
   The Serve 109
   Returns 110
   Points 110

Part 3: House of Cards   113

11 The Trumps Have It   115

Achy-Breaky Hearts 115
   How You Play 116
   How You Score 116
   Passing Cards 116
   Tricks, Not Treats 117
   Stay Away from Hearts 118
   Scoring a Bonus 119
Spades..119
   The Art of the Deal 119
   Bidding 119
   The Tricks 120
   Score! 121

Knockout Whist 121
   Let's Deal *121*
   The Knock-Out *122*
Crazy Eights 123
   Let's Get Crazy *123*
   But How Do I Win? *123*

12   Classic Cards   127

Cribbage 127
   The Cribbage Board *128*
   Playing Cribbage *128*
   Let's Go! Play and Points *129*
   Card Values/Points *130*
   The Show *131*
   The Crib *132*
Rook 132
   By Hook or by Rook *133*
   Let's Rook *134*
   Scoring *135*
Skip-Bo 135
   Miles of Piles *136*
   Get Ready, Get Set, Skip-Bo! *136*
   Keeping Score *137*
Tripoley 137
   The Stakes Board *138*
   The Play *138*
   The Final Phase *140*

13   Fun for One: Games of Solitaire   141

Solitaire's Not Always Just for One 141
So What's Solitaire All About? 142
Clocks 143
Golf 144
Forty Thieves 145
Pyramid 145
Calculation 147
Russian 147
Double Solitaire 149

14 Cards for the Kids 151

War 152

How to Play *152*

War for More *153*

Old Maid 154

Getting Started *154*

Where's That Old Maid? *155*

Concentration 155

Spit 156

Double Solitaire Gone Mad *156*

1-2-3, Spit! *158*

Making Your Moves *158*

Let the Spit Fly *158*

Spitting Tips *159*

New Tableau Layout *160*

Go Fish 160

Fishing Commercially *161*

15 Casino Games 163

Blackjack! 163

Let's Play *164*

Hitting and Standing *166*

The Dealer's Hand *166*

Insurance *166*

Splitting and Doubling-Down *167*

Basic Strategy *168*

Baccarat 168

The Play *169*

The Payout *170*

Card Combinations and Rules *170*

Hand Values *170*

Part 4: Let's Make a Deal 173

16 Rummy Noses 175

Rummy Go! 175

Basic Rummy 176

Let's Play! *177*

Keeping Score *178*

Gin Rummy 178
Luck of the Draw *179*
How to Play *179*
Who's There? *179*
Winning the Game *180*
Knock-Knock: Knock Rummy 180
Scoring *181*
Going Rum *181*
Rummy 500 181
Contract Rummy 182

17 Building Bridges   185

Bridge America 186
Let's Play Bridge 187
Tricks and Bids 188
Bidding Rules *189*
Doubles and Redoubles *190*
The Play 190
Scoring 191

18 Poker Face   195

What Is Poker? 195
Straight Poker 197
Rank and File *198*
The Bets Are On! *199*
Draw Poker 202
Ready, Set, Bet *203*
Return Policy *203*
Stud Poker: Five-Card Stud and Seven-Card Stud 204
Betting *205*
Seven-Card Stud *205*

19 A Royal Marriage: Pinochle for Everyone   207

Back to Basics 208
Two-Handed Pinochle 208
Here's the Deal *208*
Melds and Tricks *209*
The Rules of Melding *210*
Tricks and Play *211*

Card Values 212
Point-Scoring Rules 212
Declaring Out 213
Three-Handed Pinochle 213
Double-Deck Pinochle 213
Let's Bid 214
Trumps and Melding 214
Play Day 215
1, 2, 3, Score! 215
Points for Tricks 216
Points for Melds 216

Part 5: Everywhere Games   **219**

20 Road Trip: Car Games   **221**

Things You May Need in the Car 221
Let's Go! 222
The I Spy Games 223
I Spy with One Child 224
License Plate Bingo 224
What If...225
Camping Trip 226
Alphabetical Version 227
Who Am I?..227
What's Next? 227
Thumb Wrestling 227
The Purse Game..228

21 They Say It's Your Birthday!   **229**

Party Games 230
What You'll Need..231
Choosing "It"...232
Everybody Outside! 233
Red Rover..233
Red Light/Green Light 235
What's the Time, Mr. Wolf?.................................235
Indoor/Outdoor Games 236
Musical Chairs..236
Mother May I?..236
Hot Potato 237

Party Games for Little Kids 238
Simon Says 238
Duck Duck Goose..238
Telephone or Grapevine 239

22 Giggle Games   241

Names of … 241
Follow the Leader 243
Honey, Do You Love Me? 243
Sausage 244
Never Ending Words 244
Story Line...245

23 Say the Word: Word Games   247

Anagrams 247
Word Bluff 248
Hangman 249
Match Game 250
Sentence by Sentence 252
Quick on the Draw 252

24 Let's Go Team!   255

Charades 256
Charade Parade 256
What's Your Sign? 258
Ready, Set, Act! 259
Score!..259
Up Jenkins 260
Hide and Seek 261
Sardines 262

Part 6: Outdoor Games   265

25 Take Me Out to the Ballgame   267

Kickball 267
Volleyball 269
Jolly Volley..270
Join the Service 270
The Scoring 271

Touch Football 272
Croquet 273

26 Fun in the Sun **277**

Fly Away Birdie: Badminton 278
Courtside 278
What Service! 279
Keep Score 279
One Scoop or Two? 279
When You're Out, You're Out! 280
A Hop, Skip, and Jump: Hopscotch 280
Sidewalk Turned Runway 281
Getting Your Footing 281
Have You Lost Your Marbles? 282
Marrididdles, Cat's Eyes,
    and Taws! 283
The Ring Game 284
Knuckles Down 285
Jump Rope 285
Jump Rope Lingo 286
Double Dutch 287

27 Going on a Picnic: Picnic Games **289**

Tug of War 289
Off to the Races 290
Three-Legged Race 290
Potato on a Spoon Race 291
Sack Races 291
Tag, You're It! 292
Shadow Tag 292
Freeze Tag 292
Touch Tag 292
British Bulldog 293
Capture the Flag 293
Leap Frog 294
Frisbee Games 295
Ultimate Frisbee 296
Horseshoes 297

28 Water World   **299**

Water Tag 299
   Marco Polo..*300*
   Octopus Tag..*300*
Team H$_2$O 301
   Water Basketball—Splashketball! *301*
   Water Volleyball *302*
Wet and Wild! 303
   Biggest Splash Contest *303*
   In the Pool Scavenger Hunt...................................*303*
Everybody, Out of the Pool! 304
   Water Limbo *304*
   Water Gun Wars *305*
   Freeze-Up *305*

Appendixes

A Glossary   **307**

B Resources   **313**

Index   **317**

Foreword

We live in a time when families are on the move. The frenetic pace of family life involves the juggling of career responsibilities, carting children to day care and soccer practice, homework, and housework. With all that is encompassed in keeping a household moving, there is precious little time left for families to "connect," to slow down the pace and spend quality time in activities of leisure and recreation.

For so many of us, a significant portion of our "down time" is spent in front of the television, surfing the Web, or, for the younger set, spending hours playing video games. As alluring as "high-tech" recreation may seem, these activities do not bring families together to laugh, to share, to communicate, or to "reconnect" after a long day apart. *The Complete Idiot's Guide to Family Games* is a great starting point for families intent on shutting off the computer and VCR to re-explore the merits of "old-fashioned" family fun.

Families come in every possible configuration. Whether single, a "couple," newly married, divorced, remarried, with or without children, the families I see in my practice all describe the need for better communication and for opportunities to spend time together—away from the fast pace of their daily lives. Activities that promote quiet time, or that emphasize communication and outright silliness, are great places for families to begin to become reacquainted with one another. In my work with families and children, I often use games and play as a springboard to promote the development of many important skills. Games can be used to develop communication, turn-taking, and other important social skills. Whether you're 9 or 90, play, after all, is a universal language.

If you are a family who seeks the calm and quiet of "sit-down" after-dinner fun, or a family who prefers the energy of a fast-moving outdoor game, you're sure to find plenty of activities in *The Complete Idiot's Guide to Family Games*. Complete with a history of games and gaming, a note on finding time for family fun, and the art of assigning clean-up, *The Complete Idiot's Guide to Family Games* is a start-to-finish guide, which no family should be without. From Solitaire to Leap Frog, a parlor game of yesteryear to a fast-paced, silly outdoor game for tots, if you seek you can find it here, complete with rules, score sheets, and winning strategies.

Take a moment to think of the time you spend in front of the computer, of money you have spent on video and computer games, DVDs, and the like. While you're thinking of this, think about the last time you sat down with your loved ones to play a game, to laugh, to share, and to reconnect. Pick up *The Complete Idiot's Guide to Family Games* and make a date to be with your family. Shut off the computer, turn off the VCR, pop some popcorn, find the potato sacks, jump-rope, or playing cards— AND LET THE GAMES BEGIN!

Nina Cote, M.S.S., L.S.W.

—Nina Cote, a resident of Chadds Ford, Pennsylvania, is a licensed social worker in private practice. A graduate of Bryn Mawr College's Graduate School of Social Work and Social Research, Ms. Cote works therapeutically with children, adolescents, and their families to promote better interfamilial communication. She uses "play therapy" in her work with youngsters who exhibit communication and social-emotional challenges. Ms. Cote is the mother of two boys and an advocate for children with special needs and learning differences.

Introduction

I've written this book in an attempt to get you as excited about playing games with your family as I always was as a kid. I loved it when my parents cleared the table and pulled out the decks of cards or a good board game. My family always managed to have a good time with just about any game we had tucked away in the house.

I remember a brisk, cold day in autumn when my whole family took a walk to a nearby baseball diamond—bat and ball in hand. We bundled up in warm jackets, scarves, gloves, and boots, and trudged off on a long walk toward the open field. My mother brought blankets for us to huddle under as we awaited our turn at bat. I remember hitting a home run and as I ran to home plate my mother was holding open a blanket and I ran into her cozy arms.

In the summer evenings, the neighborhood streets around my house were always filled with kids playing any number of tag and ball games. We played until we were too tired to move or until the sun went down—whichever came first.

If you're not currently playing games with your kids, it will take a little time to get them into the idea. It's obviously best to start them when they are young—to have a routine already established as a family—but it's never too late. If you flip through the pages of this book, you are bound to find something that will suit the type of family you have—and when you get them started and excited, they won't want to stop. You'll have started your children on a road to wonderful memories.

How to Use This Book

This book covers every type of game your family can play: indoor games, outdoor games, car games, quiet games, games for 2, and games for 10. It is broken up into six sections to make finding an appropriate game for game time an easy and fun experience.

Part 1, "Family Fun," gives you all the information you need to set up a family fun night. From finding the time, to keeping the peace, to choosing teams, and cleaning up, all the tips you need for a successful night of family fun time are right here.

Part 2, "Parlor Games," covers all the information on indoor parlor games for rainy days you will ever need. From Tiddlywinks to Chess, Darts to Billiards, you can find rainy day fun right here!

Part 3, "House of Cards," is the first of two parts on card playing. The first section covers trump games, Solitaire, cards for tots, and betting card games.

Part 4, "Let's Make a Deal," is section two of card games. Rummy games, Bridge, Pinochle, and Poker—America's national card game—can all be found here.

Part 5, "Everywhere Games," gives you all the games you can play no matter where you are: at home, on the road, in the dentist's office … ready, set, play!

Part 6, "Outdoor Games," is all about those nice days when you want to send the entire family outside for a good day of clean air and family-fun time. From ball games to Horseshoes, Frisbee to team races—and don't forget the water sports!

Extras

Look at the little sidebars scattered throughout the text for more information that will add to your family fun:

It's in the Cards

Here are gaming definitions to help you understand the new lingo you'll be learning.

High Score

These little boxes contain gaming tips to help you score more and play better!

Winning Plays

Fun facts and tales about games throughout time. These are interesting facts you'll be sure to want to share with family and friends!

Three Strikes

Here you will find warnings: from avoiding fights to safety tips to watching out for those gaming pitfalls.

Acknowledgments

I would like to add a few words of thanks to the people who helped make this book possible. First of all to Jacky Sach, who trusted and believed in me. Secondly to my wonderful family. My siblings: Elizabeth, Nina, Chris, and Craig who always knew how to have a good time—and still do, and my mother who has always encouraged me in all my endeavors. I cherish the memories of all the wonderful games we've played together—you are my lifeline.

Many thanks also to my grandmother, Stephanie Palasek, the Romanelli family, Joan Goldsmith, Pastor Dennis O'Rourke, and Scott Warmbrand, who helped keep me focused and smiling.

I'd also like to say a special thank you to my father who beamed down upon me from heaven as I wrote, and gave me the encouragement to keep on going.

Thank you to everyone who shared their childhood memories so freely with me—you inspired me beyond words.

Trademarks

All terms mentioned in this book that are known to be or are suspected of being trademarks or service marks have been appropriately capitalized. Alpha Books and Pearson Education cannot attest to the accuracy of this information. Use of a term in this book should not be regarded as affecting the validity of any trademark or service mark.

Part 1

Family Fun

Get your family around the gaming table and start your family fun night! This section offers some tips on how to get your kids more interactive, how to start new traditions, and have some good old-fashioned, life-altering family fun. How brave you are for taking the initiative to try to change your day-to-day family life! If you take your time with it, you'll get to know your kids in new and different ways while creating wonderful memories the whole family can share.

In Chapter 1, you'll learn a little bit about what games have meant historically in terms of social behavior and interaction. You'll also learn about how to get started and how to get your family in on the idea. In Chapters 2 and 3, you'll discover ways to stop conflicts before they start and make family game night fun for all ages.

Chapter 4 gives you a good overview of the types of games you can play. There are games that require some investment—everything from buying a deck of cards to a pool table—and games that require nothing more than imagination. Flip through this chapter and decide what game might work best for your family. Then pick an evening for family game night, grab some sodas and pretzels, and play away!

Chapter 1

A Family That Plays Together

In This Chapter

➤ Games through the ages

➤ What can we play?

➤ Fitting fun in

➤ Age appropriate games

It seems that today's families spend more time in front of their television sets and computer screens than they do with each other—it makes you wonder what happened to good old-fashioned interactive family fun. We didn't have computers when I was a kid, but we probably watched almost as much TV as kids do now in the twenty-first century. It was thanks to my parents' love of good times and togetherness that I was able to play cards after dinner, board games on a Saturday afternoon, and outdoor lawn games in the summertime. They would just shut off the TV set and make room for family time. It was good fun and created some wonderful memories that I'll be able to share with my children, and my grandchildren someday.

In this chapter, you'll get an idea of why people play games and how you can easily incorporate this old-fashioned family fun into your family's hectic schedule. You'll learn how to choose the right games to satisfy everyone in the family, as well as how to make family time something that both kids and parents eagerly anticipate.

Why Play Games?

So what did families do before electricity and techno-gadgets? They were forced to use their imaginations and ingenuity. That might seem unbelievable to some modern-day, video game-loving children, and even to some gadget-loving, laptop-using adults, but if we took away all our plug-in games, we could still manage to have a good time.

By nature, human beings know how to have fun. We constantly adapt to our environments, and our creativity is the tool we use to entertain ourselves. It's the *games* we play that allow us to integrate our desire for competition with our need for stimulation and interaction. So, we hand down these games as a means to carry on a little of ourselves from generation to generation. Games are a social necessity—a way to distract ourselves from the workaday world. And, of course, they are the way we play!

It's in the Cards

A **game** is any activity used for diversion, amusement, and enjoyment.

A History of Games and Gaming

Since games predate our recorded history, it's hard to know exactly when people really became fascinated with the art of competition. Chances are that games did not derive from a simple need for frivolous entertainment; rather, historians believe that people have been involved with games since the days of the cavemen. The games we play are derived from the very beginning of our own history when we first learned as a species that we had to compete with animals—and other people—in order to survive. We may not need to play games to survive today, but it sure makes life a lot more fun!

Tag, You're It!

Since the beginning of humankind, games have been a focus of family and tribal life. The earliest known games are believed to be Tag, Hide-and-Seek, and King of the Castle—games that symbolize our basic animal instinct of survival and are a means for children to imitate adult reality. Tag: to prey and to catch; Hide-and-Seek: to display our cunning and ingenuity; and King of the Castle: to fight for our dominance over others. These are all survival games that derive from our instinctual need to stand out in a crowd as the fastest, the strongest, and the smartest. These same games exist today, and I don't know any adult or child who can say they've never played at least one of them, in one form or another. Now you're probably not playing Tag so you can learn how to catch your dinner, but winning is still as fun as it ever was.

What may have commenced as survival training for hunting and warfare—like who could throw a spear or a rock the farthest, and with the most precise accuracy—

eventually developed into a game and a cultural ritual. Survival and religion are the two founding forces behind what we know today as sports and games. As a result, games have had an enormous impact on our social evolution. Historians and sociologists believe that games are derived from our everyday life and reflect the culture from which they originate.

Today, games have a much simpler meaning, but have equally significant social importance. Games allow you to share more time with the people you love while still engaging your animal instincts for survival. (Grrrr.) Many games have, almost miraculously, been handed down through centuries without any real directions or guidebooks to go along with them. Some games are actually a cultural phenomenon. So, how do we keep them alive through the generations? Simple: We just keep playing them.

Winning Plays

Manufactured games date back as early as the seventeenth century. An example is the geographic games in which countries were cut out of maps and children were required to put them back together. These games led to the creation of the jigsaw puzzle.

Games, Games, Games

Chess is an excellent example of how games developed from our culture as well as from our survival instincts. It may be hard to imagine today's Chess player as the warmonger, but Chess is a game of great strategy and tactical skill. Although historians vary in their opinions, the general consensus is that Chess is derived from a 4000-year-old game called "Chaturanga"—a four-handed Chess game played with dice.

The pieces are elephants, horses, chariots, and foot soldiers. The game is believed to have been invented by a sixth-century Indian philosopher, and was designed as a battle between four armies controlled by four players. Each army in the game comes under the control of one leader, the Rajah (King). Two players are loosely allied against the other two and each contains four corps—infantry, cavalry, elephants, and boatmen. The board contains 64 squares and the pieces move similarly to the modern-day version of Chess. Infantry move like Pawns; boatmen can only move two squares diagonally and can jump over intervening pieces; the cavalry, or horse pieces, move like the Knight; the elephant moves like a Rook; and the Rajah has limited moves, like the King.

There are other derivations of Chess that go back to ancient China—also made of armies and weaponry. Perhaps these early Chess games were a way for ancient military powers to spend their nonbattle hours—developing military strategies while indulging in mind-boggling fun with worthy opponents.

Winning Plays

In about the year 995, as legend has it, a game of Chess spurred an argument between a Danish Earl and King Canute, King of England, Denmark, Norway, and part of Sweden, resulting in the death of the Earl. At one point in the game the Earl took a Knight from the King, and the King, returning his Knight to the board, demanded the Earl make another move. The furious Earl tipped the board over and attempted to leave the room.

When the King called him a coward, the Earl spun around and said "Thou didst not call me coward when I hastened to thy help while the Swedes were beating thee like a dog." The incensed King had the Earl murdered in the morning.

Another example of how far back games go, as well as their historical and socio-cultural significance to their countries of origin, is the *deck of playing cards*. The earliest reference to playing cards in Europe is the fourteenth century. Most historians agree that playing cards likely originated in China, where paper was invented. Cards entered Europe from the Islamic Empire where swords, cups, and suited symbols were added to the symbolic representation on the cards. It was later in Europe that symbols such as the King, Queen, and Jack were added to the decks.

Each country of origin had its preferential representation of courtly life. To this day in Italy, Spain, Germany, and Switzerland your average deck of playing cards does not have a Queen—similar to the old Islamic cards—and if you examine the history of these patriarchies, there are few women with any monarchial power. Historians have deduced, therefore, that the decks we use in North America and other parts of Europe originated from France—and not from Spain—where the Islamic deck took hold. It is believed that Christopher Columbus brought both Chess and the deck of playing cards, as we know them today, to North America in the fifteenth century.

It's in the Cards

A **deck of cards** is a set of anywhere from 24 to 78 thin, rectangular, plastic or paper pieces marked on one side to show a suit and placement in the rank of cards, and used to play numerous games. A typical deck of cards contains 52 cards, 13 cards per suit; the four suits are Clubs, Hearts, Spades, and Diamonds.

According to an article on ancient games written by Catherine Soubeyrand, one of the earliest known board games came to us by way of an ancient archaeological discovery. The game is called "Dogs and Jackals" which was discovered in the tomb of Reny-Seneb, XII dynasty, about 1800 B.C.E. Interestingly, the game is not unlike the game of Cribbage and could even be an ancient ancestor of this still very popular card game.

The game, made of ebony and ivory, was found in excellent condition and belongs to a family of games named "game of the thirty points" or "game of the fifty-eight holes." The game is actually a small piece of furniture set on four animal-carved legs. The top of the board is a rectangular wooden box on which is carved an image of a palm tree surrounded by 58 holes. Remarkably, in the drawer of the box were found 10 pawns that look like short little sticks, five carved with a dog-head and five with a jackal-head.

Although it is unclear exactly how the game was played in ancient Egypt, thanks to the discovery of the little sticks that the game today is played in the following way: It is a game for two players. Five of the dog-pawns are given to one player and the remaining five jackal-pawns are given to the other. Three coins, instead of dice, are used to determine the movements of the players. The goal is to manipulate your pegs around the board, by using coin tosses, to reach the five points (25-29) on your side of the board and win.

How Do We Start?

Just begin playing. That's really all you have to do. We get so involved in our daily routines that sometimes we forget about what really matters the most: spending time with our families. In this section, I will discuss the many ways you can organize a family game night. It's not as hard as it may seem, but you will have to be consistent if you really want to incorporate games into your family lifestyle.

There are so many games that families can play as a group, whether it's one-on-one with your spouse, or in teams as a family. You should give several games a try. It's inevitable that you'll have a great time playing at least one or more of the games, and before you know it, your routine is changed. You'll find countless games to try with your family as you read through the chapters of this book. Every family is different, so take your time and try a few varieties. Once your family finds a game they like, you'll find everyone looking forward to playing it over and over again.

Finding Time for Family Fun

Finding the time is always hard to do now that families spend so many hours at work or involved with some kind of extracurricular activity. Anyone with a teenager and a phone bill knows that kids that age want to hang out with their friends or gab on the phone all night. Prying them away from their personal lives can be a challenge. And then there's our younger kids who have aliens to blast, and levels to beat in their latest computer game craze. And we can't forget about the tremendous amount of homework to be done. Most parents nowadays work so many hours that by the time they get home, make dinner, clean up, and make sure the kids are doing their nightly chores and homework, no one has time to think about playing games. Well, it's a great way to break up the monotony of the routines we perform every night. Family time should be fun—not another chore.

High Score

If your teenager insists that the phone is more important than participating in some family fun, tell him or her to ask the friend over. The more the merrier!

Winning Plays

Technological evolution changed the way we play games, and even the games themselves. For example, the discovery of rubber led to the creation of new types of balls. Pairing these discoveries with new global trading partners resulted in the introduction of different toys and games.

The best way to get started is to get the whole family revved up. Make a big deal about a new game and set a family "game night." If you call a "family togetherness night," you may hear some grunts and groans, but if everyone knows it's a night for fun, they'll realize togetherness is par for the course.

Admittedly, it's hard to play games during the week. After all, there are meals to prepare, dishes to wash, laundry to be folded and put away, homework to be completed, phone calls to return … the list goes on and on. So I recommend weekends for family togetherness and game playing. What could be better on a Friday night than cleaning up after dinner and setting up a board game right on the dinner or dining room table? Choose your seats, get some snacks, and start rolling the dice or dealing out the deck. You can even just grab a pizza on the way home from the office, so you don't have to worry about making dinner before the games begin.

What Should We Play?

No matter what game you play, some kids are just not going to get into it. The trick is to start them young and keep the games alive. Try setting up tournaments and championships. Once you get them hooked, they'll come back to the table fast enough—after all, their survival instincts are sometimes even stronger than that of the tired and weary adult. Shut off the TV, computer, and video games and let the answering machine screen the calls. Get the kids excited about spending time with the family—even if they don't know that that's what you have in mind.

The Treasure Chest

In my family, playing cards was an after-dinner ritual. My parents kept a jar of pennies on a kitchen shelf and a deck of cards in our game cupboard in preparation for game night. Sometimes they'd even invite their own friends over and we'd have a houseful of fun. The game cupboard was full of various materials used to entertain ourselves—from board games to outdoor recreation items like balls, badminton rackets, nets, and tennis rackets. On the inside of the door were the decks of cards. My mother kept the penny jar high up on a shelf to avoid the temptation of little fingers reaching for coins for the candy store. It didn't have to be coins that we used either. Sometimes we used rocks or seashells or candy. Occasionally we even used our marble collections. And one way or another the winner always put his loot back in the jar at the end of the night … well, unless it was a candy-stakes night.

One rainy, summer afternoon in the country, my grandfather taught my four siblings and me to play Poker, using packing "popcorn" as the *stakes*. As a kid it didn't matter what you played with—just that you had the most of it by the end of the game.

Just the thought of that penny jar can still get me excited for a competitive night of family fun.

It's in the Cards

A **stake** is a prize you can win in a contest.

Fun for Everyone

There are many games that are suitable for younger and older kids alike. Sometimes it doesn't hurt to indulge in these if only to appease the little ones before bed, before the more complicated games are brought out. Games like Pick-Up Sticks, Tic-Tac-Toe, War, Old Maid, and Go Fish are great for families with youngsters and can be played around the dinner table or living room coffee table. For adults looking for a little more competitive edge to their evening but who want to include the kids, there are plenty of more "mature" card games like Spades, Hearts, Poker, or Cribbage. It's easy to get the kids involved, especially if you play in teams. The kids can help you develop strategies or even keep score. They'll be happy to just be included.

In my family, we also used to pull out Bingo cards and have a blast calling out letters and watching, in silence, as everyone focused on covering their numbers. For games like Bingo, it's best to have a prize at the end because Bingo is a reward game. When playing with kids, you can have levels of prizes depending on the amount of the card you're playing. For example, winning four corners gets a slightly better prize than a diagonal line, and a full card gets the biggest prize of all. This game requires a little bit more planning and possibly shopping on the parents' part. But everyone loves Bingo—kids and adults alike. It's a great game to play on a rainy day. You can pick up

Bingo cards at almost any store that sells children's games. You can either use chips to block the numbers or ink blotters depending on whether you are playing on cardboard or paper. If you're really inventive, try making your own cards.

Hello, Sunshine

On the weekends, when the weather is nice, get outside and play! Sunny days are a great time for families to play together. If you have younger children, there's nothing they love more than a game of Hide-and-Seek or Tag (and you thought you had to spend hundreds of dollars on a gym membership every year for that workout). Kids have boundless energy—you'll lose calories just by trying to keep up with all of their running around. There's no better way to relive your own childhood either. There are so many great games to play outside when the weather is nice—hundreds of derivations of the game of Tag, for example. There's Blind Man's Bluff, Touch Iron/Touch Wood/Touch Stone, Prayer Tag, Wolf in the Henhouse, and Mother May I. Growing up, one of my personal favorite tag-type games was British Bulldog.

My siblings, and all the neighboring kids, gathered every night to play that game. One person is "it" and everyone else lines up against a wall or other starting point. When the "it" calls out "British," everyone runs at the same time. The goal is to reach the "safe point"—usually another wall or mutually agreed upon landmark. We used to start at dusk and the household rule was that we had to be back inside when the street lights came on. We were exhausted by bedtime. It was especially fun when the grown-ups joined us. We'd squeal with laughter when a kid tagged a slow-moving parent.

Outdoor fun is a great way for families to spend time together. Some of the best games of all are the ones we play outside in wide open spaces like Softball, Frisbee, Bocce Ball, Touch Football, Volleyball, Badminton, and Croquet. There are hundreds of games to play outside and this is the best place to tire out the kids and get your own work-out into your schedule. You don't have to spend a huge amount of money on *equipment* either. In fact, the less equipment required, the better.

Three Strikes

Before beginning any game make sure you have clearly stated the rules of the game and that everyone participating understands how to play. Family fun night can turn in to family feud night if rules are not clearly stated up front.

It's in the Cards

Equipment consists of the physical resources you need to play a game. For example, you can't play Kickball without the ball and the bases.

Go Team!

Some great traditional family board games like Monopoly can be played in teams. This is especially great when you're including younger children in the fun. Kids love to be part of a grown-up's team. It makes them feel valued and special that they are considered old enough to have a say.

A Word on Ages

So you've successfully gotten the family together for game night, but before you pick what you'll play, we have to keep in mind that different games work for different age groups.

The Early Bird

If you have preschool children, you can start teaching them some of the simpler card games like War and Go Fish. There are more and more board games on the market nowadays that are specifically designed for younger kids similar to the age-old favorites like Candyland and Chutes and Ladders. Parents can really give their kids an early helping hand by involving them in some of the early childhood development games. There are concentration games, quizzes, and word puzzles that give kids some of the basic learning tools they'll carry with them through their lives. Also, if you get the kids started playing games at this age, your chances of keeping the tradition going as they get older are better.

Although there are many manufactured games that provide children with educational instruction, children love to learn new things from their parents or other adults. One way or another, play allows children to develop skills that might not be taught in school from which they will benefit later in life. Children love games that are unstructured, require little equipment, and involve imaginative play. Running and chasing games are particularly popular with young kids, and will tire them out. Sure makes bedtime a lot easier! Other games like Hopscotch, Leapfrog, and Marbles are particularly enticing to kids as well, because not only are they competitive activities, but they also involve skills of dexterity, concentration, and strategic planning.

Three Strikes

Read the warnings on all packages for games for young players. Small game pieces can be choking hazards for youngsters who like to put things in their mouths. Follow the age-appropriate warnings on all packaged games.

Winning Plays

The earliest known marbles were made of flint, stone, and baked clay. Examples have been found in archaeological sites around the world including ancient Rome and Egypt. These ancient game relics are on display in museums today.

Modern day marbles are made of glass, which is melted in a furnace and poured out. It's actually quite an intricate process—the more colorful the marble, the more complicated the manufacturing process. Different colored liquid glass is injected inside the flowing glass to make some of the beautiful inserts. Mechanical rollers shape, smooth, and dry the small game pieces. Marbles are huge collector's items today.

Time to Categorize

One game that was always good fun to play when I was a kid was a game called Categories. This is an early version of the popular board game Scattergories. But you don't have to buy the game to get the kids to play. This is the best game for long car rides because your kids will be lost in concentration as they try to fill in the blanks. If you're looking for a little quiet time, you might want to give this game a try. We played this game with every age group in my family. Even my parents got into the fun. I learned it at school and taught it to my siblings and we played it for years. It is a very simple game and it's good for all ages because it's a guessing game.

Here's how you play: You draw a chart using vertical and horizontal lines so that the page forms a series of boxes (or a grid). At the top of each column running left to right, you fill in names of categories. For example the heading of column 1 could be types of "Cars," column 2 could be types of "Vegetables," column 3 could be names of "Candy Bars," and column 4 could be names of "Countries," and so on. All the players must mutually agree on each category.

In the columns running top to bottom, on the left-hand side of the page, you fill in a letter of the alphabet. To pick the letter, have one person recite the alphabet silently in his or her head and another person say stop. Whatever letter the person stops on (and honesty is very important here) is the first letter to be written in the columns to the far left of the page. (You can also write the letters on small pieces of paper and then pull one from a hat.) From there, you have to fill in the blanks under each heading.

So if the letter is "B," each person has to find the name of a car, a type of vegetable, a kind of candy bar, and the name of a country that start with the letter "B."

Whoever finishes first says "Stop" and the game is over. This is where the fun really begins. When you go over your answers, watch the arguments and discussions abound! If you have an answer that doesn't match anyone else's and it is deemed correct by the other players, then you score two points. If you match another players' response, you each get one point. If the players decide that there's no such thing as a Beluga candy bar, for example, you get zero points—unless you can prove there is such a thing, of course. Whoever has the most points by the end of the game wins! You can either change the categories or the letter of the alphabet for the next round.

Older and Wiser

At the elementary school level, you can start getting kids into some more advanced board and card games. Have them team up with older kids or adults when playing games like Monopoly and Trivial Pursuit. You can also start teaching them the basic rules for some more advanced card games just to familiarize them with the deck. Even if they don't fully understand the games, they will start recognizing suits, pairs, and other card combinations, and before you know it, will be demanding to be dealt into the game with their own hand.

The first card game I ever learned to play was War. I played for hours with my sisters. Sometimes I'd even play alone. I'd split the deck and turn the card over for the other side just like I was playing against another person. The next game I learned was Go Fish, then Solitaire. My parents often indulged in a game of Double Solitaire, a slow moving game, until you both turn over a card at the same time that needs to be added to the growing suit on the stack of aces. Then the chaos sets in. It was fun to watch the fireworks as my parents struggled to beat the other with that card. That's a fun game for the family also, even if only two people can play at a time. And you can always offer to challenge the winner.

High Score

Include your youngest family members in the fun even if they don't fully understand what is happening. Have them deliver snacks or act as a cheering section. Ask their advice before making your next move—this ensures fun for the entire family and familiarizes them with the elements of gaming so they will be ready to go when they reach a more appropriate age.

As kids get a little older, you can pull out the stakes and start playing some of the more advanced card games like Spades, Hearts, and Crazy Eights. Those were some of the favorites in my house. We broke up into teams for these games, pairing the younger children with the adults. My parents always included the younger kids in decisions about which cards to put down and to pick up. It was great just to be included.

Teenagers tend to like a little bit more fast-paced activities, so board games like Trivial Pursuit and Pictionary could be big hits. Monopoly might not be likely to hold their attention very long—depending on the kids, of course. But, generally speaking, when dealing with teens, the faster the game the better.

Raising the Stakes

It would be very easy to get teenagers involved in a good game of Rummy if you made the stakes interesting enough for them. How about an extra hour on their curfew, or one night without having to clear the table after dinner? It can work in favor of the parents as well. How does one less hour of gabbing on the telephone sound? Or a clean room and a made bed for a whole week? Probably not a precedent you want to set—gambling your way to good behavior—but it doesn't hurt once in a while just to break up the monotony of daily chores. The kids will love it and you'll both get a break here and there.

There are some games we might know of as adults that our kids have never played. It's a great idea to pass these games down to your children—one more way to keep a tradition alive. It is traditions that build families through the generations. For example, I recently spoke to a friend about the rules of Cribbage. His eyes lit up at the very mention of the game. He had completely forgotten that his father had taught him to play Cribbage when he was a very young boy. The rules started flooding back to him as we talked about the game. It was a fond memory and he was surprised just how much of the game he remembered. These are wonderful life moments that can be shared through the ages from one generation to the next. It's not just the games we remember, but who we played them with, and the fond memories they evoke, that stay with us forever.

The Least You Need to Know

➤ Family game night is a great way to bond with your family and get everyone talking.

➤ In the past, people played games as a way to prepare themselves for war or hunting.

➤ To get your family started on game night, just pick a game, sit down, and play.

➤ Pick one night a week or one night a month for family game night and stick to it for consistency.

➤ Pay attention to the ages of the children and choose a game everyone can play.

Chapter 2

The Importance of Rules

In This Chapter

➤ Setting the rules and choosing a referee

➤ Making sure all participants understand how to play

➤ Setting the stage for peaceful game-playing

➤ Handling cheaters and sore losers

➤ Settling contentions

Rules, rules, rules! A game is only as good as its *rules,* and how well we play the game is defined by how well we follow the rules. What is so fascinating about many of the games we play today is that there are often no instruction books included—yet we somehow know how to play them anyway. We learn from family, friends, teachers, and coaches.

In this chapter, we will take a look at why rules are important and how they can make playing games more enjoyable. It doesn't matter if you follow the rules that the game came with or if you make up your own rules; it really just matters that everyone agrees on what the rules are. We'll take a look at how to avoid trouble and keep the peace, be a good winner and a good loser, and how you can settle arguments that arise in the course of playing your game. By being clear on the rules of the game, you're sure to maximize your fun at all times!

Setting the Rules

When I was a kid, we used to play a schoolyard game called Champ—otherwise known as Four Square. It was played in one large square, which was painted on the ground in our schoolyard. This square was divided into four smaller squares, with one square dedicated to the "Champ." Because our square was a permanent one, all we needed to bring along was a very bouncy rubber ball.

One person is the "Champ" and stands in the Champ's square. How you determine who becomes the Champ for the first game is up to the players. Here's some ideas for choosing a champ: You can flip a coin, pull straws, pick a number from one to ten and have the players guess it, or go alphabetically by first initial of first name. In our games, the Champ was the Champ until beaten by another player.

It's in the Cards

A set of **rules** is a prescribed guide for conduct, telling you how to proceed with your next course of action.

High Score

Create your own Champ playing field. Get a piece of washable chalk and draw the Champ grid on the pavement outside your house.

The object is to keep the ball bouncing into each square using the palm of your hand. If you hit the ball outside the line, you are out and someone else takes your place in the square. The object is to get the Champ knocked out of the game, so you can move into the Champ's square. The Champ always goes first and has certain advantages over the other players in terms of scoring points and getting other players out. If another player unseats the Champ, he or she moves into that square with all its privileges and advantages.

The most interesting thing that I remember about this game is that there was always at least one kid who knew the rules—and we made up many new rules as we went along. Sometimes the new rules stuck, and were passed on to the next group of kids. The rules were always announced at the beginning of recess and the game went on through recess. Sometimes we'd pick up where we left off the day before—we'd even mark our places in the waiting line. There was always a line; after all, only four people can play at a time.

When you decide to play any game, it's important to establish the rules in advance. Most board games come with their own instruction books, so that's easy enough. Read the rules aloud and discuss them as you go along so everyone knows what to expect when the game begins. There are many games that are passed down to us that have no written instructions. This book will help clear up the confusion on these games, so read on, and then read out loud.

Setting the rules and getting everyone to agree on the rules is the first step to avoiding arguments when the competition has begun. Sometimes it's even fun to make up your own rules as you go along, but make sure that everyone is clear on what the rule changes are. That's the way to fair play. If you're a frequent player, keep a log of the rules handy, and add to this log as you redefine the games with new rules.

Keeping the Peace

Now that you've set the rules, you're ready to play the game! Whether you're a kid or an adult, you know that when you play a game and the rules are not clear with all the players, arguments abound. So, let's try to keep the board-flipping and temper tantrums to a minimum.

High Score

Make your own book of family rules. Keep a notebook in your game closet that lists all of the specifics of the rules your family has agreed upon for the games you play.

Compromise: The Name of the Game

When you're in competition, you see all sorts of sides to people you might otherwise not have known were there. For example, if one person is on a real winning streak and getting really heated up with the thrill of competition, and then you throw a curveball his or her way—let's say they didn't follow the rules exactly as the rest of you thought fair—it's not unusual for tempers to flare. In cases when there are no guidebooks to consult, most games end with everyone getting disgusted and frustrated with all the arguing. That can ruin a perfectly good game and possibly the rest of the day.

There's only one word to keep in mind: compromise. It's not a bad idea to include the idea of compromise in the rules that you establish at the beginning of the game. You're thinking "You mean have a rule for keeping the peace?" Absolutely. When conflicts arise, a compromise must be reached, and short of one person playing the part of *referee*, it's best to establish some ground rules for conflict intervention.

This book will outline some major game rules, so you'll have the necessary guidance for most games, but there will be games not listed. What kind of rules can you set for keeping the peace? With kids, it's almost inevitable that a fight or two will break

It's in the Cards

A **referee** is someone who is chosen as the official, having final authority in administering a game. The ref makes the call when an action is questioned.

High Score

Try this: Agree before the games begin that when no compromise can be reached within a five-minute time frame, resort to the old-fashioned coin toss. If you agree in advance to such a rule, then there's no way flipping a coin can be unfair. If the coin toss does not appeal to anyone, call the game a tie and start all over again.

out in the middle of the game. But kids are easy. They argue, pout for a while, and then usually move on to the next event.

But then there are the adults. Adults already understand the concept of victory and defeat and almost always strive to win. With kids you can use some authority: Threaten that if they don't play nice, they won't get to play at all; you can always offer a reward for peaceful game playing. Adults may just require a little structure to keep the game flowing undisrupted. In the end, however, the choice is obvious: You can either argue all day or you can keep playing. Remember: The whole point is to have a good time!

Dare to Play Fair

When children play games, squabbles arise over the rules all the time. Depending on the age group, many kids are not likely to read the rules before starting the game. And there's nothing worse than having to break up a fistfight or slapfest when kids start to brawl.

Get Involved

Get the kids into good game-playing habits. Start by helping them set up the game, whether it's a board game or a lawn game. You play the role of referee. Tell the kids that all disputes will be settled by you, and maybe give them a limit of disputes they can bring to you ... let's say three disputes per game. If you hear a fourth, the game will be stopped and the kids will have to find something else to do. This is a great way to get kids to work out their own conflicts. If they know they can only bring three to the referee, the rest of the disputes will have to be worked out amongst themselves.

Cheat Sheet

But even more likely than squabbles over the rules of a game are squabbles over cheating. Kids love to sneak one past you wherever they can. I love playing board games with kids because I'm intrigued by the many ways they "strategize." It's fun to watch their creative little minds trying to sneak around the rules.

Cheating is an age-old pastime. No sporting event or game has gone through history without its fair share of cheaters, but to avoid conflict, it's best to establish a no-cheating rule. If someone is caught cheating, they will have to forfeit the game, or at the very least, forfeit a turn.

Cheating is usually considered the lowest form of sportsmanship and you should avoid it. But if it wasn't for cheating, we'd be missing out on some amazing stories and folklore. For example, Poker is the classic cheater's game—many books have been written, and movies made, about cons and cheats involved in this often high-stakes game. Cards, generally speaking, may be one of the cheater's favorite media. Cheating is so popular a pastime, in fact, that there are games based on the art of cheating. One such game is a card game called—you guessed it—"Cheat."

To play Cheat you need a minimum of three players. The more players involved, the harder the game. You deal out an entire deck of cards to all the players and each person takes a turn placing a card face-down in the center of the table—calling out the number and suit of the card as they do so. Each player must put down a card in ascending order, but not necessarily in the same suit. You must call the card aloud as you place it face-down.

Winning Plays

One of the earliest written references to Poker was made in 1834 by Jonathan H. Green. Green mentions rules to what he refers to as the "cheating game," a game he had seen being played on Mississippi riverboats. It wasn't until this time that he realized the game had never been mentioned in print before, and he decided to call it Poker.

Inevitably, you will come to one person who does not have the required card to put down. So that person must bluff and lie about what card he or she is putting down. It's up to the other players to catch the cheater. If you suspect a cheater, you must call out "cheat" on that player's turn. When the card is displayed, if the player who called "cheat" is correct, the cheater must pick up all the cards on the table. If the player who calls "cheat" is incorrect, then he or she must pick up all the cards. The object of the game, of course, is to get rid of all your cards.

Regardless of the game you are playing, you can just assume someone's going to cheat and make finding the cheater a part of the game. That's an interesting idea—a good way to make light of an otherwise sticky situation and even turn it into something fun. For example, if someone is caught cheating, he or she may be eliminated from the game after a group vote—whether he or she cheated or not. Or, depending on the game being played, if the cheater is caught, points can be deducted. Make it part of the game itself—see if you can cheat your way through without being caught! It's a good idea to make sure in advance that everyone knows this is part of the game—remember we want to have fun, not fights!

Be a Winner!

There's nothing worse than a sore loser. Sore losers are considered whiners and bad sports. The worst kind of sore loser is one who goes around accusing everyone of cheating because he or she can't face the fact that they might not have played the game very well—or that maybe luck was not in the cards for them this time. It's best to accept the loss and try to figure out a better strategy for the next game. Or better yet, accept your loss and applaud the winner.

This is an important lesson to teach your children and it's not an easy one. To teach a child to applaud the winner and accept his or her loss, you are teaching them a form of empathy. It feels good to win and isn't it nice to be congratulated for your efforts? Remind your child that the next time he or she wins, he or she will receive the same praise and that you should treat others the way you would expect to be treated in return. Life is full of tough, competitive situations and if you teach your children to stand tough when the odds are against them, you will be giving them a great gift that will help them throughout their lives—from childhood to adulthood.

Three Strikes

Accusing someone of cheating without definitive proof is the poorest kind of sportsmanship. If you can't contain your wounded pride, leave the room, get some air, but never be a sore loser.

While nobody likes a sore loser, the worst kind of game player is a bad winner. The person who wins the game should sit back and smile on the inside. To applaud yourself in front of everyone else and sing your own praises is bad sportsmanship. It's best to be humble about it—you know you won and everyone else knows you won, and therein lies the glory. I've played many a game with a bad winner. They are the ones who can only feel good about their accomplishment if they make everyone else feel lousy about their shortcomings. Those are the kind of people you might not want to play with again. It makes the game much more fun and certainly creates an atmosphere of fair and fun gaming if winners are humble and losers don't let their egos get in the way of an otherwise good game.

Settling Disputes

Many gambling men lost their lives in the Old West in Poker disputes. Gambling was no fun without a violent gun battle to solve a conflict. However, rest assured, your disputes do not have to end in bloodshed. Here are some tips for settling conflicts that arise when playing games.

Talk Amongst Yourselves

Discuss with your family how each of your actions affects the others, both positively and negatively. Show with real-life examples how sore losers and bad winners or cheating and name calling make each player feel while playing games. Is it fun or does it put a damper on the day?

If your family can see for themselves how bad behavior makes them feel and understands the negative effects on others, you may stop the wayward ones in their tracks. If, however, discussion doesn't work, agree to pick a third-party referee before the game starts. All problems can be taken to the referee; agree that the word of the referee is final. No exceptions.

Winning Plays

Doc Holliday of Wild West fame was told by his doctor to move to a warmer climate where his worsening tuberculosis might be eased by the dry heat. He packed up his dental practice and headed to Dallas, Texas. There, he rapidly found his dental offices emptying as his coughing increased. Therefore, he turned his interest toward the gambling tables, where his hacking was less noticeable among the smoking, gambling crowds. Doc's gambling career in Dallas came to an abrupt end, however, when he took out his trusty Colt and shot an upstanding citizen dead over a disagreement of a $500 pot. Doc won the argument but left town. His luck followed him around, however, and he continued to settle his card disputes with hot lead.

Discuss with your family the importance of rules and the need for having a fair way of settling disputes. When disputes arise, take the opportunity to sit down and work out a fair compromise. Stop the game and focus on the situation at hand. It's a wonderful opportunity to teach your children life skills. Discuss decisions you make and help the children learn to find that middle ground.

Try role-playing with your family to see if you can come up with creative ways of settling disputes. Role-play situations presented by your children. Discuss solutions with them and summarize the need to make rules.

Take turns at playing different roles in the game to settle disputes over who gets to be the banker, the dealer, and so on. Make new rules up as you go along. For instance, if Friday night is family fun night, alternate who gets to be the banker each Friday night. I know in my house, I never got to be the banker and it was a sore spot with me for years to come. If alternating doesn't appeal, try a coin toss, pick straws, or come up with some other random way of choosing roles.

Avoid the bloodshed of years gone by—have a fair and fun family night free of argument and discord.

The Least You Need to Know

➤ Establish the rules for your family before you start to play, and make sure all players understand the rules.

➤ Write down the rules if you're playing a game that doesn't come with an instruction book.

➤ Find a way to deal with cheating—either you can choose a referee or incorporate cheating into the actual play of the game.

➤ No one likes a sore loser or a bad winner. Be a champ and play with a good spirit—whether you win *or* lose. Remember, you're having fun!

➤ Settle disputes by discussing alternatives, or alternating game-playing roles.

Chapter 3

From Start to Finish

In This Chapter

➤ Turning off the computers and video games

➤ Including teens and starting games at a young age

➤ Picking a game and choosing teams

➤ Cleaning up and quieting down

It seems strange that kids nowadays don't play outside as much as they did in the past. Games kids play seem to take place mostly on the computer. But computer-companionship is certainly no match for human contact. Virtual reality is about fantasy; reality is about using all our senses and enjoying the physical presence of other human beings. Computers are great, no doubt, but everything in moderation!

If parents take the initiative and start family game night—and start when the kids are young—the whole dynamic of the family structure will come to life. There is very little involved in setting up for most games—it's clean-up that takes a little more time. You'll find out in this chapter that set-up and clean-up can also play a part in the fun.

A Basis for Bonding

Spending time with your children will allow you to find out things about your kids that you might not have known before. If your family dynamic is currently that everyone goes to their own space in your home to listen to music, watch TV, or play on the computer, you might have a bit of a struggle at first getting everyone unplugged—but give it a try. If you succeed, you'll be pleasantly surprised.

If you find the younger kids are more eager to play than the older kids, don't let the older kids completely off the hook. Try peeking in on them when the game is put away, and tell them how much you missed them during the game. Ask them if there are any games they might like to play in the future. How about Pool? Maybe it's worth investing in a Pool table to get them to interact with the family a little bit more. How about telling them to ask some of their friends over for family game night? Maybe that will entice them. With some teens, you won't win the battle. If worst comes to worst, ask them about the games they are playing on the computer. Ask them to teach you how to play. Maybe they'll let you watch. If you show some interest in what they are up to, maybe they'll show interest on the next family game night.

Winning Plays

Some facts from the 1998 Video and Computer Game Report Card (produced by the National Institute on Media and the Family):

➤ Video and computer games are among children's most requested gifts during the holiday season.

➤ The highest percentage of children who own or rent video or computer games is among children ages 8–12.

➤ Children who play games now do so an average of seven hours per week!

➤ A study of fourth through eighth graders in 1996 found that almost half of their favorite games featured violence.

Get 'Em Young

The trick to avoiding difficulty with teenagers is to start playing games with them when they are little kids. Keep the lines of communication with them open. Talk and listen when they are little, and never stop. Always make yourself available to them. There's no better way to establish a rapport than to get down and dirty with them in a good old-fashioned game: Chess, Checkers, board games, card games, Pool, or Darts—anything that will keep the interaction alive.

This is not only important for family interaction later on, but also for their interpersonal development. Don't let them drift away into virtual reality. Keep them stimulated. Find common ground. Find out what they like and try to be involved. If they don't want you to be involved, just make sure they know you are always there to listen, help, and guide.

Parents are busy—most parents work. It's hard to get a second to yourself and so easy to let the computer, the TV, and the music world baby-sit your kids so you can get a good hour or two of peace after a hard day. But the quality of life you build with your family is critical to their development, and ultimately everyone's happiness. Talk to your kids, listen to your kids, but mostly … play, play, play with your kids!

Keen Kids

There's no better way to engage your teenagers than with a pool table, ping-pong table, or dartboard. It's worth spending the money on these games. Most teens will love a competitive, action game. They spend so much time sitting in class and studying for exams, not to mention just trying to figure out what they want and who they are, that a game involving skill and energy will be a nice break from their daily, intensive lifestyle. You may find it hard to pull them away and get them back to the books!

Little kids will always want to play a game—so get them while they're young! Any game you teach them will be fine with them. Whether it's a board game, card game, or word game. Kids just want to be included. If you can get them to learn a thing or two in the process, go for it! If you can have fun and educate at the same time, you can't go wrong.

Chess is a good example of a great teaching tool to use on your kids. They will be forced to learn about patience, structure, and strategy. It's a great way to sit and spend some time with children too. While you're both leaning into the board, planning your next moves, you can also … talk. Chess is a wonderful game for kids of all ages, because not only does it force them to think ahead, memorize moves, and be still for minutes at a time, but it also forces them to think about what someone else is thinking—a great way to exercise principles of cause and effect. "If I do this … such and such might happen." That's a very valuable tool.

Mixed Bag

If you have a family with kids of different age groups, you can try a number of different ways to get everyone involved. There are plenty of board games and card games that are good for people of all ages. I played Hearts, Spades, and Poker as a kid. I loved a good round of Double Solitaire, and Blackjack was always a favorite of mine.

My strategy might not have been the greatest at the age of nine, but I certainly enjoyed playing. My siblings and I had stacks of board games and my sister and I even invented our own. We built the game board out of a piece of cardboard, borrowed the dice and playing pieces from another game, and used index cards for draw cards. I can't remember what the game was, but because we played so many different board games, we were savvy enough to create our own.

High Score

Invent your own game at home! Break out art supplies and put on your thinking caps. Try to come up with a new board game or create a new game of cards. The act of creating the game will probably be more fun than actually playing the game later on.

Winning Plays

The auction game Masterpiece was originally released in 1970 by Parker Brothers. In 1996 Hasbro re-released it, but it seemed to have lost a lot of its popularity. Another art auction game was High Bid, which was set in an art antiques auction. High Bid was released by 3M.

My sister's favorite board game was Masterpiece—a game where you actually bid, auction-style, on postcards of famous paintings. This game was my first introduction to art. I learned names like Whistler, Degas, Monet, Van Gogh, and Picasso for the first time in my life. The whole family used to play, and my parents, both educators, used to tell us about the paintings we were bidding on. It was educational and always fun. With a game like that, even if you don't know a lot about art, you can look up the paintings in the library with your children later. When I was older my parents took us to museums and I recognized some of the artwork from that game. That's pretty amazing!

In order not to exclude anyone from family game night, you should try organizing the family into teams. If there's a child who might be too young to play a certain game, make sure that child is teamed up with an older player. Most children will be happy just to be involved—but there will come a time when the child will notice that he or she is the only one paired up and will ask to play on his or her own. If the child is still too young, just let him or her be on his or her own and fudge the rules a little bit so they feel involved. It's not about playing a perfect game; it's about having a good time and making everyone feel good.

Take It Outside

Some of the best fun you'll have, though, is playing outdoor games with your kids, like Touch Football, Volleyball, and Kickball. For years, we've seen images of the Kennedy family playing Touch Football on the grounds of the Kennedy compound in Hyannis Port, Massachusetts. After that crazy presidential election which was too close to call, one of the first public events former Vice President Al Gore engaged in was a game of Touch Football with his family—perhaps it was their way of relaxing and re-grouping after months of a strenuous campaign. Maybe it didn't matter at that moment who had won the election … just that it was almost over and they were finally together again.

There's definitely truth to the adage "families that play together, stay together." It's important for families to let off steam, express their love for each other, and just have a good time through whatever games they enjoy playing.

Choosing Sides: Team Games

It's important to be as fair as possible when choosing sides in games. In the home, you might want to pair a child with an adult or a teen with a child. You obviously don't want two adults against two children—that wouldn't be fair. Sometimes the kids want to play against the adults, and if they insist, then go for it. It might be fun. It might be even more fun to let them win. Sometimes you'll be surprised how much the kids know, and more surprised when they beat the pants off you.

For group games, I think it's best to pull names from a hat. Write everyone's name down on a piece of paper; fold the papers and mix them in a hat or bag of some kind. Names should be pulled out one at a time and teams divided accordingly.

At some birthday parties I attended, a parent would simply divide the room in half. Wherever you were standing determined what team you were on. I don't ever remember attending a party where children were allowed to pick their own teams. Often at parties, names were pulled out of a hat at the beginning of the party and that was your team for the rest of the party games. You can pick new names for new games, but that might be a little time-consuming.

In outdoor games where there was usually no adult supervision, we used one of the rhyming methods (see Chapter 21, "They Say It's Your Birthday!") to pick who is "It." Most of these games did not require teams. However, there were games like Red

High Score

If your family is engaging in a game of skill, try to be balanced about the ages of the people on the teams. If it's a game of luck, try mixing up the age groups; it won't really matter.

Three Strikes

Avoid letting children choose teams. It's a practice that usually ends up leaving someone with hurt feelings. Remember in gym class and on the sports fields, how the kids who were tough, athletic, or just plain popular were picked first, while the smaller, less athletic, and maybe unpopular kids were left to the end? You don't want to recreate that often painful situation in your own living room.

Rover where we had to pick teams. In this case, we usually just divided up without any picking or choosing. Often there's at least one kid in every group who immediately assumes a leadership role and will tell kids what the teams are. We know that kid as the "bossy" kid. Some kids don't mind this—at least someone is making the decisions. But if the bossy kid isn't fair, kids will rebel mighty quickly.

When disputes break out and adults are called in, just tell the kids what team they are going to be on and end it there. The alternative is to tell the kids that they will have to work out a better method, and give them ideas—like pulling names from a hat (my favorite method).

What Shall We Play?

This might be the trickiest part of family game night—unless you've been playing for a while and have established the family favorites. The conflicts will arise if some family members prefer one game to another. There are a couple ways to be fair in your decision-making. It's all about avoiding conflict at this point.

Consider all the game options. If there is a game that one family member really doesn't like, but another person does, be fair and remove it from the options. Go through process of elimination until you come up with games that although everyone might not be totally excited about, they don't mind playing. Put all the names of the games in a hat and have one family member pull the name out. Whatever game is pulled is the game the family will play that night.

Another method is to put all the games in a hat—including the ones that some family members are not so excited about having as an option. Have someone pull the name of the game out of the hat, and that is the game that you wind up playing that night—no matter who likes it and who doesn't. Make sure the kids are aware of this rule in advance, or chaos is sure to break loose.

In advance of pulling the game from the hat, establish that there is to be no grumbling should the game not be preferable to one family member. If it looks like a conflict is going to brew over it, tell that child that on the next family game night, you will play his or her favorite game and no one else will be allowed to gripe about it.

You can also put a schedule up on the wall and designate each game night to one of the children. For example, Monday is Tara's night and Friday is Matthew's night. What about Joey? Well, he will get the following Monday night. Create the schedule months in advance so that the kids are clear on which night is their night.

When it's their night, they are responsible for picking the game, setting up the game, and cleaning up the game. By using this method, you are teaching the kids leadership skills. They are setting the tone for the night in the game that they choose, and in being the leader, they have certain responsibilities like set-up and clean-up. Kids do much better with structure and guidance. If they know what's coming, they know what to do and you'll avoid conflict altogether.

Another means of choosing a game is to keep track of who won and who lost the game and assign those people tasks for the next game night. Don't let the winner get special treatment—you'll just teach children that winning is the best way to go. Winning is great and everyone should take pride in his or her achievement, but losing should not mean any kind of punishment either. It's about playing the game, being together, and having a good time that matters most. The winner should feel a sense of pride—that's the best reward you can get.

Poor losers are a pain, but poor winners are undignified. There should be no gloating on family game night. Make it a practice at the end of each game for every player, including the winner, to say "good game" to every other player and "congratulations" to the winner. Perhaps the honor for the winner is that they are not required to clean up, but at the first sign of gloating, they will have to clean up completely on their own.

Winning Plays

Mary Poppins was the wonderful nanny who made every chore a game and every day a "Jolly Holiday" in the movie *Mary Poppins*. The movie went on to win five Academy Awards, including Best Actress (Julie Andrews) and Best Song ("Chim Chim Cher-ee"). It is considered by many to be one of greatest films of our time—and a fun way to quiet children down after games!

Assigning Clean-Up

"With every job that must be done there is an element of fun—you find the fun—and snap, the job's a game." So said Mary Poppins as she helped Jane and Michael Banks clean up their messy room. The same can be said for every game that must be played—there is a job that must be done. Not only do you have to set the game up—especially board games—but you also have to clean up when the fun is finished.

Playing games with your kids not only helps them develop interpersonal and cognitive skills, but they also learn about responsibility. There is no game without some element of mess. Some games require more tools than others, so there is more clean up involved. Never, ever clean up the game without the kids' involvement. This is not just about fun for them—it's a complete package.

Winning Plays

Times haven't changed that much. Those timeless classics Sorry, Clue, Monopoly, Yahtzee, and Chess are still among Amazon's top-selling family games.

It's a good idea to have the whole family clean up the game together. If it's a board game, one child can be responsible for sorting the play money and stacking it up neatly back in the box. If it's a little kid, they can use the opportunity to practice their numbers and colors. Another child can sort the draw cards and put them neatly back in the box, while yet another child or adult can put the dice and playing pieces away. It should be a group effort.

If you decide to designate a family game night to each child, you should make that child responsible for choosing the game, as well as setting up and cleaning up. Even though that child is responsible for everything, don't leave the child on his or her own to take care of it all. That could make responsibility feel very unrewarding. Responsibility shouldn't feel like a drag or a chore—it should be somewhat empowering. So what you can do is have that child be responsible for the set-up and clean-up, but make that responsibility about delegating, not isolation.

The responsible child must delegate clean-up chores to the other family members. He or she should assign tasks to all the other players, but is ultimately responsible for the whole game being put away successfully. If the game is not put away properly then that child will have to pay some sort of penalty the next time a game is played— perhaps forfeiting one of his or her designated nights. You can keep track of what games were assigned to which child on your monthly game schedules. That way you'll know who was responsible for the game the last time it was played. But have the child show it to you before you put it back on the shelf, so that you can help him or her if there is anything not quite right. They may need a little guidance.

You can start with these guidelines, and depending on how it all develops with your particular family, you may want to make up your own rules as you go along. Just get started with a plan and see how it goes.

Set-up is usually not a problem because the kids are so excited to play. Clean up is the drag—they've already had their fun and now they want to walk away. Just let them know in advance that everyone has a responsibility, and if they are not willing to clean up then no one is going to play.

High Score

The trick to set-up and clean-up is preparing your children in advance. Tell them beforehand that playing the game means you also have jobs. If they expect this, you'll have less griping when it comes time to doing the work.

Shhhh! Quiet Time

Ahh … the game is put away, the children are hooted-and-hollered-out, and you can finally put your feet up and relax. Well … not quite! The game is put away, the kids are wired and dying for another game, and you're pulling your hair out. Again—it's all about preparing your kids in advance.

Before you play any game, make sure the kids are fed, homework is done, they are bathed and in their pajamas ready for bed. When the game is put away, maybe it's early enough for a half-hour of TV, or maybe you want to pull out a book and read to them for a little while. One way or another, you have to set a few rules for family game night.

Here's a list that might help:

➤ If family game night is on a weeknight, homework must be done, and everyone must be clean and in their jammies ready for bed.

➤ Everyone helps set up.

➤ Everyone helps clean up.

➤ There is one game allowed per night.

➤ The game must end by a certain time.

➤ If there's still time before bed, it is called "quiet time" where everyone mellows out until it's time for bed.

➤ If kids do not adhere to quiet time, there will be no family game night next week.

It's all about establishing a routine, setting rules, being clear, and sticking to all the rituals. If you do, you'll find that the kids will get used to it and settle in pretty easily.

When the kids are finally tucked away after a good night of playing, you can finally kick back and relax—or, you can pull out the cards and have an adult game night. The kids will never have to know!

The Least You Need to Know

➤ Start playing games with your children while they are young to avoid trouble interacting with them later.

➤ Be as fair as possible when choosing sides for teams. Break up the age groups and equalize the talent on each side.

➤ Find a fair way to pick a game each time you play. Pick suggestions from a hat or take turns choosing games.

➤ Be clear on the clean-up and set-up before you start family night. You don't want everyone running when it's time to put the games away. Delegate responsibility.

➤ Find a way to quiet down together if there's time after your game. Kids can get wired during all that fun, and you don't want to send them to bed raring to go another round.

Chapter 4

The Name of the Game

In This Chapter

➤ Types of games

➤ Indoor games

➤ Outdoor games

➤ Games on the run

Games have been around as long as humans, and there are so many different types of games it boggles the mind. There are indoor games, outdoor games, quiet games, rowdy games, solitary games, games for teams, and so on. Let's take a look at all the different kinds of games available to you so you can pick and choose to suit the occasion.

This chapter takes a look at parlor games—such as various table games, dice games, Dominoes, Darts, and board games—as well as games to play outside, games you can play anywhere at all, and many, many card games! Whether you are alone on a quiet rainy night or surrounded by six family members at a picnic, there's a game waiting for you!

Come into My Parlor ... Parlor Games

The very word "parlor" evokes images of lush country manors with tapestry-lined walls, silk-covered duvets, ladies and gentlemen lounging with a good book after

It's in the Cards

A **parlor game** is a game that is meant to be played indoors.

It's in the Cards

Board games are any games of strategy—such as Chess, Checkers, Backgammon, or Monopoly—that you play by moving pieces around on a board.

Winning Plays

Dice have been found all over the world. Did you know that dice marked with dots were found in Egyptian tombs, and ancient Greek and Roman literature contain many references to dice-playing?

supper with warm glowing embers flickering in the hearth. Well, this might not exactly be what the average American living room looks like today, but it's in these old-fashioned rooms that some *parlor games* originated.

Parlor games are games that are played at a table or in a comfortable room in your home. Some parlor games have their origins in taverns and pubs where friends and family gathered for an evening. Nowadays, parlor games find their niche in a family recreation room, on the kitchen table, or in the den or living room. No matter where you play the games, they are supposed to be played in your leisure time in the room of your choice. The name of the game in this instance is comfort.

Set the Table

Table games are meant to be played by two or more and consist of games like Chess, Checkers, Backgammon, Pick-Up Sticks, and Tic-Tac-Toe. They are slow, leisurely games that involve a certain amount of quiet concentration, strategizing, and patience. There are countless *board games* on the market to be purchased today, but there are also these timeless classics that have been played for centuries. Chess, Checkers, and Backgammon are perfect examples of parlor table games. They can get intense, but rarely get loud.

On a Roll

Dice games have been part of human culture since ancient times. They may have originated in Asia and migrated across the globe. Now they can be found in nearly every culture on Earth. Dice are small cubes that are marked with dots on each side; these dots represent numbers from one to six. The small playing pieces are usually made of plastic in most modern games, but in the past have been made of bone, wood, stone, fruit pits, seeds, ivory, and clay.

Dice are thrown from a player's hand or dice cup and the total number showing face-up after the dice have settled determines the value of the throw. Dice are used either on their own in games of chance, such as Yahtzee, or as part of another game, like in various board games.

Ebony and Ivory

Dominoes is a game played by two or more people using small rectangular blocks made of plastic or wood. Older versions of the game contained blocks made of ivory and bone. It is a game that dates back to ancient China, but was not introduced to the western world until the eighteenth century. Historians think that the name of the game originates from the way the blocks looked in its early form: an ivory front backed by ebony, giving it the appearance of a hooded cloak called a "domino."

Each domino is divided in two by a line or ridge. Above and below the line is a combination of spots. The dominoes are numbered in a specific sequence. There are many derivations of the game. (See Chapter 6, "More Table Games.")

Bull's-Eye!

The origin of Darts is a bit of a mystery, but we know that it existed in British folklore. The English apparently played Darts before defeating the French at the Battle of Agincourt in the fifteenth century, and the Pilgrims supposedly played the game as they traveled to America in 1620.

Despite its buried roots, Darts is hugely popular in modern times. It is a game that is played in almost every British pub and American bar. There are clubs, organizations, tournaments, and championships held all over the world. It is so popular that the real enthusiasts consider it a sport to be reckoned with, and not just a game for fun-seekers.

The object of the game is to score as many points as possible by throwing a metal-tipped dart at a round board that is divided into sections representing points. There are many variations on the sport, but this basic premise is the key to most of the games.

Three Strikes

Don't play Darts when the little ones are around—save it for the more grown-up crowd. Those heavy darts can be quite sharp and little hands love to get involved in adult fun.

High Score

Skill is needed in order to play Darts successfully. For example, the way the dart is held and thrown and the concentration involved in hitting the target are important factors.

Rack 'Em Up

It is believed that Billiards derives from the Croquet family, with its green table-lining representative of the village green. The game is several centuries old and was originally played on a table with six pockets, Croquet-type hoops, and an upright stick. The balls were pushed rather than struck. Over the years the rules have changed and varied drastically, but in 1885 the Billiards Association changed all that by setting standards in the rules of the game.

Winning Plays

Neville Chamberlain claims to have named Snooker, which for many years was referred to as Snooker's Pool. It bore more relation to the existing Pool games of the time than the game of Snooker that we know today. Fewer pool balls were used, they took different positions on the table, and the values, scoring, and rules were different. The modern-day Snooker probably evolved in the British Army garrisons, where it is thought to have originated.

Winning Plays

It is believed that the earliest table soccer games date back as far as the late 1800s. The first patented Foosball game was registered in 1901, but it wasn't until the latter half of this century that the game really gained widespread popularity.

Common games in the Billiards family are Pool, Pyramid, and Snooker. The general object of the game and its variants is to hit a colored billiard ball into a pocket, clearing the table of all the balls before your opponent. Pool tables can be very expensive and are purchased in specialty shops and sporting goods stores.

Table Games

There are two different types of table games: There are table games that are played on a table, like cards and board games (but they could just as easily be played on the floor) and then there are table games that *are* the table. Table games like Foosball and Air Hockey are played on a specially designed table and became popular in the United States as coin-operated arcade games in the early 1970s. Foosball originated from the German table soccer game "Fussball" meaning, literally "football."

In 1976, the first table soccer organization made up of different countries united to form the European Table Soccer Union, which holds an annual championship. The problem with such a union, however, is that each country has its own table size, ball types, and different playing figures. This makes it difficult to switch successfully from table to table. The United States is the only country that holds a tournament with a large cash prize given to the winner. This money tournament has brought many other countries to compete in the United States, thus regulating some of the varying rules and playing variants. Sure is a good example of how money is a motivator!

Air Hockey is another table game with a huge following in North America. Designed for two players, it is a game that requires a fast hand and a quick eye. Played with two Air Hockey paddles, the object is to keep the "puck," or playing piece, on the board and eventually into the opponent's goal.

The playing surface is glossy and looks like a miniature hockey rink. The goal is usually a slot in the board on either end. Your hand, which holds the paddle that hits the "puck," should slide backward and forward in an effort to protect the goal. The person who scores the most goals is the winner.

There are several other variations of table games. The games are taken rather seriously by their ardent players and tournaments are played worldwide on an annual basis.

Later on, we'll also take a look at other parlor games such as Ping-Pong, Uno, Rook, Skip-Bo, and many more!

Let's Make a Deal: Card Games

Although the earliest known reference to a deck of playing cards dates back to the fourteenth century, it's believed that cards actually go back to ancient China, where paper was invented. Today we play with the standard English deck of 52 cards. Cards came to Europe by way of the Middle East. The face cards vary in their representation of King, Queen, and Jack from deck to deck, and there are many specialty decks on the market today with variations—sometimes even humorous ones.

High Score

Foosball tables, air hockey tables, and other such games can be purchased at toy stores and sporting goods stores.

Winning Plays

The English deck of cards uses suits of Spades, Clubs, Hearts, and Diamonds, while in other countries suits differ. Hearts, Leaves, Bells, and Acorns are found in Germany; Shields, Roses, Bells, and Acorns in Switzerland; and Coins, Cups, Swords, and Clubs in Spain.

Most card games played in North America can be played with this standard 52-card deck, but games like Pinochle require a special deck of cards. Uno, Skip-Bo, and Tripoley also require specially manufactured decks that can be purchased at game and toy stores. Cards can be played alone as in *Solitaire*, in groups as in Poker, Hearts, and Spades, or in teams and in tournaments as in Whist and Bridge. Then there's the ever-popular game of Blackjack, which is good fun at the casino.

It's in the Cards

The name **Solitaire** refers to any of a number of card games that are played by one person, alone.

The standard deck of cards can be purchased almost anywhere. Recently, I needed to pick up a deck for a friend who was having a backyard BBQ and was looking for a deck of cards at the last minute. Was I so surprised when I asked the gas station attendant, on a whim, if they sold cards. He said they did, and I bought my deck right then and there. I've also seen cards sold at convenience and drug stores. Playing cards is a very popular past time. There are groups of people on my train ride home who play Poker every day. I think the stakes are pretty low, but while others sleep or read, or gaze out the window, these folks are having a good time, and can often get pretty rowdy.

Everybody Outside!

Then, of course, there are the outdoor games. These games will be seasonal for people living in colder climates, but for those living in fair weather most of the year these are games you can play on a regular basis. Some of these games require a ball that is suitable to the sport, others require nets and racquets, and some require specialty equipment that must be purchased in an outdoors or sporting goods shop.

Break Out the Equipment

Bocce Ball, for example, requires special equipment and is usually sold as a complete set. A Bocce Ball set can be purchased at sporting goods supply stores. Volleyball will require a tall net that reaches several feet high and a special ball—also available at sporting good stores. Frisbees can be purchased in toy and game stores or sports supply stores, as can horseshoes, croquet sets, footballs, softballs, and mitts. Badminton will require a net, racquets, and a birdie.

Just Bring Your Sense of Fun

Outdoor games kids play tend to be a lot simpler and only require some imagination. Games like Tag, Red Rover, Mother May I, Hide-and-Seek, and Leap Frog are examples of imagination games. But then there's Hopscotch, Marbles, and Jump Rope that will require a trip to the toy store. Hopscotch is a great game for city kids. They just need a piece of chalk to draw the Hopscotch board on the pavement. You can use a bean bag or small pebbles for the toss before the jumping begins. Marbles will have to be purchased, but the game board can be drawn in the sand or dirt. It can also be drawn with a piece of chalk if the kids are playing on the pavement.

Kids amaze me with Jump Rope—not only because of their ability to jump effortlessly for hours, but also due to the fact that they know all the jumping rhymes that used to be so much a part of my daily life. I've forgotten most of the sing-song rhymes I used when either jumping by myself or using a longer rope and jumping in groups. But you go to any schoolyard today and the kids seem to have picked up right where I left off. You hear those same old rhymes again.

Picnic games are other great examples of outdoor fun. Tug-of-War and the Three-Legged Race just re-quire teams and some good strong rope. Games like these need very little preparation or purchase of supplies.

Everyone into the Pool!

Pool games require a backyard pool and very little else unless it involves a ball. There's Marco Polo, Chicken, Water Ballet, Biggest Splash contest, and more. It's not advisable to play these games in a public pool because other swimmers might find it disruptive. But if the games are played in the privacy of your backyard, then there's no harm done.

Games Are Everywhere!

Thank goodness for "everywhere games." These games have been handed down through the ages and are great for kids' parties and long car trips. Car games are inspired by the imagination and can be played just about anywhere (and had to be the brainchild of desperate parents on long road trips with bored children). For these games you don't need any accessories—just a creative mind and the ability to keep the kids interested for lengthy peri-ods of time.

I can't imagine that there's a single adult who can't think back to some of the games they played as

Three Strikes

Water games such as Marco Polo, Chicken, and Biggest Splash re-quire a certain amount of safety. There should always be a life-guard or trained adult on hand in case of an emergency, but that's all you really need to have a wet and wacky water-fun day.

High Score

Before embarking on a car jour-ney of any length with young children, make sure you plan ahead and prepare some fun car games. Keeping young minds oc-cupied in the car will make your trips more enjoyable for the en-tire family and you won't have to hear the ubiquitous, "Are we there yet?"

kids. There's "I spy," a great one for the car that often adults get bored of before the kids do. "I spy with my little eye, something starting with the letter 'L'," or "I spy with my little eye, something that is pink." The kids will guess forever and revel in their opportunity to "spy" something and have you figure out what it is. This is where the parental stamina must take hold!

Then there are the party games like Broken Telephone—no kid's birthday party is complete without games like this one. When the kids are seated eating their slices of birthday cake, have the first kid at the table think of a sentence and whisper it to the person next to him or her. The sentence should be passed all around the table in the form of a whisper. The last person to get the message should speak it aloud and see if it is the same as the original whispered sentence. You'll find that 9 times out of 10 it has taken on a whole new form and meaning. Kids will squeal with laughter over that game.

Musical Chairs is a timeless classic in the party game realm. Kids get really excited to play it and you may have to pull one kid off another as they fight over a chair. You'll have to play referee, but you'll find in the end that everyone has had a good time.

Party games like these will be outlined in Chapter 21, "They Say It's Your Birthday!" There are so many great ones and even if you never get to incorporate them into your family games, you'll have a great time remembering the games you played as a kid!

Whether you opt for a parlor game, a card game, an indoor game, an outdoor game, or a game you can take on the road, don't forget to pack your sense of fun!

The Least You Need to Know

➤ There are many different types of games to play—you are limited only by your imagination!

➤ Parlor games are meant to be played indoors.

➤ Card games are great since they can be played indoors or outdoors and rely on little equipment. You can buy playing cards almost anywhere.

➤ Most games are very safe and require few safety measures. However, whenever water and swimming are involved, you should have a lifeguard or other adult supervision.

➤ Try making up your own games as well—let your imagination take you to great heights of fun!

Part 2

Parlor Games

On rainy Sunday afternoons or cold winter evenings, you'll really appreciate the board games you have around the house. Now is the time to raid the basement or attic and see what you have stashed away. If you don't have any games on hand, check out the chapters in this section, grab a pen, make a list, and head to your local toy store.

There are so many games you can play with your kids from the educational to the strategic. You'll find Chess, Checkers, and Backgammon. These games are must-haves and will teach your kids some valuable tools—not just about how to play the games, but in logic and reasoning. The Dice and Dominoes games are great fun, too. You can even use these games to show your kids that playing a game is not always about brain power, but sometimes just plain old luck!

Some of the games are a bit rowdier, like Darts, Pool, and Ping-Pong, and will require some financial investment on your part. But it will be money well spent when you find yourself involved in hours of good, fun, family competition.

Chapter 5

Hands on the Table: Table Games

In This Chapter

➤ Understanding Chess pieces and the way they move

➤ Setting up the Chess and Checkers boards

➤ How to play Checkers

➤ Capturing and crowning

The games discussed in this chapter as well as Chapter 6, "More Table Games," are timeless classics with rich histories, and are played all over the world. Games like Checkers and Pick-Up Sticks are usually played in the home, but Chess and Back-gammon are played competitively and are taken quite seriously by the more ardent players. But no matter how or where you play the games, there's no doubt as to their popularity. You'd be hard-pressed to find an American household without at least one of these table games in a closet, attic, or basement.

Most of these games are played by two people in a quiet room in the house. Why a quiet room? Because they are games of strategy and skill and require a certain amount of concentration. These games don't often get too rowdy, but they can be frustrating. I'll bet many a board has been flipped over through the centuries in a moment of heated anger over a lost Queen in Chess or someone calling "King me" in Checkers. But don't be intimidated; it's all good fun in the end.

Checkmate!

The game of Chess today is played by two people and is renowned the world over for complicated maneuvering and strategic planning. You can learn the basics of Chess and have a good time playing it, or you can learn Chess notation and find out how the great players of the world think.

The goal of Chess is to maneuver your pieces in an effort to remove your opponent's pieces and ultimately capture his or her King. That might sound easy enough, but don't forget your opponent has the same goal in mind, so while you're strategizing your win, you also have to strategize your defense. There are some hard and fast rules in Chess, but there is also an art to achieving the ultimate goal of "checkmate" (winning the game). The art is in the movement of your pieces and the way you strategize the win.

History of the Game

The history of Chess is a much-debated topic amongst historians, but the consensus is that it has its origins in Persia or India. The oldest ancestor of Chess is a 4,000-year-old game called Chaturanga—a game played with dice and playing pieces consisting of elephants, horses, chariots, and foot soldiers. The most recent ancestor of Chess, as we know it today, is a 2,000-year-old game called "Shatranj," which was played by Persians and Arabs. The current game of Chess was designed by a champion player of his day (the 1840s) named Howard Staunton.

It's in the Cards

A **Grandmaster** is an expert player who has consistently scored high in international competition.

There are many arguments floating around today—with some very good evidence to back them up—that Chess did not originate in Persia or India, but rather in China. Still other researchers claim that Chess was invented by women of ancient times and that the game is actually one of fertility and procreation rather than battle and war.

We Are the Champions

The most famous living Chess player today is Garry Kasparov. He is currently the highest-rated Chess player in the world—otherwise known as the *Grandmaster*. Kasparov continues to play Chess with one of his latest opponents—the IBM computer chip known as "Deep Blue," reportedly the fastest microcomputer chip in the world to date. Kasparov also spends his time educating people about the game. In addition to starting a Web site dedicated to Chess education, he opened a Chess academy in Israel in 1997—a nonprofit association dedicated to worldwide Chess education.

Winning Plays

The hope of Garry Kasparov and many Chess education proponents is to integrate Chess as a regular subject in schools. Many schools that teach Chess use Kasparov's techniques, and his Web site and electronic game development have proven to be great assets to the teaching curricula. The theory behind Chess education is that it stimulates the growth of concentration, multidimensional thinking, discipline, focus, and responsibility.

American-born Bobby Fischer is another world-famous Chess champion. He became Grandmaster in 1972—the first American ever to win the world championship. He is considered by many to be the greatest Chess player of all time due to his astronomical IQ. Fischer became a recluse for 20 years because the International Chess Federation for championship competition did not accept his desire to change the way Chess was played. He reappeared to play a match against previous rival Boris Spassky in 1992. He won 10 games to Spassky's five.

Piece by Piece

In a standard Chess set, you usually have white and black playing pieces. Some fancier sets have dark and light colored pieces in all different shapes and sizes, but it's usually easy enough to identify who is who and which side is "black" or "white."

Here is a list of the different pieces and the moves they can make on the board:

The King: This piece is the most important piece and, ironically, one of the least powerful. The King can only move one square in any direction and usually doesn't journey too far into the board as a means of self-protection. But don't be fooled! The King is the key player in the game because when the King is captured, the game is over. The primary objective of Chess is to capture your opponent's King while keeping your own well-guarded.

Winning Plays

In the royal courts of Europe, human chessboards were not uncommon. The pieces were human beings dressed in costume to represent various Chess pieces. The game was played on a huge chessboard in a courtyard or lawn. The human pieces took their places on the board. Monarchs and courtiers called the moves and the "pieces" moved where they were told to go.

When your King is trapped and cannot avoid capture, your opponent calls "check-mate" and the game is complete. If your King is threatened with capture, your opponent calls "check" and you have to figure out how to move out of that position. A King cannot move into a "check" position, but if your opponent says "check," you must move out right away, and there are only three ways to accomplish this:

➤ Capture the piece that is threatening your King.

➤ Block the path between your opponent's threatening piece and your King. (Don't forget that Knights cannot be blocked.)

➤ Move the King away.

The Queen: Ah ... the Queen, your most valuable player. She is the most powerful piece on the board with her ability to move forward, backward, and diagonally for as many squares as you want her to go—as long as her path is not blocked. Watch out though ... if you lose this piece to your opponent, your offense and defense will be severely hindered.

The Rook: This is another very powerful piece due to its range of mobility. The Rook, often shaped like a castle, can move forward and backward along any row as long as no other piece is blocking its path. The Rook cannot, however, move diagonally.

The Bishop: This piece, like the Rook, is very powerful due to its range of motion. Unlike the Rook, the Bishop can move on a diagonal and can move as many spaces as needed, provided there is no other piece in its path.

The Knight: The value of the Knight usually applies to the early stages of the game. It is a powerful piece that moves in an L-shape on the board. The reason it is so powerful in the beginning of the game is because it can jump other pieces on a crowded board.

Pawns: These are the least powerful pieces due to their lack of mobility on the board. A Pawn can only move one square at a time (if its path is not blocked), except on the first play when it can move two squares forward. Pawns can only capture opposing pieces when moving on a diagonal, and even then this piece can only move one square at a time. If the Pawn manages to survive its way to the eighth row (because these pieces don't last on the board very long), it can promote itself to any other piece except the King. When a Pawn is promoted, it is then replaced by that piece, so it is possible to have more than one Queen, two Bishops, two Knights, or two Rooks on the board at the same time.

Setting Up

The first thing you need to do to play Chess is set up the board—that's half the battle as each piece has a specific place on the board. Make sure that in placing the board, the white corner squares are in the lower right-hand corner on both your and your opponent's sides.

The pieces should be placed on the board in the following way:

➤ First row closest to you from right to left—starting on the black corner square: Rook, Knight, Bishop, Queen, King, Bishop, Knight, Rook.

➤ On the second row place your Pawns. There should be eight Pawns on each square.

The starting positions on a chessboard.

From Antiques to Computer Games

Chess sets can be purchased at any retail toy and game store. They also come in travel sizes for long trips, and there are countless computerized versions on the market today. Some of the computer games are extremely challenging and fun. Even today's Grandmaster, Garry Kasparov, has his name on one of the computerized versions of the game. You can also play interactive Chess matches with anonymous opponents on the Internet or watch matches between other online players. It's a hugely popular game—and its popularity seems to grow on a daily basis.

The price of Chess sets vary from as little as fifty cents for miniature plastic sets to priceless sets found only in museums. There are sets made of precious stones played by kings and queens, and then there are the hokey sets that depict cartoon characters like the Simpsons.

Basic Moves and Rules

The rules of Chess are very strict and there isn't really any room for change, but there are ways you can lighten them up a little so they work better for you at home. There are the hard-line Chess players who will stick to tournament rules, so just be aware of whom you're playing with and how you both want to use the rules. You don't want to get into any arguments when the game is underway, so be clear with each other before the match begins.

For example, in professional tournaments, if you touch a piece that can be legally moved, you must move it. This rule is often ignored in casual games or home matches. When I played Chess, we usually used the rule that you can touch the piece, but you cannot move it and return it to its old position. If you move the piece, the play must be carried through. Be clear on these kinds of rules before the game begins. We don't want anyone getting riled up at the beginning of the game. That should come later, when your King is in check!

You may never move a piece into a square already occupied by another one of your pieces. However, you may move into your opponent's square by capturing one of his pieces.

Most plays begin by moving the Pawns. The Pawns advance upon each other in an effort to capture each other and make way for the advancement of other key pieces to make their moves.

These Chess moves will take some time getting to know.

Tournament Moves: Playing with the Pros

Here are some basic moves to get you started:

Castling: This is an important move because it affords the King the necessary protection and places the Rook in a position to do some serious battling. Castling is usually done early in the game and savvy players will do their best to prevent their opponent from castling their own King. This play is usually the first battle you'll experience in a game of Chess between two knowledgeable opponents. Castling occurs when you move your King two squares from one of your Rooks and then move that Rook to the opposite side of the King. You cannot use this maneuver if your King or your Rook has already made a first move. That is why this play is usually made near the beginning of the game. The King cannot castle out of or into check and there can be no other piece between the Rook and the King when castling.

En passant: The play *en passant,* which is French for "in passing," allows a player to capture an opponent's Pawn *en passant.* This is usually done to prevent a player from using the "two squares first" rule for Pawns. You don't want your opponent's pawns to pass you without a chance to capture. The play is made when your Pawn (the one that was passed) removes your opponent's Pawn (the one that moved two squares) from the board. This maneuver is optional and is useful if there's a reason you don't want your opponent's Pawn to move ahead of your own.

Check and Checkmate

If your King is trapped so it cannot move in any direction without capture, your opponent declares "checkmate" and you've lost the game. A King can never move into "check"—meaning it can never move onto a square where it can be captured by an opponent's piece. If a King is not in check, and no other move is possible, then the game is called a "stalemate" or a tie.

In casual games, it is common for one player to call "check" or "checkmate." In fact, I remember playing Chess games where if you didn't call it, the game is declared a tie.

But in tournament conditions, it is considered rude and illegal to speak aloud, let alone call out when your opponent's King is in jeopardy. Tournaments are usually played in a roomful of people, and if a player speaks aloud (especially to utter such a threatening word to the ears of other Chess players) he may be penalized by the Tournament Director. Calling "check" or "checkmate" is rude in the Chess world because it assumes that the other player isn't paying enough attention to notice that his or her King is in danger. The correct etiquette is to let your opponent discover the danger on his or her own.

If the player in check doesn't realize the danger and then proceeds to make an illegal move (for example, not moving the King out of danger), the opponent should point out that an illegal move was made and the player in check will usually realize what's happening.

The Tournament Director (TD) acts as a kind of referee. At home, when disputes arise, a third party can be called in to moderate. If you do call in a third party, make sure that person knows how to play the game.

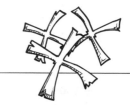

Three Strikes

In professional tournaments, there is no need for the one player to explain the rules to the other. If you've made it as far as a tournament, it's understood that you both know the rules. Explanations of rules can only be spoken aloud by the Tournament Director. If one player takes it upon himself to explain the rules, it is considered interference and he or she can be penalized.

Stalemate

Stalemates do not happen that often in Chess matches, but there are a few exceptions. Most matches will be played until the King is taken, but even the pros have been known to confront this rarity.

Here are a few examples of a game being declared a stalemate (or tie):

➤ If a King is not in check and no other move is possible

➤ If 50 moves are made without the advance of a Pawn

➤ If the same position (recurring plays) occurs three times

Let's Get Going

Now that you know the basic rules (and even some of the etiquette) of the game, you're ready for your first match. Find a worthy opponent (or maybe someone in the learning stages like you) and start making your moves. You will figure out strategies as the game moves along. All you need to know are the basic moves of the pieces, and you can get started.

If you're playing at home, you may want to go over the standard rules with your opponent just so that you're both clear on whether this is a casual or tournament-style game. It's probably best to play casually unless you have a third party on hand who can act as the TD. After the first move is made, each player must alternate turns. No turn can ever be skipped or passed.

High Score

Just remember: The white player in Chess always moves first. You can determine who is white and black by flipping a coin.

Chess Notation

If you decide you like the game enough and want to try and get really good at it, you should study up on game playing tactics. There are many of them. To do the necessary studying, you will have to know a little bit about Chess notation.

When studying the games, you will notice that all the plays are described in a coded language. One of the most popular forms of Chess notation is the Algebraic System. This system identifies each square on the chessboard by number and letter. Each column or file is labeled with a letter (ranging a to h from left to right) and each row is labeled with a number (going from one to eight up the rows when the white corner is on your bottom right). So you identify the players on the board according to where they sit in the grid. For example, at the start of the game, once the board is all set up, your Rooks sit on a1 and h1 accordingly. You will need to know this system if you want to study previous matches or follow matches played on the Internet. There are so many interactive Chess matches on the Web, and if you follow these games closely, you will eventually learn more about tactics. Notation can get very complicated, but here are some basic examples that will be helpful to you as you study:

Basic symbols in notation:

K King

Q Queen

R Rook

B Bishop

N Knight

+ check

++ checkmate

x capture (This symbol is often omitted when recording the capture of Pawns. For example, cxd5 means the Pawn on c4 captured the piece on d5. Sometimes this is shortened to cxd or even to just cd.)

High Score

Some suggestions to becoming a more advanced player can be found on many Web sites. One very good site I came across: www.chess.liveonthenet.com/ chess/beginner/lessons/tactics/ tactics.html

Checkers

Checkers is one of the first games I ever learned how to play. It is supposed to be lighthearted and fun, but there are some serious players out there who abide quite strictly to the rules of the game. Checkers (or "Draughts" as it is called in the United Kingdom) is played in many pubs and taverns throughout the world. It can be as serious or as silly a game as you want it to be. It is not as involved or as complicated as Chess, mainly because all the pieces on the board must abide by the same rules of movement—you can only go forward unless you're a King. In this section, you will find some of the fun and serious rules that govern this game. But in the end, it's all just fun.

The game of Checkers, as we know it today, is believed to date back to about 1400 B.C.E. But an even older relative of the game was found in the ruins of an ancient Iraqi city called "Ur" and is believed to date back as far as 3000 B.C.E. Checkers today is a two-person game. The object is to move one's pieces (round red and black disks often made of plastic or wood) across the checkered board. The goal is to jump the opponent's pieces, and remove them from the board, in an effort to win back one's players and remove every opposing piece from the board.

Checkers sets can be purchased at any retail toy and game store and come in a variety of sizes. There are standard boards, travel-sized, and computerized versions of the game.

The Board

The standard checkers board is the same as the chessboard. It's comprised of 64 squares of equal size and alternately colored light and dark (sometimes black and white, sometimes black and red). The board is set up the same way as the chessboard, with the light colored square in the bottom right corner facing you.

Piece by Piece

Checkers pieces are also light and dark in color. They are round disks made of plastic or wood in most store-bought games. The standard playing piece is about an inch in diameter, but the travel games have smaller, often magnetized pieces so they don't slip around when you're in a moving vehicle.

Setting Up

With the light-colored square in the lower-right corner facing you, place your playing pieces on the alternate black squares. You opponent should do the same. When the board is set up and ready to go, you should both have your Checkers on the first 12 squares of the board on both your sides. You should choose who gets to be black or white (or red, depending on the set you own) by flipping a coin or any other means agreeable to both players. Unlike Chess, black always goes first in Checkers.

It's in the Cards

A **capture** is a move made in Checkers where you "jump" your opponent's piece and remove it from the game board, thereby "capturing" the other side's checkers piece by piece.

Making the Moves

In Checkers the moves are made on diagonals, so the first player moves his black piece one square on the diagonal. The pieces can be moved in either direction provided there is a vacant black square.

There are very few ways to move the checkers across the board in the beginning of the game, but the game can really heat up once you've made it from one side of the board to the other. Here are some of the ways you can move your pieces during the course of the game.

Capturing

If your opponent's piece occupies one of the adjacent squares and there is a vacant square immediately behind it, then you can, and must, *capture* your opponent's piece. You can never move your piece onto an occupied square.

You can capture more than one piece at a time if there are vacant squares behind each of these pieces and you can make the jumps in one consecutive move. If you can make a capture, you must do so. However, if you have a choice of more than one capture, you don't have to choose the one that will capture the most pieces. You can choose whichever capture you want. But if you begin the capture, you must complete it. You can't decide halfway through the play that you want to stop or go back. You must capture all the pieces that are available for the taking in your move. You can only make captures in a forward direction unless your piece has been crowned.

A play is complete when you remove your hand from the playing piece.

Crowning

When a piece reaches the opposite extreme end of the board, that piece becomes a King. To recognize the King, the piece is "crowned" by the opponent with one of the captured pieces. So, for example, if you are red and your piece makes it to the opposite side of the board, your opponent (the player with the black pieces) must place a captured red piece on top of your piece—like a crown. When the player is crowned, the play is complete. That crowned piece cannot move until your opponent makes his or her play. Once a piece is crowned, it has the power to move backward and forward on the board, but like any other piece, the King must capture when the occasion arises.

When I was a kid we used to get very excited when we had the first piece to make it to the opposite end of the board. We shouted "King me! King me!" and clapped our hands in excitement. There was nothing like that little thrill of power, knowing that you now had the only piece on the board that could move in any direction. It became a little less novel when there were several Kings on the board from both sides, however. That's when you really had to concentrate.

Huff or Blow

Because a play is complete when you remove your hand from your piece, if you fail to capture all the pieces from the board that should have been captured, your opponent may remove the piece that should have done the capturing. This is called the "huff" or "blow" and is not considered the opponent's move. So be very careful not to "blow" it and be sure to think out your moves carefully before you remove your hand from your piece. One false move and you will not only have blown the move, but forfeited a potentially valuable piece. The opponent in this case also has the power to "huff," meaning that he can choose to let the piece stay on the board. Watch this maneuver—it may mean the opponent has a trick up his sleeve.

Don't Touch!

In most Checkers matches, played casually at home or on a car ride, many of the stricter rules are not really enforced. But there are some rules in Checkers that you should be aware of should you begin a match with a savvy opponent.

You may not touch any of the pieces on the board in an effort to arrange them on their squares. Sometimes the checkers move around on the board and there's a temptation to set them straight. The rules say that you cannot touch any piece out of turn unless you both agree to it. If one player touches a piece without a previous discussion, then the player may be required to forfeit the game.

When it is your turn and you touch your piece, you must play it or forfeit the game. When the piece is not playable, the game must be forfeited according to the rule on arranging the pieces on the board. Be very careful before you touch a piece! Your opponent may not know this rule, but because you know it now, you may want to discuss this and other rules with your opponent before you start to play. It all depends on how seriously you want to play the game.

Three Strikes

A player must move his piece within five minutes of his turn. If you can't move or can't decide on a move, you must forfeit the game due to improper play.

The Win

The game is won when you capture all your opponents' pieces or when you force him or her into a position of immobility.

A draw is declared when neither player can force a win and no other moves are possible.

The Least You Need to Know

➤ Chess and Checkers are games of strategy and skill that require concentration.

➤ The goal of Chess is to maneuver your pieces in an effort to remove your opponent's pieces and ultimately capture his or her King.

➤ While you're trying to win at Chess, you also have to strategize your defense and watch your opponent carefully.

➤ The goal of Checkers is to jump your opponent's pieces and remove them from the board.

➤ The two key moves in Checkers are capturing and crowning.

Chapter 6

More Table Games

In This Chapter

➤ All about Backgammon

➤ Pick-Up Sticks

➤ Xs and Os: mastering Tic-Tac-Toe

➤ Tiddlywinks!

Chess and Checkers aren't the only fun games of strategy to play around the house. As mentioned in Chapter 5, "Hands on the Table: Table Games," you can always break out the Backgammon set, some Pick-Up Sticks, or Tiddlywinks! Or, take out a pen and paper and start a game of Tic-Tac-Toe. It's always fun to see if you can beat the pants off a family member in that old-time classic.

In this chapter, we'll take a look at these ever-popular parlor games. We'll concentrate on the intricacies of Backgammon and how to score this often befuddling game.

Backgammon

Backgammon has many different historical derivatives. Games of its type were played in Ancient Egypt, Greece, and Rome, but the closest predecessor to the one we know today is a game called Nard or Tables which was probably brought to England by men returning from the Crusades. The game was hugely popular in the Middle Ages, but was replaced as the game of choice in about the fifteenth century by the game of Chess. Interestingly, Backgammon made a comeback around 1970 as a popular parlor game.

The game is basically a race between two armies moving around a track made up of 24 dagger-shaped divisions called "points." The board is divided down the middle by a partition called "the bar." The bar divides the two sides of the board into the outer and inner "tables." The inner table is also called the "home" table. The side nearest you is your outer and home tables while the other side is your opponent's inner and outer tables.

The object of the game is to move all your pieces onto the board and then to move them off the board. The first player to get all his or her pieces off the board first is the winner.

Winning Plays

Did you know that the name *backgammon* is derived either from the Welsh back-gammon (little-battle) or the Saxon "bac-gamen" (back-game)?

Picking Up the Pieces

The game consists of the following pieces of equipment:

➤ Backgammon board

➤ 30 round stones (similar to checkers), 15 of each color

➤ A pair of dice (one die is used by each player)

➤ A dice cup

➤ A doubling cube which is marked with the numbers 2, 4, 8, 16, 32, and 64. This cube is used to keep track of the number of units at stake in each game and to mark the player who last doubled.

Backgammon sets can be purchased at any toy or game store.

The Point of It All

The backgammon board may look a little unusual to you if you've never played before. The spaces on which you move are pointed stripes that look like elongated triangles. There are 12 pointed stripes on each board: 6 to each side of the board. Your "points" are on your side of the board and your opponent's on the other side. The bar does not count as a space. Although the points are not numbered on the board, the plays are often described with numbers to indicate the points. The points are numbered 1 through 24 with 1 being the point from which you begin play and 24 being the last (directly across from point 1). A move from your 10 point to a 6 point is 4 spaces (don't forget: the bar does not count as a space) but a move from your opponent's 12 point to your 12 point is only considered 1 space even though it crosses from his or her board to yours. These 2 points are considered to be next to each other even though they are on opposing sides of the board.

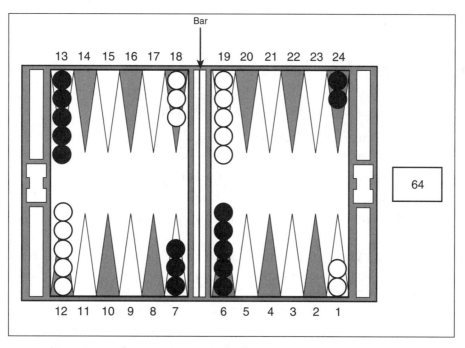

The starting positions on a backgammon table.

Getting Started

Each side has a set of pieces similar to checkers. The pieces are usually white and black. Each side has 5 pieces on his or her 6 point, 3 on his or her 8 point, 5 pieces on the opponent's 12 point and 2 pieces (called "runners") on the opponent's 1 point. The players advance in opposite directions from each other. The runner has to move along the entire track while the other pieces have shorter distances to travel.

The game begins with the roll of two dice. If you roll a 4 and a 2, you may move 1 piece 6 spaces or 1 piece 4 spaces and another 2 spaces. If you choose to move just 1 piece, you are actually making 2 moves with 1 piece.

It's in the Cards

A **doublet** is two thrown dice with the same number of dots on the upper face of the dice.

If the same number appears on both dice—for example, a 2 and a 2 or a 3 and 3—you can actually move your piece 4 spaces instead of 2. This is called a *doublets*. If you roll a 3 and a 3, for example, you can move up to 4 men, each move consisting of 3 spaces.

The players continue to roll the dice alternately throughout the game. A player can pass if no move is possible.

Language of the Game

There are some key words in the Backgammon vocabulary you will have to learn in order to become a savvy player. Here are just a few of them:

➤ **Points:** The triangular-tipped lines on the backgammon board on which you move your pieces.

➤ **Prime:** When a player has made 6 consecutive points.

➤ **Blots:** A single piece that is sitting on a single point.

➤ **Closed Board:** A player who has made all 6 points in his or her home board is said to have a "closed board."

➤ **Bearing off:** When a player has brought all his pieces into his home board, he or she can begin to bear-off, meaning you take your pieces off the board and they cannot be reentered in play. This is the goal of the game. The first person to bear off all his pieces is the winner.

➤ **Gammon:** If you bear off all your pieces before your opponent has removed one single piece of his or her own, you win a gammon—or double game.

➤ **Backgammon:** If you bear off all your pieces before your opponent bears off one single piece of his or her own and he or she still has pieces on your home board, you win a "backgammon," or a triple game.

➤ **Cocked dice:** You should always roll the dice on your home board. Both dice must come up flat in that board. If one die jumps the board or comes to rest in the other board, the dice are considered "cocked" and must be recast.

➤ **Doubling:** You can choose to double the stakes if you feel you have an advantage during the course of the game. You can do this at the start of your turn before you've rolled the dice. Your opponent may accept or refuse the double. If he or she accepts, he or she becomes the "owner of the cube," plays for the higher stakes, and may make the next double. If he or she refuses, he or she must concede the game. A doubling cube with the numbers 2, 4, 8, 16, 32, and 64 is used to keep track of the stakes. Subsequent doubles in the game are called "redoubles."

Scoring Points and Making Primes

You score by positioning 2 or more pieces on a single point, thus claiming that point. Your opponent cannot land on that point, nor can he or she touch down on it when using the combined total of his dice with 1 piece. This means if your opponent rolls a 4 and a 2, but uses 1 piece to move 6 spaces, he or she cannot complete that move if your piece is on the 4 point space, the 2 point space, or the 6 point space. The player who makes 6 consecutives points (spaces) has completed what is called a "prime."

Blots

A single piece on a single point is referred to as a "blot." If you move a piece onto your opponent's blot, or touch down on it during a move made on your total cast, you remove the "hit" blot from the board and place it on the bar.

High Score

Completing a prime is exactly what you want to do to keep your opponent at bay. Your opponent will be trapped behind the prime because he or she cannot move more than six spaces at a time—the highest number to appear on a die.

A piece that has been hit (and thus placed on the bar) must reenter on the opposing player's home board. The player cannot move any other piece until his piece on the board has been brought back into play. You reenter the game if there is a point available that is equal to the number rolled on the die. In other words, you can reenter if you roll a 2, provided there is not 2 or more of your opponent's pieces on the number 2 point at that time. If the number 2 point is occupied by a blot, you may take the blot's place and move your opponent's piece to the bar. If the point is not open, the player loses his turn. A point is not open if it has 2 or more pieces on it.

Closed Board

If you have made all 6 points on your home board you are said to have a "closed board." If, at this time, your opponent has any pieces left on the bar, he or she will not be able to reenter these pieces into play since there is no vacant spot to land on your home board. The opponent must therefore forfeit his or her turns until you have cleared a point on your board.

Bearing Off

Bearing off is the goal of the whole game. This process commences once you've brought all your pieces onto your home board. The player who bears off first is the winner. You cannot bear off if you have any pieces remaining on the bar or outside your home board.

If you've begun bearing off and your opponent hits one of your blots, you cannot continue to bear off until you reenter that piece onto your own home board. But remember: When you reenter you must do so on your opponent's home board, so you may have a long way to go before you can continue the bearing off process.

Bearing off is done in accordance with the number shown on the dice that you roll. In other words, you remove pieces from the points that correspond to the number on the dice. However, you do not have to remove a piece after you roll the dice; you may choose instead to move a piece inside your home board.

If you roll a number higher than the highest point on which you have a piece, you may apply that to your highest occupied point. For example, if you roll a 5 and a 3, but your 5 point is vacant, you can move the pieces on your 4 point instead.

Doubling

Each face of the doubling cube bears a number starting with 2 and doubling that 2 until 64. At the beginning of the game, the doubling cube sits on the bar and serves as a means to double the stakes. For example, if at any point during the game you feel you are far enough ahead, you may propose to your opponent that you want to double the stakes by turning the cube to a 2. You must do so, however, on your opponent's turn before he or she rolls the dice.

Your opponent can decline the offer to double, which means he or she forfeits the game and loses a point, or he can accept the double and the stakes increase by two units. The player who accepts the double now owns the cube and can redouble the stakes at any point during the game. The owner of the cube now has the advantage and the original doubler faces the same choice. If you are the original doubler, you can choose to decline the redouble and lose 2 points, or accept and play for 4, and then you'll own the cube again.

You can choose to double even if you're on the bar and your opponent has a closed board. Even though you can't roll the dice because you can't move, you still have the option to double.

An interesting note: Gammon doubles and backgammon triples the stake of the cube.

Pick-Up Sticks

This game was one of my favorites as a kid. We made up most of our own rules, though. We poured the sticks onto the floor and they were to stay where they fell. We usually used a coin-flip to determine who went first. You had to be very careful not to move any of the other sticks while attempting to lift the stick that you think will move, unhindered, the easiest. If you moved another stick, you had to forfeit your turn to your opponent. Sometimes it was best to forfeit your turn just to move a stick. The challenge comes when it's almost impossible to move one stick without moving several others.

You don't have to play until there are no more sticks left in the pile. If all players determine that no further moves are possible, then you count up your sticks. The person with the most is the winner.

Pick-Up Sticks was a game originally played by Native Americans using straws of wheat. The game was passed to the pioneers and is still played to this day by children all over North America. The object of the game is to pick up a stick from the pile without moving any of the other surrounding sticks. The person with the most sticks by the end of the game is the winner.

You can buy Pick-Up Sticks in most toy stores, but you might have fun making your own. You can use any lightweight stick—even twigs from outside. You can try doing what the Native Americans did and use pieces of straw. The pioneers made their own Pick-Up Sticks, often carving them into thin sticks from birch trees or other lightweight woods.

You should have at least 25 sticks to play the game. The sticks should be about 10 inches long.

Tic-Tac-Toe

The origins of Tic-Tac-Toe are a bit of a mystery. The earliest game that even slightly resembles our modern-day version was a game played by the ancient Romans called Terni Lapilli. This board game was found throughout the Roman Empire—scratched on walls and floors, but no Xs and Os markings were found accompanying the boards. Researchers have concluded that game pieces were probably used in place of Xs and Os, so it's hard to tell how closely related the games actually are.

The object of Tic-Tac-Toe is to outwit your opponent by marking three Xs and/or Os inside six connecting squares, either vertically, horizontally, or diagonally.

Tic-Tac-Toe is not a game for adults—they get bored very quickly because there's not much to it. But for kids this is a really great "first" game. Most kids don't think that the game is boring because it does require a small amount of strategy for beginners. It is a good game to introduce to kids before they move on to tougher strategy games like Checkers, Chess, and Backgammon.

Three Strikes

Tic-Tac-Toe has often been referred to as the "unwinnable" game because the only way to actually win is to hope that your opponent isn't paying close enough attention and misses their mark.

Tiddlywinks!

I don't know many people who didn't play Tiddlywinks in their youth. But I bet you didn't know that this game is actually taken quite seriously in some parts of the world. It is considered to be a game of skill, strategy, and luck. It has quite a popular following in the United States, England, and Scotland with its origins at universities like Cambridge and Oxford in England and MIT and Cornell in the United States.

The origin of Tiddlywinks is unknown. One researcher, Fred Shapiro, on a quest to seek some ancient derivative, found reference to an ancient Chinese game called "t'an ch'I," which appeared to be sort of Tiddlywinks game with the exception of one key factor: the *squidger*.

There is no evidence that this Chinese game had a squidger, and without a squidger, determines Shapiro, it just couldn't be Tiddlywinks. However, Shapiro did learn from a professor of Chinese at Cambridge University that in Chinese "ch'i" means chess and "t'an" means to snap, flick, or shoot down. But with all the possible English translations of Chinese, there's no way to be sure.

It's in the Cards

A **squidger** is a piece used to press down on smaller pieces in attempt to propel the smaller pieces forward.

Most people believe that Tiddlywinks was invented in England sometime in the early 1800s. My guess is that it started as a university drinking game similar to the games that college kids play today. Whatever its roots may be, the game is played today and has quite an elaborate set of varying rules and ardent followers.

The rules indicated here were established by The English Tiddlywinks Association.

Piece by Piece

These are the pieces in Tiddlywinks:

➤ **Winks:** Small round discs usually made of lightweight plastic.

➤ **Squidger:** A larger disc used to propel the smaller discs into a pot (to squidge is the act of propelling the discs with the squidger).

➤ **The pot:** The container into which the discs are to be squidged.

➤ **The mat:** The surface on which the game is played—it should have two lines drawn at either end to indicate the baselines and indicate the boundaries of the playing field. The mat is usually 6 feet by 3 feet. The mat should always be placed on a flat, smooth surface.

Let's Play

Your winks should come in four different colors: blue, green, red, and yellow. Blue and red always play as partners against green and yellow. Partners are located diagonally across from each other on opposite corners of the mat. When played in teams, each player has one partnership color, and in singles games, the two players use both colors. There are six winks in each color—two being smaller than the other four.

The "squidger" is used to play the winks. This squidger is larger and thicker than the other winks. The pot is placed on the center of the mat.

The object of the game is to get as many winks into the pot as possible. The game begins with a squidge-off, to see who can get his winks into or closest to the pot. If you get your wink closest to the pot, you are the winner of the squidge-off and you get to go first. The plays then continue in a clockwise motion.

All winks are played from behind the baseline. A play is made by placing the squidger on a wink and putting pressure on it to propel that wink forward. Sometimes a wink may wind up on top of another or directly below it on the mat, making it difficult to squidge. This is when the game gets a little trickier and the rules a little more difficult to decipher.

When a wink lands on top of a wink or too close to a wink, the wink on the bottom or directly below another wink is referred to as "squopped." It is even considered squopped if it is not touching the wink directly ahead of it. When this happens, according to the official rules, you can only touch the topmost wink in your color sequence, and a squopped wink can never be the first wink played in any sequence. This means that if all the unpotted winks are squopped, the game is complete. The score is calculated and a winner declared.

Potting Out

The official rules say that the game of Tiddlywinks should be timed, giving 25 minutes to pairs matches and 20 minutes for singles. The clock starts after the squidge-off and at the time of the first play. A game is over before the time limit when one color is completely squidged into the pot and the score is settled by potting-out. Potting-out means that the pot is emptied and points are scored based on its contents. The first color to pot-out receives 4 points; the second to do so receives 2 points; the third and remaining colors do not get any points. Partners' points are added up and 1 point from the losing side is given to the winners. At this time, all squopped winks can be unsquopped as long as they are kept at the same distance from the pot, leaving a distance of about two millimeters from one wink to the other.

The game can be continued until all winks are potted. Otherwise, the game is over when the clock says it's over. In this instance, each color has three "tiddlies" for each potted wink and one tiddly for each unsquopped wink. Unplayed winks do not count. The color with the greatest amount of tiddlies scores 4 points. The color with the second highest number of tiddlies scores 2 points. The third gets 1 point and the fourth does not get any points. Partners' scores are totaled and a winner is declared.

There are many variations to playing this game so you should be clear before you start as to which set of guidelines you will follow. You can even have a little fun making up your own rules. But one way or another, be sure to use the right words when referring to the pieces. They are fun words, after all, and you'll surprise your friends when you say "winks," "squidgers," and "tiddlies."

The Least You Need to Know

➤ The object of Backgammon is to first get all your pieces on the board and then to get them all off the board.

➤ Backgammon comes with its own language that is good to know if you are to be a savvy Backgammon player.

➤ You can create your own game of Pick-Up Sticks by using twigs from your own backyard or even Popsicle sticks.

➤ Tic-Tac-Toe is considered by many to be unwinnable unless your partner isn't paying attention, and may be suitable only for younger children.

Chapter 7

See Spot Run

In This Chapter

➤ Break out the dice or the dominoes

➤ Yahtzee is good family fun

➤ Play Poker Dice with older family members

What else can you do when you've decided to stay home and play some games with the family indoors? Why not break out the dice or the dominoes! There are many different dice games to choose from; however, we often don't think of playing with only the dice or the dominoes.

Dice are the ultimate symbols of chance in the gaming world. You take two small cubes in your hand or a cup, shake them, and let them fall where they may! Or, how about digging out that old box of dominoes? Playing Dominoes as a kid, for me, meant stacking them up and building towers, or lining them up in rows and watching them topple over ... the infamous "domino effect." I was quite surprised when I learned that the game of Dominoes is actually a chance game. There's much more to Dominoes than watching them fall into each other in a graceful flow!

In this chapter we'll take a look at different Dice and Domino games. It's amazing how much fun you can actually have with such little equipment! Some games described here will be for more mature audiences, but kids of any age can play Dice or Dominoes. Even if it is just stacking up those chips and watching them fall in a zigzagging pattern all through the living room.

Dice Games

There are countless games that use dice to determine plays, scores, moves, and, well, plain old luck. And we'll take a look at many of them here.

The history of dice is unclear, but we know that the use of dice as a betting device goes back at least to 3000 B.C.E. One of the earliest references to dice comes from Greek mythology where Zeus, Poseidon, and Hades tossed "lots" to divide the universe. According to researchers, "tossing lots" most likely refers to an ancient form of dice called "astragal," rectangular cubes with rounded edges made from sheep bone. The sides of the astragal were decorated with symbols similar to the dice we roll today. Dice are also referenced in ancient Egyptian writings, and we know that the Romans played a dice game, similar to Craps, called "Ten."

High Score

There are 36 number combinations that can be rolled from a pair of dice. The combination totals range from 2 to 12. Each die has spots that represent numbers 1 through 6.

It's in the Cards

The official word for the "spots" on the dice is **pips.**

Let's Play Yahtzee!

Yahtzee was invented by a wealthy Canadian couple in the 1950s. When friends were invited aboard their yacht, they were often called upon to engage in a few rounds of the dice-based game. At the time, they called it "the yacht game." Their friends enjoyed the game so much that they wanted copies of their own, so the couple decided to seek a manufacturer. Today, Yahtzee is manufactured by Milton Bradley and is available in any toy and game store.

Here's what the game consists of and the dice configurations you need to roll. It's really quite simple.

How to Play

Yahtzee is a game played with five dice. Each player has a scorecard and a pencil and takes turns rolling the dice up to three times. On the first roll, all five dice must be rolled, but on each subsequent roll, any number of dice may be rolled. The dice that are not rolled are placed aside facing up with the last numbers rolled and recorded.

The object of the game is to create the highest scoring configuration using five dice. At the end of each play, each player scores his or her points on a scorecard. The person with the most configurations and points wins the game. Each configuration may only be recorded once on the score sheet (with the exception of Yahtzee). If the player does not roll a remaining configuration, a zero should be entered in the configuration of choice.

You can play without purchasing the product from Milton Bradley, but it is nice to have the whole game ready to go in one box.

The Scorecard

The scorecard should be divided into fields. At the top of the card, you should have fields one through six. You can enter a roll of the dice in one of these fields by adding up the faces of all dice containing that number. For example, if the dice rolled show 1, 2, 2, 3, 5, you can enter a 1 on the "ones" field, a 4 in the "twos" field, a 3 in the "threes" field, and a 5 in the "fives" field.

The rest of the fields are as follows:

➤ **Three of a kind:** Three dice are rolled with the same number on them. The sum of all dice may be entered in this field.

➤ **Four of a kind:** Four dice are rolled with the same number on them. The sum of all dice may be entered in this field.

➤ **Full house:** This roll consists of three of a kind and two of a kind. The score for this field is 25 points.

➤ **Straight:** A sequence of four numbers is rolled: 1 though 4, 2 through 5, or 3 through 6. The score for this roll is 30 points.

➤ **Large straight:** A sequence of five numbers is rolled: 1 though 5, 2 through 6. This roll scores 40 points.

➤ **Yahtzee:** All dice rolled have the same number facing up. "Yahtzee" is the only roll that can be recorded more than once. The first player to roll Yahtzee scores 50 points. Any Yahtzee's rolled after the first, by any player, will score 100 points. Yahtzee can also be recorded as another roll elsewhere on the scorecard if it's beneficial to do so.

➤ **Chance:** The sum of all dice regardless of what they read. You can use your Chance field when you don't roll any other configuration.

Let 'Em Roll: Poker Dice and More

The game of Poker Dice is not unlike the standard 52-card Poker game except that it's played with dice instead of cards. The dice look like regular dice only instead of spots on the face of the cubes, you will find markings representing playing cards: Ace, King, Queen, Jack, 10, and 9.

High Score

You can play Poker Dice by using regular dice: just make one the Ace and the rest of the numbers (2=6) the face cards (2=9, 3=10, 4=Jack, 5=Queen, 6=King).

It's in the Cards

The **doubter** (or **caller**) is the person in a game of chance, such as Liar Dice, who calls the bluff of another player.

It's in the Cards

The **boneyard** is the draw pile in a game of Dominoes. Players pull from the boneyard when they can't play any of the tiles in their hand.

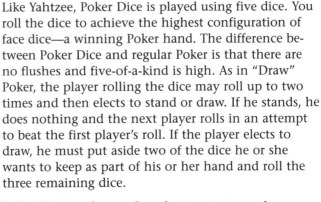

Like Yahtzee, Poker Dice is played using five dice. You roll the dice to achieve the highest configuration of face dice—a winning Poker hand. The difference between Poker Dice and regular Poker is that there are no flushes and five-of-a-kind is high. As in "Draw" Poker, the player rolling the dice may roll up to two times and then elects to stand or draw. If he stands, he does nothing and the next player rolls in an attempt to beat the first player's roll. If the player elects to draw, he must put aside two of the dice he or she wants to keep as part of his or her hand and roll the three remaining dice.

Poker Dice can be purchased at toy stores and gambling supply stores. It is very inexpensive to buy.

Other Dice Games

Here are a few other dice games (mainly versions of Poker Dice) you can try:

➤ **Horses:** This is a version of Poker Dice, only in this version if a player rolls five Aces, he loses.

➤ **Liar Dice:** This game must have been designed with "the cheater" in mind. In this version of Poker Dice, the art is in the bluff. In this game, you roll the dice and hide the dice from your opponents and then announce your roll. You can either tell the truth or bluff.

It is up to the next player (otherwise known as the *caller* or *doubter*) to call the bluff or take you at your word. If the doubter decides to take your roll as the truth, he or she must roll the dice and try to beat your roll. If the caller is correct, he or she wins. If he is incorrect, you win.

Dominoes

Dominoes is played the world over and there are many different versions of the game. The game is divided into two categories: draw games and block games. Draw games allow players to pull from the *boneyard* (or draw pile) when they cannot play any of the tiles (domino pieces) in their hand. In block games there is no boneyard to draw from and you have to work with the tiles you're dealt.

Dominoes are long, usually black, tiles with white spots on them. Some sets are made of natural wood with black inset spots, and even older sets are made of ebony with ivory inset spots.

When I lived in England, I visited a local pub and made the fatal error of sitting on a bench along the back wall to admire a glassed-in display of domino sets. What I didn't know was that I had just sat in the seat where a local has sat for over 30 years playing the game of Dominoes with whomever cared to join in the action.

No one else had sat in that seat for 30 years because it was Joe's seat, and, apparently, his lucky charm. It felt as though all eyes were upon me as I moved out of the way and Joe took his seat—his luck, or lack thereof, was now on my shoulders. Joe won and he bought me a pint of lager to celebrate. Although I lucked out that time, it taught me to never mess with a serious Domino player!

Winning Plays

Believed to be a derivative of Dice, the game of Dominoes probably has its roots in ancient China. The oldest set of dominoes has been dated as far back as C.E 1120. The word "dominoe" is French for the black and white hood of a priest's cloak, so that's possibly where the name derives. Dominoes migrated to Europe in the eighteenth century and the game changed as it was adapted from Chinese to European culture. North American Eskimos also play a tile game similar to Dominoes, so some researchers ponder that Dominoes may go as far back as the early land-migration from Asia to North America.

Here is a glance at some helpful definitions and terms you will need to know when you sit down to play a round of Dominoes:

➤ **Tiles:** The playing pieces. Even though we often hear the pieces themselves referred to as "dominoes," technically, this is not correct. The pieces are called "tiles," "bones," or "stones."

➤ **Blank:** An end piece that contains no spots (pips).

➤ **Double:** A tile that has the same number of spots on the bottom as it does on the top.

➤ **Double Sixes:** The highest-ranking tile in a 28-tile set as well as the name of the set itself.

➤ **Double Nines:** The highest-ranking tile in a 55-tile set. Also the name of the set itself.

➤ **Double Twelves:** The highest-ranking tile in a 91-tile set. Also the name of the set itself.

➤ **Shuffle:** To mix-up the tiles face down on a table.

➤ **Draw:** Picking your "hand" of tiles from a pile.

➤ **Draw Pile** (also known as "bone pile" or "boneyard"): The leftover tiles that are still facing down on the table after everyone has drawn their hand. The boneyard is used in draw games. You draw from the boneyard when you have no other tiles in your hand to play.

➤ **Heavier:** A tile with more spots on it than another tile is said to be "heavier" than the other tile.

➤ **Lighter:** A tile with fewer spots on it than another tile is said to be "lighter" than the other tile.

➤ **Block Games:** The object of these types of Dominoes games is to play all your tiles while preventing your opponents from playing any of theirs.

➤ **Point Games:** Similar to block games only you score points as you lay your tiles.

➤ **Match Games:** These types of games are similar to Rummy card-playing games. The object is to set aside sets of tiles and score points for the sets once all the tiles have been laid.

Here are some of the many Dominoes game versions you can play. I'm not sure which version was Joe's game of choice, but I'm sure he knew them all.

The Draw Game

The object of this basic game is to score 100 points. That is the standard score that players aim for, but if you're looking to play a shorter match, you can make the win a 50-point score. You should decide how many points you're going to play for before the game begins.

The Draw Game is designed for two to four players and is often played with a 0–6 set. Some sets contain tiles that have spots that go higher than six, and many people prefer a larger set for more of a challenge. If you're playing with a larger set, the structure of the game alters. For example, if you use the 0–6 set, you will play the game in a straight line, leaving two open ends at all times. If you play with a 0–9 set, the tiles are added to both long and short sides of the first tile—giving four open sides at all times. With the 0–12 set, tiles are added to all four sides and four corners of the first middle—leaving eight open sides at all times.

Getting Started

The game begins with the shuffle of the tiles. Place all the tiles face down (so you cannot see the spots) and mix them up. Each player should draw seven tiles when playing with two people and five tiles when playing with three to four people. The remaining tiles stay face down in the middle of the table as the boneyard (draw pile). The number of tiles drawn varies all over the world.

The tiles drawn by the players should be kept secret. You can place your dominoes in front of you, on their sides, with their spots facing you and their backs facing your opponents. The play begins after the draw. To start the ball rolling, after the tiles are drawn, one person (you can decide in advance who this will be) asks if anyone has double sixes. If someone has double sixes, he or she places the tile face up in the center of the table, thus commencing the game. This play is called "setting the highest domino."

The following plays continue to the left of the player who sets the first tile. If no one has double sixes, the caller then asks who has double fives, then double fours, until zero. The caller continues to ask until the highest tile is found and set. If no one has a double, then the tiles are returned to the pile, reshuffled, redrawn, and you start again.

The Plays

The dominoes are placed according to matches. For example, if a double five is placed as a first tile, the next tile placed must have five spots on it to match the original tile. On the same tile as this newly set five tile there will be another set of spots in the other section of the tile—this becomes the new number to match. So let's say the other number on the newly placed five tile is a two, then the next player must match the two and so on. The game is always double-ended, meaning there are always two sides to which you can match a tile.

If you cannot match a tile, you must draw from the boneyard until you find a matching tile—even if this means picking up every tile in the boneyard.

You cannot play a tile until both sides of the initial tile have been matched.

Let's Go Domino

When you place your last tile, it's referred to as "going domino," which signals the end of the game and means it's time to add up the points. When no more tiles can be placed and every player has to pass, the game is over and points are tallied. The person who has no tiles left scores points by adding-up the number of spots on all remaining tiles in the hands of the other players. If the game ends due to everyone being forced to pass, then the player with least number of spots on his or her remaining tiles collects the points.

Rules to remember in this draw game:

➤ Doubles are always played crosswise as opposed to lengthwise.

➤ Tiles may be pulled from the boneyard even if a player is able to set a tile. The strategy behind this is that you may want to save a valuable tile for a later play—but be careful that you rid yourself of these tiles or you won't stand a chance of "going domino."

➤ In this game you may play the long and short sides of the domino.

The Block Game

Block games differ from draw games in that all the tiles are distributed to the players so that there is no draw pile. Like draw games, most block games are designed for two to four players and are usually played with the 0-6 set of tiles. You can also play to the score of 100 or cut the game short at 50 points. Just make sure everyone is clear, in advance, what score you're playing to.

How to Start

The tiles are shuffled face-down as usual. Each player pulls his or her tiles from the boneyard.

The tiles should be distributed as follows:

2 players = 6 tiles

3 players = 5 tiles

4 players = 4 tiles

In other words, eight tiles minus the number of players are distributed. The rest of the tiles go to the boneyard and are never used. Other rules say (Hoyle's) that the deal should be seven tiles for two players and five tiles for three or four players. It's up to you how many tiles you decide should be in a hand; the trick to this game is in the absence of the boneyard.

The Rules

The rules are pretty much identical to the draw game only this time there is no boneyard to fall back on. The bones must be matched to a free end and the plays are made lengthwise so the game always has two open ends. Players who cannot set a tile must pass. Doubles are, as always, played crosswise.

The point scoring system is also the same in the block game: The game goes on until someone "dominoes" or everyone has passed their turn and no more plays are possible. The points are scored based on who has the least spots in his or her hand. If someone dominoes, he or she is automatically the point-earner.

The Domino Effect

What kid with a set of dominoes hasn't dreamed of building the highest tower or the world's longest "tipable" line? In fact, that's all I thought dominoes were good for in my younger years. I had a set of dominoes, but I never played any of the games. It's not just kids who imagine the magic of building with dominoes; everyday someone builds some amazing creation hoping to beat the latest existing world record.

It's in the Cards

The term **domino effect** comes from the idea that one action can cause a whole series of actions. For example, a little white lie can turn into bigger and bigger lies if you're not careful, or a tornado can cause a fire that can burn a house and evict a family. It's a metaphor for a chain reaction. But the domino effect is also a literal placing of dominoes in a line—tip one, and the rest will fall, too.

There are world records set for the tallest domino towers and the builders are very serious about their "art." There are also worldwide tournaments and championships for the tallest, longest, most imaginative pieces of domino architecture.

For years advertisers have used dominoes to market products by building logos out of colorful dominoes that, when toppled, spell out a phrase or other marketable slogan to sell the product. There's nothing more mesmerizing than watching the line of dominoes topple over—one after the other—and advertisers have jumped on the bandwagon in an effort to find yet one more way to captivate an audience and sell a product.

There are companies that do nothing but set up dominoes for movies, trade shows, and advertising agencies. These are the professional tippers! One company even set up an around-the-world topple once. The topple spanned six different continents and the first topple was linked to the second and so on. The first group on one continent tipped their dominoes and when the last domino fell in that group, the next group on another continent began to tip theirs … and so on until all the tiles had fallen.

The current world record for a successful and complete domino tipping, as of this writing, dates back to August 1998 when one group of people in the Netherlands erected 1.6 million dominoes only to tip one and watch the whole thing fall to the ground. A long set-up for a short-lived thrill.

The most ambitious attempt at setting the record was another group of people who set up 2.25 million dominoes, equal to 40 miles when laid in a straight line. They used multicolors and the tiles were distributed to over 75 projects. They set up eight images to represent past, present, and future. But this undertaking, which took 10 weeks to set up, failed. The dominoes did not fall continuously as the project organizers had hoped. These competitions are set up to very detailed specifications.

The Least You Need to Know

➤ You don't need a lot of equipment for a fun night at home—just break out the dice or the dominoes.

➤ You can play Yahtzee at home without purchasing the game at a store: Use your own dice!

➤ There are other fun Dice games, such as Poker Dice, Liar Dice, and Horses.

➤ There are two kinds of Dominoes games: draw games and block games. Draw games allow players to pull from the draw pile, but in block games there is no pile to draw from and you have to work with the tiles you're dealt.

Chapter 8

Bull's-Eye!

In This Chapter

➤ Discovering the language of Darts

➤ Understanding the board and setting it up

➤ Learning the rules for Darts

➤ Exploring various games of Darts

Darts is historically a British game. With its origins dating back to the Middle Ages, it is said that soldiers shortened spears and arrows fashioning them into darts, and used tree trunks—their natural rings made perfect markers for scoring purposes—and keg bottoms as their targets. They tossed these mini-spears to wile away their idle hours—inventing point combinations to keep the competition lively. In colder weather, the game moved indoors.

Fortunately for us, we no longer have to fashion our targets from trees in our back-yards (although that could be fun!). There are plenty of beautiful dart sets at our local sporting goods stores. In this chapter, you'll learn about the proper way to hang a dartboard, what those markings on the board are all about, the rules for Darts, and different types of games you can play.

Learning the Lingo

In most games, you have to know the lingo in order to play. But in Darts, you should learn the lingo just because some of the language—true to British form—is just plain fun. Some of the terms have a rich history, while others seem to have just come out of the nature of the game. You'll have fun using the jargon and teaching it to your teammates.

If you go pro, you'll be able to play with the best of them when you can throw some of these terms around. You may have to do some memorizing, or if you start playing the game, listen to the other players and see if they are using the jargon. You'll pick up on it as soon as the darts start flying.

Here's a primer on the lingo used in Darts:

➤ **Annie's Room:** Number 1.

➤ **Arrows:** Another term for darts.

➤ **Baby Ton:** The score of 95 (usually achieved by scoring five 19s).

➤ **Bag O' Nuts:** The score of 45.

➤ **Barrel:** The part of the dart right behind the point (the part you grip).

➤ **Basement:** Double-3.

➤ **Breakfast:** This Dart slang word has an interesting history. "Breakfast" comes from a bed and breakfast price of 26 pence. The Dart term means a single-5, single-20, single-1 (adding up to a total of 26). This is used in the game "x01."

➤ **Bucket of Nails:** Hitting all three darts in the 1s.

➤ **Buckshot:** When your darts land all over the board.

➤ **Bust:** Hitting over the required score in the game of "x01"—the darts don't count.

➤ **C:** Term used in the Dart game Cricket—Refers to high scores based on the number of darts scored. Example: Triple-20, single-20, single-20 would be called "C5" because five scores were made with three darts.

➤ **Chucker:** A player who doesn't aim at the board, just throws wildly without care.

➤ **Circle It:** Player scores a single digit (under 10) with three darts. This player's teammates would shout "circle it" to emphasize the disastrous throw.

➤ **Clock:** The dartboard.

➤ **Cork:** Center of the board. Again, a little interesting history on this term: The bottoms of kegs (which were made of cork) were used as targets in the early days of Darts.

➤ **Diddle for Middle:** A term for the opening throws to see who gets to shoot first in the game. The goal of the first throw is to hit the bull's-eye in the middle of the board. The person who hits closest goes first.

➤ **Double:** On a dartboard you will see several metal rings that wrap around the board. The thin outer ring on the board counts for twice the number hit or a "double."

➤ **Double In:** Term used when a double is needed to start the game.

➤ **Double Out:** Term used when a double is needed to win the game.

➤ **Double Top:** Double-20

➤ **Double Trouble:** When a player is unable to "double out."

➤ **Downstairs:** The lower portion of the board. A term normally used in the game of "x01" to refer to the 19s.

➤ **Easy In:** A term meaning that no special shot is needed to begin scoring.

➤ **Feathers:** The wings at the end of the dart also known as "flights." The term "feathers" also refers to the number 33.

➤ **Half-a-Crown:** Score of single-5, single-20, single-1 (in the game of "x01").

➤ **Hat Trick:** Three bull's-eyes.

➤ **The Throw Line:** The line behind which you throw the darts. Also referred to as the "Toe" line or "Hockey." The term hockey has an interesting lore: It is believed that the distance from the throw line to the dartboard was measured using crates from a brewery called "Hockey and Sons." The crates were three feet long and three crates were used, making the distance from the line to the board a total of nine feet. Eventually, the Hockey crates were reduced to two feet and four were used—for a total of eight feet, which is today's standard playing distance (with a few exceptions).

➤ **Island:** The playable area on the dartboard (inside the doubles ring). If you miss this area, someone might say you're "off the island."

➤ **Leg:** Used in terms of a Darts match—the "leg" is one game in the match.

➤ **Mad House:** Used in game "x01" in reference to double-one. It can drive you mad trying to hit it.

➤ **Monger:** A person who scores more points than needed to win the game—usually a deliberate maneuver.

➤ **Mugs Away:** This is used when the loser of the previous game goes first in the next game.

➤ **Murphy:** Again, a term used in the game "x01" to refer to the score of single-5, single-20, single-1—based on "Murphy's Law" (whatever can go wrong, will go wrong).

➤ **Popcorn:** Darts that land so close together that they knock each other off.

➤ **Right Church, Wrong Pew** or **Right House, Wrong Bed:** When you hit a double or a triple, but not the right number on the board.

➤ **Robin Hood:** When you shoot a dart into the shaft of another dart.

➤ **Shaft:** The part behind the barrel of the dart when the darts are mounted.

➤ **Shanghai:** Single, double, and triple in the same number (in some games, this score is an automatic win). This is also the name of a particular Dart game.

➤ **Shut Out** or **Skunked:** When you lose a game without ever scoring.

➤ **Slop** or **Splash:** Darts that land and score, but not where you intended them.

➤ **Spider:** The metal ring that wraps around a dartboard resembling a sort of spider web.

➤ **Straight In:** A game that does not require a special shot to begin.

➤ **Three in a Bed:** Term used when you throw three darts in the same number.

➤ **Ton:** In the game of "x01" the score of 100. Scores over 100 would be referred to as a ton-ten (110) or a ton-twenty (120), and so on.

➤ **Triple:** Thin inner ring on the dartboard—usually counts for three times the number hit.

➤ **Upstairs:** Upper portion of dartboard. Usually used in reference to the 20s.

➤ **Wire:** Darts that land on the other side of the spider—just missing where you aimed.

➤ **X:** A double-1 out.

So now that you know how to speak like one of the pros, let's learn how to play.

Winning Plays

Professional dartboards are made of sisal (a strong and durable white fiber). The fibers are compressed to make a nice, stiff, woven surface and then the material is bonded to a backboard. The surface is sanded to a smooth finish and printed with the appropriate colors. The wires are then stapled on and the numbers are attached with clips. Most dartboards are made in England, but the highest-quality brand is Puma, which is made in New Zealand. The darts themselves are made of a heavy metal—usually steel or brass.

The Playing Area

Where you set up your dartboard is of utmost importance. The dartboard should be placed on a wall that doesn't have anything else around it and where you don't mind if it gets banged up a bit (a dart can fly at least eight feet in any direction if it doesn't hit the board).

The Proper Surroundings

You have to be very careful where you decide to put the board if you plan to play in your home. You don't want it to be in a place that is heavily trafficked because darts are made of metal and are extremely dangerous if they hit anything but that board. You might want to consider hanging a scoreboard on the same wall as the dartboard.

Another important factor is the floor on which you will stand while playing the game. Darts can damage wood and linoleum surfaces. If you play on carpet, be prepared for a lot of wear-and-tear. Concrete, tile, and other hard surfaces can damage the darts. So what kind of flooring should you use?

The best thing to do is to buy a dart mat. You can buy these from sporting goods stores or specialty shops that sell darts and dart supplies. These mats are rubberized and darts will bounce lightly off their surface. This is the best route to go if you plan to play the game often. Leave ample space for spectators also—there's always some that won't be playing, but will enjoy watching the match.

You'll also need proper lighting to play Darts. Not only do you want to be able to see the board to make your best shot, but you'll also want to be able to read the board once your dart hits it. The best way to light the board is to hang two lights on either side of it—one on the left and the other on the right. If you don't like this look, try hanging one of those tiny "piano lights" over it—the same kind of light that people use to light paintings. That won't be too unsightly and should provide adequate light for visibility and practicality.

Three Strikes

The scoreboard should be the only thing near the dartboard on the same wall. But *please* don't throw any darts until the person marking in the scores is out of range!

High Score

If you don't have any place to hang a board, don't compromise safety—leave the kids at home and go to a local pub or bar and play the game there. You'll have just as much fun and you might even be able to get involved in a few matches and eventually join a local team.

Hanging the Board

Get out your tape measure because hanging the board is pretty specific business. The board must be hung five feet, eight inches from the floor to the center of the dartboard.

Dartboards are designed so that they hang from the *bull's-eye,* so measuring the required height is really pretty easy to do. But if you do wind up with a board that hangs from the top, you should measure the distance from the center of the bull's-eye to the hanger and add that to the height.

Marking the Throw Line

The throw line or "hockey" should be three feet wide and it may be drawn with anything you want depending on what surface you are playing on. Many people just stick a piece of tape to the ground. Specialty stores may have a throw line sticker that you can paste to the floor. The throw line should be placed seven feet and nine-and-three-quarter inches from the face of the board when playing with steel-tipped darts. With soft-tipped darts, the throw line should be eight feet from the board.

Understanding the Board

When you look at the dartboard, it may seem a bit confusing at first, but it's really pretty simple. There are numbers around the board and metal rings. There's an outer ring, a middle ring, and an inside ring. The goal is to throw your darts in the number and ring corresponding with the amount of points you need to score in a given game. The outer ring is made up of single points, the middle ring doubles your points, the inner ring triples your points, and the center is the bull's-eye. Which game you are playing and how many points you require to win the game determines where you aim your darts.

Let's Play Darts: The General Rules

There are some basic, general rules for playing Darts that exist for most games. Before you start playing, though, be sure to check with the other players on the rules you're going to stick to. Darts is played differently all over the world and you'll be amazed by some of the new rules you'll learn from other players. Don't be surprised if you find yourself making up some new games from all the varying rules you encounter. Just be sure you're all on the same page before you begin playing.

Darts is usually started with the "diddle for middle," where each player throws a dart to determine who goes first. The goal is to hit the bull's-eye, but if no one manages that on the first throw, then the player who throws closest to the bull's-eye will be the player, or team, to go first in the game. If the first player hits the bull's-eye, the second player has the option to remove that first dart in order to try and hit the same mark. But if the second player hits the bull's-eye without removing that first dart, he or she automatically wins the throw. If the dart is removed, then a tie is declared and throwing begins again in reverse order.

The winner of the throw gets to choose which Dart game will be played.

If you are playing in teams, the team that wins the initial dart throw goes first. The teams then alternate.

The teams alternate turns and players. Be careful not to throw out of turn, because you may forfeit the game—or at least your turn. It depends on how strictly you want to enforce the general rules.

Each player throws three darts per turn.

You cannot step over the throw line when it's your turn or your darts will be voided and you will lose your turn to the opposing team. You can lean as far over the line as you want, but don't let your foot cross over.

High Score

You might want to designate numbers to each player so you know who is up at the throw line at a given time.

If your dart is knocked out of the board, even if it sticks at first and then falls out, the dart does not count and may not be thrown again. You can go up to the board and catch a dart before it falls out but only if all the darts in that round have been thrown.

Be careful not to pull your darts from the board (or let another player pull your darts from the board) before the score for that round has been agreed upon and marked on the scoreboard. If you pull the darts before the score is marked, you might lose your points.

Scoring is sometimes the trickiest part of any Dart match. You want to make sure you choose a reliable scorekeeper and one that is not on either team. That will help when making some tricky scoring decisions. It's good to have an impartial party involved.

There are several different Dart games you can choose to play. Here are just a few.

x01

The name of this game is pronounced "x-oh-one," and it is one of the easiest games to play and a good one for beginners. The rules are pretty simple and allow new players to develop their throwing skills without having to worry too much about complicated rules and scoring.

The Object

The object of the game is to score a zero. It sounds a little strange to play a game where your object is to lose points, but that's the name of the game here. The game starts with a score of 301, 401, 501, 601, or 1,001 points—it's up to you what point value you decide to start with. The goal is to subtract the total of your darts thrown from any of those values, until you eventually get down to zero.

You can start the game by throwing either a double-in or a single-in (see the lingo list for the details on these terms). You can also play using double-out or straight-out. It's up to you and the preferences of the other players. Usually, people don't play this game with a straight-out; playing a straight-out is rather uneventful. It's much more challenging to play a double-out. Games 301 and 601 are usually played as double-in/double-out while 401, 501, and 1,001 are played straight-in/double out.

Scoring

The score that you agree to start with, let's say "301," is written at the top center of the scoreboard before the game begins. A vertical line should be drawn down the center of the board and underneath the "301" the letters "DD" or "SD" should be indicated to show the agreed upon start and finish rules. DD: double-in/double-out and SD: single-in/double-out. After each round (throw of three darts per player) the total points from that round is written on the board along with the remaining score on that player's side of the board.

The score of 100 is called "Ton" and is written as a "T" on the scoreboard. Scores over 100, are a "Ton" plus the extra score. For example, a score of 120 is a "ton-twenty" and is written on the board as "$_2T_0$."

Winning Plays

Pubs in the United Kingdom often measure eight feet or eight feet six inches from the board when using steel-tipped darts. Sounds like they must really know their darts if they need that extra foot or so.

The initials of each player are marked in vertical columns on the scoreboard with the winner of the initial throw written on the left.

So, as you can see, scoring does require one's undivided attention, and it's best to have someone dedicated to that job alone. If you don't have someone, it's okay to use one of the team players, but make sure it's just one person and that that person speaks the scoreboard lingo; otherwise, you could wind up with a muddled board and you'll never know who won the game.

Getting Started

You start the game with the usual round of "diddle for middle." Each player throws a dart in an effort to hit the bull's-eye and go first. You've already read the rules for this procedure, so your next step is to start playing the game!

If the game is called a straight-in game, the person who threw the winning opening dart goes first. The goal is to score as many possible points with your first three throws (the opening round). Each dart is scored by the number it hits on the board. If you hit in the outer ring, the score is the face value of the number. If your dart hits the middle ring, your score doubles the value of the number you hit, and if you hit within the inner circle, your score triples. The highest possible score in one round is 180 or three triple-20s.

If the game is called a double-in, then the first player to throw the darts must score a double in order to start the game. If you are the first player up and you hit any number in the double ring area, you will have officially started the game, and the scores add up from there. If you don't hit a double, then the play goes to the player number one on team two and that thrower tries to hit a double. This keeps going until someone hits a double and the game can commence.

If player number one hits a single, then a double, and then another single, the first single doesn't count toward the points. The second throw—the double—does count, as does the third dart thrown. The opening round is the only round that requires the players to hit a double. After the first double is hit, all other scores are valid.

Getting Out

Because you are scoring backward in x01, meaning subtracting points from the initial score, you will have to begin to think how to strategize your out. Expert players don't have much of a problem hitting exact numbers to get out. They probably start rounding out when they get to about 160, but if you're a novice, you may want to figure your out when you get down to about 40. You won't have to be as precise with the numbers you hit.

If you're playing straight-out, you'll be able to hit single numbers to get to zero, but if you're playing double-out, you'll have to be a little more precise with your throws. With a double-out in this game you will have to throw a double to get to exactly zero, in order to get out of, and win, the game.

Double-out example:

Let's say you are at 32, you will need to hit a double-16 in order to end the game. If you don't hit a double-16, but hit a single-8 instead, you now have 24 points. If you score 23 points with your remaining two darts, you have busted, because you will only have 1 point left and there's no way to throw half of one. If you "bust," none of your darts counts for that round and you pass your turn to the next player. You also bust if you score less than zero, or exactly zero if you hit zero but your last dart was not a double.

The only way to bust in a straight-out game is if you wind up with less than zero as your total score.

There are many strategies for getting out of the x01 double-out games. There are actually scoring charts that show you what you need to throw to win the game. These scoring charts can be located online or through a sporting goods supply store. You may even be able to find these charts in local bookstores. Experts use these charts, so don't be too bothered if you can't understand the charts right away. The longer you play, the easier it will be to catch on to some of the scoring techniques. Even if you did understand the techniques, practice makes perfect, and if you're new to this, you'll need to do a lot of practicing before you learn the art of the double-out.

Cricket

My brother was a big Cricket player in college. It was the first Dart game he learned to play. He said he got pretty good at it by senior year. It was how he and his frat buddies blew off steam during exam time. It is the most common game played in bars across America, so I have to wonder how much studying my brother was actually doing. This game requires a little strategy, so it gives an advantage to the more clever player who is perhaps not the strongest player.

The object of the game is to close all numbers from 20 down to 15 plus the bull's-eye and wind up with more, or at least as many, points as your opponent. You must hit three of a number in order to close it.

To keep score, you should write the numbers 20 down to 15 and bull's-eye in descending order down the center of the scoreboard. To score, you must throw your dart at any of the game numbers 20 through 15 and bull's-eye. Again, the outer ring counts as two of that number (double) and the inner ring counts for three of that number (triple).

Scoring for one dart is indicated with a slash "/" next to the number scored. Scoring for two is indicated with an X placed next to the number, and scoring for three is indicated with an O next to the number. These symbols are written to indicate that the number is closed. When three of a number is hit in any combination, the number is closed, and you should use these symbols to indicate this on the scoreboard.

Each player throws his or her darts, alternating between teams and/or players, to try and close a number. Each round is the throw of three darts. You keep playing until you score more, or an equal amount of, points as your opponent.

Keeping score is the really fun part about this game. Cricket gets interesting when you deal with the points.

If you close a number and your opponent has not closed that same number, any dart that lands in that number goes to your side of the scoreboard total. If, for example, you close your 15 and your opponent has only one 15, if you throw a triple-15, you have 45 points added to your total. If your opponent throws a triple-15 at this point, only two count to close the number—the third 15 does not count because you have already closed that number. However, if you have all your numbers closed, including your bull's-eyes, but have fewer points than your opponent, you have not yet won the game. You have to keep throwing until you have more points than (or an equal amount of points as) your opponent. If you only have bull's-eyes left, then you must throw extra bull's-eyes, which are worth 25 points each or 50 points for double bull's-eye.

So the art of Cricket is in strategizing the plays. You have to think ahead and try to outwit your opponent. You have to have a good aim, but the real key is in the brain.

A good trick is to close your highest numbers first in descending order. Why? Because the player with the highest numbers closed first has an advantage. This is the great part of the game: If you close your 20 and score 20 points in your first round, your opponent will have to throw two 19s after he or she closed just to make up the points and score 38.

Winning Plays

One of the early versions of Darts was a game called Huff and Blow. In this game, the dart was blown from a pipe at the target. A folk tale dating back to 1844 says that one man actually drew the dart inward instead of blowing it out. Needless to say, he died just a few days later.

The Least You Need to Know

➤ You will want to pay attention to the floor area where you hang your board. Darts can harm many floor types. A dart mat is recommended.

➤ Your dartboard should be hung from the bull's-eye.

➤ It's a good idea to mark your throw line on the floor.

➤ The game is usually started with the "diddle for middle," where each player throws a dart to determine who goes first.

➤ There are several different Dart games from which to choose, but x01 is a fairly simple, straightforward, and fun game to start learning the basics of Darts.

Chapter 9

Rack 'Em Up

In This Chapter

➤ The history of Billiards and Snooker

➤ Billiards and Snooker today

➤ Pocket and pocketless Billiards games

➤ Snooker games

Moving right along with our parlor games … let's take a look at the various games of Billiards and Snooker. The nice thing about modern-day Billiards and Snooker—and many games that fall under the sporting category of table games—is that there are no gender or age issues to contend with. Everyone has an equal advantage! You don't have to be fast or strong, you just have to be able to strike the ball.

If anything, a good eye, a steady hand, and a certain sense of logic are the key factors to being good at these games. Not to say games of Billiards and Snooker are not serious business; Billiards is taken very seriously in the sporting world. You can either pocket the balls or you can't. Anyone can play!

Cuing Up the Past

Believe it or not, the game of *Billiards* originated from a fifteenth-century outdoor lawn game resembling Croquet played by all classes of people in Northern Europe.

It's in the Cards

Billiards derives from the French "billart" referring to the wooden stick used to strike the ball. "Billiard" may also derive from another French word, "bille," meaning "ball." Today, it is any of several games played on a rectangular table where you hit balls with a stick, called a cue, against one another into pockets.

Winning Plays

Originally, women were not "permitted" to use the handle side of the stick to hit the ball in Billiards, and were required to always use the larger end. The reason given? The male Billiards players felt the women might rip the cloth on the table if they used the thinner end of the stick. I think the men might really have been afraid that if women used the thinner side of the stick, they might win!

While peasants played it in open fields and side streets, the nobility played in landscaped gardens. The outdoor game was later miniaturized to a table version, probably because it was so popular that enthusiasts wanted to play it indoors. In fact, the green table lining was designed to emulate the green grass on which the outdoor version was played!

Instead of using their hands to roll the balls like they did in the original outdoor version, players used a wooden stick called a "mace." The mace was wide on one end and thin on the other. Interestingly, it was the wider end that was used to strike the ball. The thinner end was originally the handle.

However, as the game evolved, players found that it was easier to use the thinner end of the stick to hit the ball—especially when the ball was nestled by the table rail. So while players generally used the wide end, if they needed to strike the ball out of a difficult place on the table, they flipped the stick around and used the handle. Now it is standard practice to use the thin end of the cue stick—you'd look really silly if you tried to hit the cue ball with the wide end.

Billiards has undergone many changes over the years, and it seems that much of the game evolved through trial and error—the use of the wide end versus the handle is one such experiment that revolutionized the cue stick. Another similar development was the use of the table edges to pot the ball.

Originally, billiard tables had walls just to keep the balls from flying off the tables. The walls were called banks because they reminded players of riverbanks. Players began to use the walls to make their shots, thus the term "bank shot" (deliberately aiming a ball into a wall to make a shot). Nowadays, the walls of the pool table are padded to give the ball a little spring.

How Billiards came to America is somewhat uncertain, but it is said that George Washington played Pool in his lifetime. In the early nineteenth century, pool halls started popping up all over the country and the rest is, well, history.

But What About Today?

Billiards, more commonly known as Pool, has an interesting history, but maybe even more interesting is the place the game—or sport—has taken in popular culture. It is anything from a gambling game, to a game of logic, to a professional sport. There isn't that much luck involved—it's all about experience and skill.

Pool is a great game for people ages 13 and up (that's my personal opinion). I don't think Pool is safe for children younger than their teen years. The cue sticks are large and cumbersome, the balls are heavy and move quickly, and the table is too high. Little children could get hurt.

Your teenager, however, will love it. In fact, if you can afford it, I can't think of a better way to engage your teenagers than to invest in a pool table. The tables aren't that expensive and it's well worth purchasing one if you have the space because it really is a fun way to get the family together. You can play in teams or one-on-one. You can just leave your teens alone and let them play with their friends (you know they'll appreciate that). It's the perfect thing for a rainy afternoon.

High Score

Children might have a harder time maneuvering the cue sticks, so you might want to avoid getting really little kids involved. You can ask them to referee or keep score—give them some role in the game so they don't feel neglected. It might be best to play with your teens when the little ones are in bed, however. Adults and teens can really have a great time with the various Billiard game options.

Your Own Pool Hall

Before you start playing, there are some basic things you need to know about equipment and the rules of the various games. There are several different rules using standard Billiards and then there are special tables and rules for games like Snooker, but we'll get into that later in this chapter.

Of course, you'll have to start by purchasing a table or finding a local place for your family to play. You can buy some relatively inexpensive tables—it's the equipment that could run you the extra dollars. Start small and inexpensive and see how much you enjoy it before buying the fancy stuff. If you want to play outside the home, you might have to leave the kids behind with a sitter as there aren't that many pool halls that will allow children.

Winning Plays

Did you know that in 1600 William Shakespeare made reference to Billiards in his play *Anthony and Cleopatra?* That means the game must have been popular enough for the masses to understand the reference.

It's in the Cards

The **footspot** is the little white dot on the green cloth where you put the apex of the rack.

The Truth About Tables

The table is rectangular in shape and the top is slightly inset with a green cloth covering its surface. The official measurements of the table (according to the Billiards Congress of America) should be 3½' by 7', or 4' by 8', or 4½' x 9'. The height of the table should measure (from the bottom of the leg to the playing surface) 30" to 31".

The table has six "pockets," which are actually holes in the four corners and on two of the long sides of the table. The cloth is marked with a spot called the *footspot.* The sides of the table and the surrounding pockets are cushioned, so the ball has a softer impact. There are several different regions on the table that designate play—some of which are not marked visibly on the actual cloth, but are indicated by the diamond markings on the rails.

Billiard Basics

The rack, in most Billiard games, is a triangle made of wood or plastic and is used to group the balls at the beginning of the match. The balls are placed in the center of the triangle and placed with one point of the triangle (or apex) on the footspot. The ball in the apex should be sitting on the footspot before the rack is lifted. The balls must be touching each other when the rack is lifted before the first player can strike.

The white cue ball is the focal point of the game and is used to strike the other balls—the cue ball must be struck (with the cue stick) so that it hits other balls into the corner and side pockets. In other words, you don't hit the balls directly, but you use the cue ball to hit the other balls on the table.

The cue stick is the stick you use to hit the balls into the pockets on the table. Cue sticks are usually made of wood and are wide on one end and taper into a thinner end with a dulled pointed tip (usually padded with a small piece of leather). Sometimes, chalk is used on the tip of the stick to allow for better friction and control when the stick hits the cue ball.

The numbered balls, or "object balls," are usually made of a hard synthetic material and are half solid colored and half colored with stripes. The balls are heavy (another good reason to keep little fingers away from the table). In regular Pocket Billiards, one player (or team) will play the solid colors and the other will play the striped. This means that one side will try to hit the solid-colored balls into the pockets, while the other side uses the striped balls as their targets.

A frame is one complete game of Billiards. A match comprises a number of frames of a Billiards game mutually agreed upon by all players involved before the game begins.

Pocket Billiards Games

Let's first take a look at the general rules of Pocket Billiards. Playing a few rounds of Pocket Billiards is probably the best introduction to Pool in general; by playing, you will come to understand the basic rules and terminology that apply to most games of Pool. There are, of course, many different Pool games you can play. But let's start with the basics.

Racking and Breaking

The game commences by racking the balls and subsequently "breaking" them. To break, the cue ball can be placed anywhere on the table in back of the *headstring*. When you have your shot in sight, using your cue stick, hit the cue ball so that it knocks the neatly compacted balls all over the table. Congratulations! This is your first break.

High Score

When you rack the balls, the 8-ball should be in the center of the triangle. The apex of the rack should be on the footspot (any ball can be placed in the apex), and a striped ball should be in one far corner of the triangle and a solid ball should be in the other corner.

It's in the Cards

The **headstring** is the line on the head end of the table between the second diamonds of the long rails, passing through the head spot.

Some experts believe that the break is the most important shot of the game because it determines the placement of the balls on the table for the opening round. Hopefully, on this first break, you'll manage to get some of the balls into the pockets. Often on your first try, you either wind up missing the cue ball and fouling or thinly spreading the balls around the table without potting anything. Not to worry—that's the standard beginner's shot. Before you know it, you'll be potting balls all over the table. However, keep in mind that in Pocket Billiards, if you don't pot a ball on your *visit* to the table, you pass to your opponent.

It's in the Cards

A **visit** to the table consists of a shot, or a series of shots, that comprise a player's turn at the table. The visit lasts until a player fails to pot a ball, he or she fouls, or the frame ends (all the balls, except the cue ball, are potted).

The terms "pot" and "pocket" are used interchangeably. While modern day tables have pockets fitted in the tables, some of the earlier tables had little pots at the corners to hold the balls.

Lagging for the Break

How do you determine who gets to break first? There's an old technique called "lagging for the break." Each player stands at the head of the table. Using your hands (as opposed to your cue stick), simultaneously shoot one of the balls across the table so that it hits the opposite edge and rolls back toward your end of the table (opponents should watch their fingers—especially if you're playing against an aggressive "lagger").

The ball that rolls back and comes closest to the edge of the table is the winner. The ball can hit the cushions more than once, but it must hit the foot end at least once. You might want to get a ruler for close calls.

The Play

A play is considered "scratched" when you strike a ball and the cue ball lands in a pocket. You must return the cue ball to play by putting it on or near the dot on the head end of the green cloth. Your opponent can then take the cue ball in hand and move it around in the space closest to him or her behind the headstring. In other words, you miss your turn and your opponent can choose from where he will hit the cue ball (as long as the cue ball is placed within the headstring). Some people play that if you sink an object ball with the cue ball, you must return the object ball to the table on the footspot.

When playing from the headstring on a scratch, you may not strike another ball directly inside this area. If you want to pot a ball inside the headstring, you must first hit a ball outside of the headstring that will return to strike the ball within the headstring. Any ball directly struck by a spotted cue ball within the headstring is considered a foul.

If you fail to pot a ball on your visit to the table, your visit is over and your opponent is up. Don't forget that the object of Billiards is to pot as many balls as possible with each visit to the table.

Pool Game: Eight Ball

Eight Ball is a Billiard game played with a total of 15 object balls numbered 1 through 15. The goal of each player is to pocket all of his or her group of object balls 1 through 7 (or 9 through 15) and win the game. You will either play the solid-color balls or the striped balls. You'll establish who plays which at the beginning of the game after the break.

You don't pocket the 8-ball until the end of the game. When you have pocketed all your balls, you take aim at the 8-ball. The first player to pocket all his or her balls and then pocket the 8-ball is the winner.

If you're making a "bank shot" or "combination shot"—two types of *call shots*—you should inform your opponents of your intended shot because those shots are not considered obvious. Name the ball and pocket for which you intend to aim. You don't have to give any more detail than the object ball and the intended pocket.

It's in the Cards

Eight Ball is generally played as a **call shot** game, which means that before you hit a ball, you must call the shot. First you pick your shot, then you say it aloud so your opponent can hear you: "Five ball in the corner pocket" or whatever the shot is that you're about to make. If the shot is obvious, you don't have to call it, but your opponent is entitled to ask if he or she is not sure. If you pot a ball that you did not call (called "slopping"), official rules say to leave the ball in the pocket. However, many people prefer to return the slopped ball to the footspot. One way or another, your turn is forfeited to the next player.

The Rules

Here are some general Eight Ball rules:

➤ The opening break is never a called shot.

➤ If you are making the break, you may make another shot as long as at least one ball on the break was legally pocketed.

➤ If you fail to make a legal break (no ball is pocketed), then your opponent may decide to shoot the balls as they rest on the table after the break, or the opponent may choose to rebreak.

➤ If you pot the 8-ball on a break shot, all the balls stay potted except the 8-ball, which is returned to the table. The opponent can rebreak if the 8-ball is pocketed or can spot the 8-ball on the table on the footspot.

➤ If you shoot a ball off the table during an opening break, you forfeit your turn. Your opponent then takes position at the table and may continue shooting or take the cue ball in hand and play from behind the headstring.

➤ The table is considered "open" after the break shot, meaning that stripes or solids have not yet been determined. The table is always considered open immediately following the break shot. You may strike any object ball at this point, whether it is striped or solid. It is even legal to strike the 8-ball when the table is open—but don't pocket the 8-ball.

You can only hit the 8-ball as part of a combination shot at this point during the game. If you make a direct strike on the 8-ball, you lose your turn and any pocketed balls remain pocketed. Your opponent can continue play on the open table at this point.

Stripes or Solids?

Now that the table is open, it's time to pick your group of object balls. Your selection is determined only after you pocket a called shot. The solids are numbered 1-7 and the stripes are numbered 9-15. The 8-ball is black. So if you call "9-ball in the corner pocket" and you manage to pocket that called shot, then you will be stripes for the remainder of the game.

Making Contact

All this sounds pretty easy, right? Well, not exactly. Here's the catch: On all shots—after the break and not when the table is open—the player must hit one of his group of balls first, and either pocket a ball, or make a ball (or the cue ball) contact the side of the table. You can make the cue ball bounce off the side of the table (bank shot) before striking the object ball, but the object ball must be pocketed, or it, or the cue ball, must contact the side of the table. If either of the balls does not contact the side of the table, the shot is considered a foul. Your opponent may then play the cue ball in hand from anywhere on the table (this does not necessarily have to be from behind the headstring—that just applies to the opening break) .

Fouls and Ball-Jumping

A shot is considered to be a foul if it is jumped off the table. Jumping a ball off the table means you lose your turn to your opponent. Your opponent may spot the balls in numerical order from any location on the table (that means he or she can place the ball anywhere on the table before taking his or her next turn).

Illegal Pocketing

A ball is considered illegally pocketed for the following reasons:

➤ If you pocket a ball while lobbing another ball off the table (shooting a foul)

➤ The object ball that you called does not go into the designated pocket

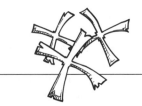

Combination Shots

Combination shots are legal shots, but you can never use the 8-ball as the first contacted ball. In other words, you can use the 8-ball in combination with another object ball to pocket an object ball, as long as you don't strike the 8-ball first.

Scoring

You keep playing your object balls on your visit to the table until you fail to pocket a shot. Once all the object balls of your group are pocketed, you try to pocket the 8-ball. The first person to achieve this wins the match.

Losing the Game

You can forfeit the game for the following reasons:

➤ Pocketing the 8-ball (except on the opening break) before your object balls have been pocketed

➤ Pocketing the 8-ball on the same shot as pocketing your remaining object balls

➤ Jumping the 8-ball off the table

➤ Pocketing the 8-ball at the end of the game in a different pocket than the one you call

➤ Pocketing the 8-ball when it's not the legal object ball

Pool Game: Nine Ball

Nine Ball is played with nine balls numbered 1 through 9 (plus the cue ball). The object of Nine Ball is to pocket the 9-ball. Sounds pretty easy, but you can't just pocket the 9-ball at the beginning of the game. The lowest-numbered ball on the table must always be the first ball contacted by the cue ball. That doesn't mean you have to pocket the balls in order of 1 through 9, but at the very least you have to hit the lowest ball in order to pocket another ball. For example, after the break, the lowest ball on the table will be the 1-ball. Let's say you want to hit the 5-ball into a corner pocket; you can't hit the 5-ball without contacting the 1-ball first. So you'll have to find a way to hit the 1-ball into the 5-ball in order to make the shot you want.

Nine Ball is not a call-shot game, so you don't have to worry about not making the shot you had in mind, but you still have to pocket a ball in order to continue your turn at the table.

If you miss or foul a shot, you forfeit your turn to your opponent and your opponent must pick up play at the table where you left off. That means that the opponent has to stand in the same position occupied by the previous player. He or she doesn't have to attempt the same shot, but must stand in the same place. Your opponent can place the cue ball anywhere on the table after a fouled shot.

Racking the Balls

The balls are racked in a diamond shape. The 1-ball should be placed at the top of the diamond on the footspot and the 9-ball in the center. The placement of the other balls is not relevant. The game begins with the cue ball in hand and shot from behind the headstring.

Break Shot

In a legal Nine Ball break shot, the 1-ball must be the first ball struck and a ball must be pocketed as a result, or at least four balls must be struck to the edge of the table. If the break is fouled—which means that the cue ball is pocketed or driven off the table (or another ball jumps the table)—or the 1-ball is not the first ball struck, the player forfeits his or her turn. The opponent may take the cue ball in hand and play from anywhere on the table. If the object ball jumps off the table, it is not spotted. If the 9-ball jumps the table, it *is* spotted.

No pocketed object balls may be spotted after being pocketed on a foul—with the exception of the 9-ball.

Push Out

A push out can be played immediately after a legal break. The goal is to move the cue ball into a better position to make a better shot. This means that you can hit the cue ball without hitting any other object ball or a rail. Before you play a push out, however, you must announce that that is what you're doing. If you pocket an object ball on a push out, it does not count and remains pocketed unless, of course, the 9-ball is pocketed. After a push out, the next player can shoot from the same position or pass the shot back to the player who shot the push out. You cannot play a push out if a player scratches on the break.

The game continues until all object balls are pocketed—the last ball to be pocketed will be the 9-ball.

Snooker

Snooker is hugely popular in the United Kingdom and perhaps a little less so in the United States. With its origins possibly in India, it was a game played by British soldiers stationed overseas in the late nineteenth century. Its popularity increased through the years—if you're ever in the United Kingdom, you can catch a Snooker match almost anywhere you go.

It's in the Cards

Snooker is a word that refers to the position of the cue ball in an "impossible" shot. For example, if it's your turn and you need to pocket the pink ball, but your cue ball is in a position on the table that makes that shot virtually impossible, you are said to be "snookered."

Getting Started

Snooker is not unlike other Billiards games in that it is played on a similar size table (12' x 6') with similar markings, but it is played with 22 balls. There are 15 red balls (one point each); one yellow ball (two points); one green ball (three points); one brown ball (four points); one blue ball (five points); one pink ball (six points); one black ball (seven points); and, of course, a cue ball.

The object is to pocket the balls, score the most points, and win the game. It's how you get to the end of the game that makes Snooker so much fun.

There is a certain amount of set-up involved before play begins. This is how you should arrange the balls on the Snooker table:

➤ **Red Balls:** Set up in a pyramid formation on the pyramid spot

➤ **Black Ball:** On the billiard spot near the foot of the table

➤ **Pink Ball:** Should be touching the apex of the red-ball pyramid

➤ **Blue Ball:** Placed on the center spot

➤ **Green, Brown, and Yellow Balls:** Placed at the left, center, and right of the straight line of the "D" (a region of the head of the table shaped like a semicircle)

Opening Break

You make the break with cue ball in hand at the "D." A red ball must be contacted and pocketed after the break, or at least two red balls and the cue ball must contact a side rail after contacting the racked red balls. The beginning of the game is all about pocketing the red balls.

The first shot of each turn is always on a red ball. You alternate shots: first the red and then a colored ball. Once the red balls are all pocketed, you can start to shoot for the colored balls one after another. You continue to play until you either fail to pocket a ball or foul. If you don't make a legal break, your opponent can choose to play the table as-is, or have you rebreak.

Playing the Game

Although Snooker is not considered a "call shot" game, when you plan to strike a non-red ball you must indicate which ball you are targeting. However, you do not have to say where you plan to pocket the ball. If you happen to pocket a non-red ball before all the red balls have cleared the table, you must spot the pocketed non-red balls (but first give yourself the points scored).

High Score

Bonus! If the colors are all pocketed during one player's turn, that player receives a bonus of 100-points.

All red balls stay pocketed. After the red balls are pocketed, you must aim for the non-red balls in ascending numerical order. The game is not over until all the balls are pocketed. Points are tallied and the winner is selected based on the highest score.

Non-red balls must be "cleanly" pocketed, which means they cannot touch any other ball on their way into the pocket.

If the points are tallied and the end result is a tie, then the black ball is spotted on its designated spot and players lag to see who shoots at it first. The first person to pocket the black wins. If a player fouls on attempting to pocket the black, the opponent wins.

Here are the fouls for Snooker:

➤ Scratching (cue ball is pocketed).

➤ Missing the targeted ball.

➤ Pocketing two balls at a time (other than two reds).

➤ Non-red (colors) must be pocketed cleanly without hitting any other balls.

➤ Pocketing more than one ball on one strike.

➤ An illegally pocketed color must be spotted prior to that player's next strike—failure to do so is a foul.

➤ When a player fails to alternate pocketing red and color balls.

➤ If the tip of a cue stick touches the felt on a "masse shot" (curve shot made by elevating the cue stick), it is considered a double-foul and the penalty will therefore be doubled.

And the penalties:

➤ When a player fouls, the opponent receives seven points per foul.

➤ The opponent may take his turn at the table with the balls as-is, or the opponent may choose to have the player who fouled shoot again. As in most Billiards games, fouls result in a forfeiture of your turn and you don't score any points.

The Least You Need to Know

➤ In order to play Billiards you need a pool table, rack, cue stick, cue ball, and object balls.

➤ There are many different games of Pocket Billiards, such as Eight Ball, Nine Ball, and more.

➤ Snooker is more popular in the United Kingdom than the U.S. It is not unlike other Billiard games in that it is played on a similar-size table with similar markings, but it is played with 22 balls.

Chapter 10

Direct Hit!

In This Chapter

➤ Air Hockey

➤ Foosball

➤ Ping-Pong

The table games in this chapter are a far cry from the slow-moving strategy parlor games you've just read about. The games in this chapter are for those rainy days when you're stuck inside and need to unleash some raw energy.

Many of us have played these games over the years without any real instruction manual to guide us—we just stood up at the table and shot the puck or hit the ball. No one really cared about rules when I played Air Hockey or Ping Pong—you just hit to score by any means necessary. In fact, I have a friend who tells me that his older brother's whole position in Air Hockey was to shoot and aim for his opponent's hands in the hopes that my friend would drop his playing piece, and therefore his defenses, and lose the game.

Well, that's not fair play and would never go over very well with parents or with tournament officials, but it's basically how we were all introduced to action table games. These games are all about action, but there are also those who adhere to some very strict rules. While we may have knocked around in our basement smashing fingers and whooping and hollering with each goal or point, these games are actually played on a professional level with tournament regulations.

Air Hockey, Anyone?

It's hard to talk to any die-hard Air Hockey fan without seeing the gleam in their eyes and the puck in their brain. Air Hockey has long been an addictive pastime. It's a fast and furious game and really gets the adrenaline flowing. When I was a kid, Air Hockey came in several different table sizes. You had the little miniature home games that were really hard to maneuver around without getting a finger or two smashed, or without watching the puck fly through the air rather than on the board. And then there were the bigger, arcade-size tables.

Most of my friends had an air hockey table stashed away in the basement. We'd play on and off—the addiction passed over us in waves, and then when we moved on to college most of those old tables were sold in yard sales. In this day and age, the best air hockey tables can be found in arcades. These tables are monstrously large with a surface so smooth the puck wouldn't dare to leave it and fly through the air. The game is the same, but the tables are pretty impressive with their high-tech glitz and sleek angles. It's really fun just to stand by and watch—even if you're not into playing.

Air Hockey is often called the world's fastest table game. Depending on how skilled the players are, the puck has been known to travel at speeds of 80 mph—so it's very unwise to play with a big brother who gets his jollies out of finger-smashing as a means to score a goal.

First of all, if you've never seen an air hockey table, take a peek at one in your local mall's arcade. Almost every arcade has one or two tables. The playing board looks pretty much the same as an ice hockey rink. You have a centerline and two goals at either side of the table.

Three Strikes

A fast-moving puck can really sting, so you may want to be careful when up against an opponent. Some finger-smashing may be inevitable in the beginning stages, but once you're used to the game, you'll find the puck hits the mallet more often than your index finger.

How to Play

The game is very simple—it's just like Hockey, only you have two players, you're not skating on ice, and you don't have a stick. What you have is a very slick surface, a round mallet (playing piece), and a round, lightweight puck (the puck is what is shot across the board in order to score a goal).

The surface of the table is so smooth that it will seem as though the puck, and your hand, is gliding over an icy surface. This is what makes the games so fast and so much fun. At first, it will seem impossible to be able to hit the puck at the speed that it flies, but after a few rounds, it will come more naturally to you. The trick to the game is in the types of shots you apply in order to make a goal. The goals are located at either end of the board. You stand on the side of your goal and use your mallet to hit the puck away from and into your opponent's goal (located directly across the board from you).

The best way to start a game of Air Hockey is to flip a coin to see who gets possession of the puck first. Once you've established that, then you can begin the game. In tournaments, matches are based on the best two out of three games.

A win occurs after a player scores a predetermined number of goals (typically seven or ten). So you can keep going for best two out of three, or you can stop with one—it's up to you. Just make sure everyone is clear on how many games they are obligated to play. If you do play best two out of three, then you should alternate who gets the puck first from game to game.

To begin play, the puck must start out flat on the table. You should have someone on hand to give the signal to begin play.

When the signal is given, keep one eye on the puck and the other on your goal. You want to be able to move quickly enough to stop the puck from entering your goal. Now you begin to hit the puck back and forth, and it is at this point that you will discover that the art of the game is in the sleight of the hand.

The Rules

As with most of these types of games, the rules aren't really documented in any easy, identifiable way. Most people still just stand up at the table and shoot the puck back and forth. But the tournament rules are very clear, and I'll use these rules to help guide us through the action. It's up to you how seriously you want to play. You can adhere to the pros' rules or just make them up as you go along, but these rules will be a good place to start.

➤ Players cannot reach across the centerline and strike the puck.

➤ No *palming*.

➤ If you hit the puck off the table, your opponent gets possession of the puck.

High Score

Because this is such a fast game, it is critical to assign a referee—someone who is objective and is familiar with the rules of Air Hockey. As a player, you're so busy watching the puck and concentrating on your own shots that there are times you won't be able to judge a foul or a penalty without a third party.

It's in the Cards

Using your hand to stop the puck is known as **palming.** Palming will result in forfeiture of the puck.

103

➤ When a violation of the rules occurs, the opposing player should always receive possession of the puck (this is called a penalty).

➤ You cannot hold the puck with your mallets for more than seven seconds. (If the puck decides to spin on its side, then the seven-second rule only applies once the puck has stopped spinning and can be put back into play.)

➤ No *topping*.

It's in the Cards

Placing your mallet on top of the puck is known as **topping** and is considered an offense resulting in forfeiture of the puck.

High Score

The experts believe that varying your puck speed is the best way to improve your level of Air Hockey playing. It's easy to want to make that puck fly, but that can get a little boring and repetitive. You want to keep your opponent on his or her toes. Keep 'em guessing!

Footing

The most important thing to remember in Air Hockey is, believe it or not, where you place your feet on the floor. Real pros know that the use of your leg muscles is key to your offensive and defensive strategies.

For example, I read one player talk about how he will use a kneepad, so that he can lean his right knee against the table while keeping his left leg about two feet from the table for support. His back foot remains firmly planted on the ground. This stance allows him to balance himself in such a way that he can make quick moves backward when necessary. But this same person points out that this is more of a defensive stance because you cannot lunge forward using this technique. If you try moving your left leg in a little and put the balance on your toes rather than on your whole foot, you will have more maneuverability to be on the defense and on the attack at the same time.

The Puck

The puck is the life of the game and does seem to take on its own persona as it whips across the board. But if you learn to use it right, you can have complete control over where it goes.

One shot known as an "exaggerated release shot" is just what it claims to be. The player moves his or her hand in such a way that it makes it look like he or she will hit the puck really hard, when in fact the play is actually just a tap, causing their opponent to flinch and perhaps move their own hand in the wrong direction. This is a common technique used in regular Ice Hockey as well. So ... watch the puck and be on your guard for such clever tactics.

The Board

You can stand on any side of the board (playing surface) as long as you are on your side of the centerline. The board is very simple. There are two goals on either end, and across the center of the board you will see a line (usually a red line, but it depends on what board you are playing on).

The centerline has a circle through the middle of it. The circle is where opponents face off at the beginning of the game. Most boards do not have any other lines to worry about.

The centerline is the key focal point of the game and there are a few rules you need to know in relation to this line. You cannot cross the line with any part of your body at any point during the game. This will result in a penalty (usually forfeiture of the puck).

If your opponent has possession of the puck completely on his or her side of the board, you cannot reach over to the opposing section to strike the puck or opponent's mallet. If, however, the puck touches any part of the centerline while in the possession of your opponent, either side may attempt to strike it. The mallet may never extend further than its diameter across the centerline, but it may partially touch the centerline. All these rules apply at time of face-off as well.

Score!

Points are scored when one player hits the puck into his opponent's goal. The puck must break the horizontal plane in order to be considered a goal. In other words, if the puck lands in the goal, but on a tilt still half touching the board, then it is still considered a goal. But if the puck lands in the goal area, but does not tilt in, then play continues and no points are scored.

If the puck rebounds out of the goal, then no point is scored—but if the puck rebounds off the mouth of the goal, hits the defending player's hand, and lands back in the goal, then a point *is* scored.

If the puck goes into the goal after bouncing off a player's hand, then it counts as a point, as long as the point would have been scored had the hand not been in the way. This is where you may need a referee, because it could be cause for an argument. It's hard to be objective sometimes, especially when the score is 6-6.

If a player hits the puck, the opponent doesn't touch it, and it flies back into the striking player's goal, it is considered a foul and the puck is forfeited to the other player. However, just for fun, you can bend the rules and make it a goal for the opponent—that will certainly add some spice to the action.

The Shots

Here are a list of terms you'll need to know to play like a pro. The more you play, the more you'll become familiar with the lingo.

➤ **Off-Goal:** The best way to win Air Hockey is to have a deceptive offense. One good shot to lead you toward this is the off-goal. The purpose of this shot is to trick your opponent into thinking you will always shoot from a certain angle in order to score a goal. But in reality, the off-goal is not used to score a goal at all. It is used to make your opponent think you want to score a goal. So, if you make the shot repetitively, your opponent will automatically start defending himself on that side. But your real goal will be scored completely differently. Remember, you can only hold the puck for up to seven seconds.

➤ **Drifting:** What drifting means is that when you are in possession of the puck, you only have seven seconds to hold it before you make your shot. That means you have to keep it moving on the board, but you have to shoot it before the seven seconds are up. After seven seconds, you forfeit the puck to the opposing player. You don't want to sit there with a frozen puck for seven seconds; you have to keep it moving. In the same way that an Ice Hockey player keeps the puck in motion, looking to pass it to another player or attempt a goal, in Air Hockey, you're essentially doing the same thing. You want to keep the puck moving and keep your opponent guessing.

It's in the Cards

Foosball originated in Germany and the word is actually a derivation of the German word "Fussball," meaning "football" in German.

Winning Plays

Did you know that Foosball players refer to themselves as "Foosers?"

Are You Ready for Some Foosball?

Most of the world refers to the game of Soccer as "football," which is what *Foosball* is—Soccer played with miniature players, controlled by hand-rods, on a table. No one really knows when Foosball hit the European scene, but since the real game of Soccer became an organized sport in about 1860, it is assumed that Foosball is a little younger than its predecessor.

One of the oldest manufacturers of Foosball is a Swiss company called Kicker. They also used the same name for their table. This is what most Europeans call Foosball: "Kicker." So, Kicker is to most of Europe what Foosball is to North America.

Tables

Like Air Hockey, Foosball is played on a table, and the object of the game is to keep your opponent's ball out of your goal and vice-versa. The table is deep set, and inside, running along metal bars, are rows of plastic players of opposing teams, dressed in Soccer uniforms. If you follow the metal bars to the ends of the tables, you will see that the bars extend through the sides of the table to the outside where handles are connected. The players stand on either side of the table and turn the handles to move the players.

Full-size foosball tables range in price from about $250 to $1,000. If you are buying a starter table or a table for kids, it's best to buy one of the lower-range tables. If you really want to start playing and maybe even get into tournaments, you should probably buy a table in the $400-$500 range. You will, of course, need a good-size room to fit the table. Table dimensions are 56" long by 30" wide. The rods stick out on the sides, so you will need at least a seven- to eight-foot space.

> **Three Strikes**
>
> Don't put the foosball table in a room where little children play. You could put an eye out!

Let's Play!

For many of us, Foosball was another basement game—good for a rainy Sunday afternoon. But for even more people, Foosball is addictive and good fun. It is also taken very seriously in the world of professional table games. It's a game that requires quick reflexes and control. In this game, it's not so easy to keep your eye on the ball when you also have to juggle so many players.

Foosball begins with the serve. To determine who gets the ball first, a coin flip is the best way to go. Whoever wins the coin toss gets the ball and may place it in play. Most foosball tables have a duct on either side of the table. All you have to do is drop the ball into the duct and it will roll onto the table and play begins. Some of the older tables may not have a duct, in which case you may drop the ball onto the table, but this is the only time your hand may approach the playing area. The ball is in play once the serve is made and the first rod is turned.

If the ball leaves the table, it is returned to the player who initially served the ball. The ball is then put back into play with a new serve.

A "dead ball" is a ball that is on the board, but is not reachable by any players on the rod. If a ball is considered dead between the goal and the two-player rods, it should be put back into play in the corner nearest the spot where it "died." If the ball "dies" anywhere between the two-player rods, it should be put back into play with a new serve by the team that served the ball in the first place.

It is illegal to deliberately cause a dead ball. If you have a referee and he or she declares this to be true, the player who causes the dead ball will forfeit the ball to the opposing team for a re-serve.

One point is scored when the ball enters the goal. If the ball bounces into the goal but then bounces out again (even if it leaves the table), it is still considered a goal and therefore scores one point.

No more than three time-outs should be called by either side during a game.

One overly used technique you will see in Foosball is "rod spinning." Most of the professional players do not recommend this action in Foosball, and in fact, it is actually illegal in a professional tournament. Players who use this method usually wind up spinning the rods out of excitement, hoping to get a strong hit of the ball. In actuality, you may wind up missing the ball and damaging the table instead.

Winning Plays

Did you know that you can play Foosball doubles? In a doubles match, each player may play only two rods and must stick to those two rods until a point is scored or a time-out is called. The players may switch rods between points or games, and during time-outs.

Ping-Pong Party

Ping-Pong, otherwise known as Table Tennis, is a relatively young game. It is unclear exactly where it has its origins, but the earliest known form of the sport was called Indoor Tennis.

Ping-Pong came to the United States in about 1900. It is believed that an Englishman named James Gibb, pocketing a handful of celluloid balls, brought the game across the Atlantic coining it "Ping-Pong" after the sound the ball makes upon hitting the table and the racket. The name "Ping-Pong" was registered in 1901 by an English sporting goods manufacturer named John Jacques, and later sold to Parker Brothers, who manufactured a new kit under the new name.

High Score

The best way to shoot the ball is to stop it, aim it, and hit it. If you try to hit the moving ball, you may wind up losing it to the other side.

I don't think I know a single person who hasn't at least attempted a round of Ping-Pong in his or her lifetime. It's another one of those table games that winds up in a basement loaded down with old magazines and cartons.

Well, uncover the table and dust it off, because Ping-Pong is a great game when you learn how to hit that ball. With this game, I think a referee is mandatory. There is no way you'll be able to learn how to concentrate on your game if you're trying to watch for a score or a foul. In tournament Ping-Pong, the referee is actually called an umpire. Get an umpire for your games; you'll be happy you did.

Winning Plays

British soldiers in India and South Africa played the game in the late nineteenth century. The rackets were fashioned out of lids from cigar boxes and the rounded edges of bottle corks were used as the balls. Books lined up across the middle of the table acted as the net. This invention probably originated from a strong desire to play tennis, combined with a lack of space from being cooped up in a barracks somewhere waiting for the next battle. Perhaps this popular modern-day sport is actually the brainchild of boredom—hours of restlessness while serving one's duty of maintaining the old British Empire.

The Setup

Ping-Pong is a game that is very much like tennis, but played with a little ball and small rackets. The ball is super-lightweight and is made of a celluloid material. The table is rectangular, about nine feet in length and about five feet wide. The playing surface is usually a flat green board with white lines painted on it. A net fits low across the center of the table, dividing the two sides.

The Ping-Pong racket is a flat, rubber-matted board, usually made of a thick natural wood. It comes in many shapes, but most of the time you'll find it is square with slightly rounded edges.

The Serve

To figure out who serves first, it's best to flip a coin. In this game it is important to pay attention to the service, because, like in most racket games, it is the server who scores the point. Serving is also one of the hardest things to learn when you're just starting. The serve is definitely a learned skill. It's not hard—it just requires some hand-eye coordination.

This is how it's done: Hold your racket in your racket-hand and the ball in your free hand. Toss the ball into the air, straight-up—but not too high (six inches is about right)—and when the ball comes down from your toss, hit it downward so that it first strikes the table in your own court and then over the net and into your opponent's court.

If you're playing singles, it doesn't matter whether it strikes in your right or left court, but in doubles, upon serving the ball, it should first strike the server's right-hand court and then bounce into the receiver's right-hand court.

Now, you better practice the serve before you get involved in any real matches with people who really know how to play. If you miss the ball when it comes down after your serving toss, your opponent will score a point. However, if you hit the ball but it hits the net, you can re-serve and there is no limit on how many times you can do this. There might be a limit to your opponent's patience, but no regulation to stipulate a legal limit on this kind of bad service.

High Score

Did you know that the ball is still considered to be in play if it passes around the net and the net supports rather than over the net?

The serve that everyone dreams of making is the "crashing serve." This is achieved through a great deal of practice because it is the fastest serve you can make. The serve happens so quickly that it almost appears as though you are hitting the ball to your racket and the ball to the table in one single maneuver. Of course, this isn't possible, but it's that fast.

Whatever serve you decide to learn, be prepared to learn how to return them as well. Often, they are not possible to return. But if you are learning them, be assured that your opponent knows the same tactics.

Returns

Okay, so the first ball has been served—now how do you hit it back? That's the easy part—you have to return the ball so that it goes back over (or around) the net and touches down in your opponent's court. Even if the ball touches the net on its way over to you after the initial serve, it is still considered in play and you will have to hit it back.

Many times you'll find yourself face to face with a spinning ball. Balls that are spun by your opponent are often tricky to return. The best maneuver is to try to brake them by using your racket to spin them back in an opposite direction. Braking the spin is referred to as "rubbing." You should use this technique for side- and top-spin balls that come flying at you. I know, you're thinking, how the heck will I know which direction the ball is spinning? Well, you'll learn. One of the reasons you have the pitted rubber mat glued on the racket is for friction.

Points

Points are scored in a variety of different ways. A point is scored when ...

➤ A player does not make the serve.

➤ An opponent fails to make a good return.

➤ An opponent obstructs the ball in play.

➤ The ball touches an opponent's court more than once.

➤ An opponent strikes a ball twice.

➤ An opponent strikes the ball with the side of the racket blade.

➤ An opponent's free hand touches the playing surface while the ball is in play.

➤ An umpire decides upon a penalty point against a player.

➤ The ball passes over or beyond the court without touching the playing surface, after being struck by an opponent. The point goes to the player who did not strike the ball.

The first player to score 21 wins the game. If you are both tied at 20, then you have to get 2 points more than your opponent to win. This rule applies to doubles matches as well.

The Least You Need to Know

➤ Table games such as Air Hockey, Foosball, and Ping-Pong are action-packed energy users, good for getting some exercise indoors on a rainy day.

➤ Air Hockey is often called the world's fastest table game.

➤ Foosball is similar to Soccer, but played with miniature players, controlled by hand-rods, on a table.

➤ An interesting way to learn to keep your eye on the ball in Ping-Pong is to do the following: When the ball hits on your side of the table, say aloud the word "ping." When it hits your racket, say aloud the word "pong."

Part 3

House of Cards

When I told friends and family that I was writing this book, I couldn't believe how many people wanted to share a memory about the card games they played when they were kids, or in the clubs they joined in college. One person told me that he started playing Hearts in graduate school as a means to let off steam and that he and his friends still gather a few times a year to continue the tradition.

There are wonderful card games that kids can play together, like Old Maid, Go Fish, and War. When you teach them the basics, they'll be teaching their friends—and before you know it, you can leave them to it and get back to that novel you were reading. Your older kids can play some of the tougher games like Spades, Cribbage, and Solitaire. You can even set up your kitchen or basement as a mini-casino night with games like Baccarat and Blackjack!

Try a few of these games on a family game night and you're bound to find a favorite. When you do you'll be on your way to building some of your own great memories.

Chapter 11

The Trumps Have It

> **In This Chapter**
>
> ➤ Hearts
>
> ➤ Spades
>
> ➤ Knockout Whist
>
> ➤ Crazy Eights

How many family members and friends do you have for your card game? This chapter takes a look at card games that are appropriate for two to four players. Some of our all-time favorites appear here, such as Hearts, Spades, and Crazy Eights.

Hearts was a favorite family-game-night event in my house growing up. My parents taught us several card games, but I think Hearts, Crazy Eights, and Spades might have been the favorites. When we were very little, we weren't dealt a hand of Hearts or Spades; we had to team up with an adult. That's probably the best way because those games may be a little too complicated for children under seven or eight years of age. Young children might have more fun playing Knockout Whist or Crazy Eights. With cards, there's always a game for every family member!

Achy-Breaky Hearts

Hearts is a very popular game in the United States. A lot of people pick up the Hearts habit in college, and I know a few friends who've continued to use the game as a means to get together with that same old crowd many years after graduation. When you start playing the game, you won't want to stop. It really is a lot of fun!

Winning Plays

Did you know that people have actually devised mathematical formulas to figure out the odds of winning a round of Hearts given a certain hand?

It's in the Cards

A **trick** in card games is the group of cards collected in a round of a game that is used as a scoring method. In games such as Hearts and Spades, you take tricks by playing a card that beats all other cards in a particular hand, thereby "winning" that hand.

It's in the Cards

A **trump** is a card of a suit that will beat any card of another suit that is not a trump suit, regardless of hierarchy.

What is Hearts? Hearts is a *trick*-taking game, and the object is to score the lowest amount of points. The game is over when someone scores 100 or more. The game is always played with four people (not necessarily in partners) and a 52-card deck. The idea is to get rid of all your point-scoring cards, especially your Hearts and the Queen of Spades.

How You Play

Each player is dealt 13 cards and the game consists of 13 tricks. Because there are four players, each trick consists of four cards. Points are given based on the tricks you win. The highest-ranked card in the suit originally played (the lead suit) wins the trick.

In other words, if the card led is a 3 of Diamonds and each player puts down a Diamond but you put down an Ace of Clubs, the highest Diamond wins the trick. There is no *trump* suit. Play continues to be guided by the first suit played in each trick.

You must follow suit whenever you have that suit available in your hand. If you don't have any more cards in your hand that match the lead suit, then you may play any card in your hand. The player who wins a trick, leads the next trick.

How You Score

You will need to keep score when you play Hearts, and it's really quite easy. Here's how it works.

> ➤ All Hearts = 1 point
> ➤ Queen of Spades = 13 points
> ➤ All other cards = no value

So, if you add up the value of all the Hearts cards plus the value of the Queen of Spades, the total amount of points in a game is 26.

Passing Cards

At the beginning of the first round, you pass three cards—face-down—from your hand to the player on your left. On the second round, you pass the cards in the same manner to the person on your right; on the third round, to the person across from you; and on the fourth round, no cards are passed. You may only pick up the cards passed to you after you've passed your cards to another player. You cannot pass a card that was passed to you. In rules pertaining to more than four players, the passing configuration varies.

High Score

Passing is an important part of the game—if not *the* most important part of the game—because it's your chance to get rid of any "bad" cards in your hand. "Bad" cards consist of Hearts, the Queen of Spades, and any other high card that might make you win tricks in the trick-taking part of the game. You want to hold on to low cards, non–Hearts cards, and you certainly want to get rid of the high-scoring Queen of Spades.

Tricks, Not Treats

The player who has the 2 of Clubs starts the first trick. Each player must follow suit and lay down their lowest card in that suit. Aces and face cards are high, 2s are low.

The whole point is *not* to take the trick because you don't want to score any points. If you don't have any cards in the suit, you can play your lowest card of another suit. You take the trick if you play a card that is the highest card of the suit originally played. The player who takes the trick leads the next trick.

You can never lead with a Heart until a Heart has been discarded in a previous trick. When a Heart is discarded, it is called "breaking Hearts." That just means that in discarding a Heart, you are allowing Hearts to be played as a lead card in the future. Breaking Hearts can be used as an important strategy. Discarding a penalty card in a trick-taking card game is called "painting the trick."

High Score

Pass the Queen if you don't have enough Spades in your hand after the first deal. Always pass the King and Ace of Spades because those cards beat the Queen in a trick, and if you have those cards it's almost inevitable that you'll get stuck with the Queen.

It is standard practice to lead with Spades. This is usually done to drive another player to play the Queen, otherwise known as "smoking-out" or "fishing-out" the Queen.

At the end of each round, you count the points you have in your trick pile. You keep playing until someone scores 100. That player is the loser. If one player gets all 26 points in one round, it's called "shooting the moon." But don't be fooled—that player doesn't get all the points added to his or her score. It's added to everyone else's score! So as the "shooter" you can either choose for everyone to add 26 points to their total or you can have 26 points deducted from your own total.

There are some people who really strategize this maneuver because it's quite a challenge. There are even strategies to recognize and counter such a maneuver. Phew ... it all gets pretty competitive if you really know how to play this game.

High Score

Watch out for the Queen! Believe it or not, most Hearts enthusiasts believe that the best way *not* to get stuck with the Queen of Spades is to hold on to her for as long as you can. If you have a lot of Spades in your hand *and* the Queen at the beginning of the game, you are in the best position to get rid of her. Because most players will play to "smoke-out" or "fish-out" the Queen, they will keep playing their Spades until they run out—then someone will have to lead with another suit.

Stay Away from Hearts

It is, of course, always tempting to rid your hand of Hearts right away, but you might want to hold on to a couple of low Hearts if you have any in your hand. If you have some low Hearts, you can play them when a trick is led with Hearts.

Remember, Hearts are worth one point each and you don't want to get stuck with any of them when you're adding up the score at the end of a game. If you keep the low ones, you can lose the Heart-led tricks. The ideal hand is to have at least one low Heart, one medium Heart, and one high Heart.

Scoring a Bonus

Some people like to play that the Jack of Diamonds (or 10 of Diamonds) is worth negative 10 points. In other words, if you have the Jack of Diamonds at the end of the game, you get to subtract 10 points from your total score. Make sure that all the players are in agreement on this because you'll also need to decide if you have to have the Jack of Diamonds in order to shoot the moon. If a player does shoot the moon, you should handle scoring in the standard way—meaning that the player who took the Jack of Diamonds has 10 points deducted from his or her score (that includes the shooter!).

Spades

Winning Plays

Did you know that Spades is an American game? It seems to have originated in the United States and doesn't have much of a following in the rest of the world.

Spades is usually played with four people. It is possible to play with fewer, but the preferred number of people is four (not necessarily in teams).

The game requires a standard 52-card deck. It is a trick-taking game where Aces are high. The object is to score 500 points. You can vary the end-game rules and point values, but the standard rule is 500 points.

The Art of the Deal

Cut the cards to choose the dealer. The person who gets the highest card gets to deal. The dealer should deal the cards in a clockwise direction (starting to his or her left). Play also commences to the left of the dealer. All 52 cards are dealt to each of the four players, so that each player winds up with 13 cards.

Bidding

Bidding usually opens a trick-taking card game and occurs immediately after the deal. Each person goes around the table and bids a certain point value. If you are playing as individuals (not teams), you look at your cards and, basically, try to guess how many tricks you think you'll be able to take. If your hand is a good one, you might think you can take five or six tricks. If your hand is a little low, you can bid one or two. There is also a time you can bid nothing at all (called "nil"), but we'll get to that in a minute.

If you are playing in partners, you have to bid as a team. You each have your own hand, but you cannot show each other your respective hands. You can, however, communicate to each other about how many tricks you think you can each take. For example, you can say "I think I can take three tricks, possibly five." But you can't say

"I have an Ace of Clubs and a 6 of Hearts." When you both agree upon a number, you write it down and that is your official bid. The side that did not deal the cards gets to bid first.

There are two different types of bids:

➤ **Nil:** This bid is declared if a player thinks he will not be able to win any tricks during play. This is a tricky bid (no pun intended). You have to have a pretty bad hand to bid "nil." If you succeed in not winning any tricks, you will score 50 points, so if you think you can pull it off—go for it. However, be prepared: Your opponents will work really hard to make you win a trick. If you are playing in teams, however, your partner will do his or her best to see that you don't win any tricks. If you wind up winning a trick, you lose 50 points. Sometimes it's a little less risky to bid at least one, since that way you will only lose 10 points—instead of 50!

➤ **Blind Nil:** This type of bidding is usually used in teams only. It means that you bid "nil" without looking at your cards first (thus, you're making a "blind" bid). If you pull off the Blind Nil, you will score 100 points. Some people play that if you bid Blind Nil, you and your partner can swap one card. This is considered a safety net in case you look at your hands and discover the dreaded Ace of Spades (the highest card in the "trump" suit). You can pass it to your partner and he or she, in turn, can pass you a low card. Sometimes people even allow two cards to be passed between partners—just be sure you have the rules straight for all players involved before you start passing cards around.

The Tricks

The player to the left of the dealer plays the first trick. You cannot lead the first trick with a Spade. In fact, you can only lead with a Spade once a Spade has been played as a discard in a previous trick. The only other time you can lead with a Spade is if you have no other card in your hand with which to lead. When you lead with a Spade, it's called "breaking Spades" (you have to admit that's not quite as catchy as in the game of Hearts: "breaking Hearts").

The players must follow suit according to what the lead player puts down. If the lead player puts down a 2 of Clubs, you must play another Club. The highest card of the suit takes the trick. If you don't have a card in the suit, you may play any card in your hand.

If a trick contains a Spade, the highest Spade wins the trick. If no Spade is played, then the highest card of the lead suit wins the trick. The winner of the trick leads the subsequent trick.

Score!

The round is over when you've exhausted all your cards. The winner of the round is the person who bid closest to the amount of tricks won. If you take at least as many tricks as you bid, you receive a total of 10 times your bid. Then you count the *overtricks*—otherwise known as "bagging" or "sandbagging."

On the other hand, if you don't make your bid, you lose 10 points for each trick you bid. So if you bid 4 and you only win 2 tricks, you will lose 40 points. You can see how important a good bid can be.

There are countless variations on the rules of Spades. It has been such a popular game that new variations come up all the time. The variants have been derived from years of heavy-duty enthusiasm. Don't be surprised if you come up with a few ideas of your own as you and your family catch on to the fun.

It's in the Cards

An **overtrick** (sandbagging) is the difference between what you bid and the tricks you actually take. So let's say you bid 4 (4 multiplied by 10 equals 40) but you win 6 tricks (6 minus 4 equals 2)—you have 2 overtricks (or sandbags) and would therefore score 42 points.

Knockout Whist

Knockout Whist (otherwise known as Trumps) is a great trick-taking game for kids. It is a good introduction to the more difficult games like Hearts, Spades, and Rummy because this game teaches the basic rules of trick-taking. Knockout Whist is simple and can be played by two to seven players. Make sure the kids have some stamina, though, because this game consists of seven hands.

The game is played with a 52-card deck and Aces are high. One player deals the cards and you can choose the dealer at random or cut the cards to determine who should deal. I like the idea of cutting cards when playing with kids. It is a lesson in fairness and luck of the draw.

Three Strikes

Some people play that if you get more than 10 overtricks over the course of a few games, then you will have 100 points deducted from your score. So watch those overtricks or you might see your point score going down, not up!

Let's Deal

The dealer hands seven cards to each player in a clockwise direction (meaning starting with the person to his or her left). The remaining cards are turned face-down in the middle. The top card is turned face-up to determine the trump suit.

The player to the left of the dealer plays the first trick. Each subsequent player must follow suit whenever possible. If a player doesn't have a card in that suit, then that player can play any card in his or her hand. The idea is to win the trick, so you want to play your higher cards in the suit in an effort to take the cards. Each trick is won by the highest trump card played—or by the highest card played of the suit led.

The winner of the trick leads the next trick. The player who wins the most tricks is the winner of the hand. The winner of the first hand chooses the trump suit on the next hand. If the hand results in a tie, the players should cut cards to determine who gets to call trumps on the next hand—another good lesson on fairness, cooperation, and plain old dumb-luck.

This is where the game gets interesting. After the first hand is played, the next hand is dealt by the next person seated to the left of the dealer—this time, however, the dealer deals one less card to each player. The play continues like this until each player is dealt only one card.

The Knock-Out

A player who does not take any tricks is knocked out of the game and cannot continue on to play the next hand—a process of elimination.

The exception to the knock-out rule is being awarded the "dog's life." This means that on the next hand, the "knocked-out" player can be dealt one card and has the option on which trick to play this one card.

There is a little humiliation tactic for this poor player. If you are awarded a dog's life, you can play the card on a given trick or you can choose to play it later. But if you choose to play it later, you must knock on the table indicating that you're going to hold on to it for a later trick. If the dog's life player is seated to the left of the dealer, he or she is not obligated to lead the next trick (that wouldn't be quite fair, now would it?) But he or she still has to knock to pass the play on to the next player. There is only one dog's life per game, but if two people tie on one trick (meaning neither one of them take a trick on one deal) then they can each get a dog's life. Players who cannot take tricks after a dog's life has been used in the game will be "knocked out" right away.

If a dog's life player manages to take a trick with his or her one card, he or she will be dealt a normal hand on the next deal. If he or she doesn't take a trick, then the knock-out applies and there are no chances left.

If all players are knocked out, the surviving player is the winner. Otherwise, the winner is the player who wins the last hand.

Crazy Eights

Crazy Eights was perhaps the most popular card game in my family. It was easy and all the kids could play. It is played by two or more players; the object is to exhaust your hand by placing your cards in a discard pile according to number (or rank) and suit. There are many variations to the game but here are the basic rules to guide you.

Let's Get Crazy

The dealer is chosen at random and deals five cards to each player. If there are only two players, then each player gets seven cards. The remaining cards become the discard pile and the first card of the pile is turned face-up and placed beside the pile.

The play begins with the player to the left of the dealer and continues in this clockwise pattern around the table. After the deal and the placing of the discard pile, the play begins. The options are to play a card face-up on the discard pile or pull a card from the face-down deck.

You can place a card on the discard pile face-up as long as it matches either the rank or the suit of the previous card. For example, if the top card is an Ace of Diamonds, you can either play another Ace or you can play any Diamond. If the top card is an 8, you must play the suit called by the player who called the 8. If the 8 is on the discard pile at the beginning of the game, you must play to the suit of that 8. An 8 is sort of a wild card in this game. For example, if you don't have any Diamonds or the rank of the card on the pile and it's your turn, you can play an 8 and call a suit that works better for your hand.

Winning Plays

Crazy Eights is such a popular game that there is even a commercial version of the game with a whole host of its own rules. That game is, of course, UNO, manufactured by Mattel. But rather than go running out to buy a deck of commercial cards, try some of these variants first—they are just as much fun.

But How Do I Win?

The person who gets rid of his or her cards first is the winner. The idea is to score no points at all. The other players will score points depending on the cards remaining in their hands:

➤ 8 = 50 points

➤ Face card = 10 points

➤ All others receive points according to their face value (2 card = 2 points, 3 card = 3 points, and so on); an Ace scores 1 point

So those are the basic rules to get you started in Crazy Eights. Because it is so simple, it is easy to come up with variations. People have added rules and made up new procedures throughout the years to create a variety of new games in the Crazy Eight family. Here are just a few:

➤ **Drawing cards:** One variant on the theme of Crazy Eights is to be a little bit more strict on when a player can draw a card from the pile. For example, try playing so that you can only draw a card if you have no other playable cards in your hand. If you can play a card in your hand, you must play it and you cannot fall back on the discard pile just because you don't *want* to play a certain card. Some play that you must keep drawing cards until you have a playable card, while other games allow you to pass after one draw.

➤ **One Card:** You can also play that you may have to say "Crazy Eight" when you have one card left. If you forget to say it when you have only one card, you must then draw eight additional cards.

Whatever you decide, just be sure all players are aware of the rules of play.

To really liven things up, you can change the meaning of certain cards to play a bigger part in the action of the game. Here are some ideas:

➤ **Skip:** You can designate any card as a Skip card—let's say a King. When a King is played, the next player loses a turn and play continues to that player's left.

➤ **Change Suit:** You can play that an 8 can change the suit of cards at any point in the game, or you may choose a tougher rule that says that an 8 must match a previously laid 8 or at least the same suit as the previous discard. Try playing so that if the 8 matches the previous suit, you can change the suit, but if it does not match the suit, you cannot change it.

➤ **Reverse:** Try an Ace or a Jack or some other card of note to be a reverse card. This means that when the designated card is played, the play reverses in the other direction. So if you're playing clockwise, the play switches to counter-clockwise.

➤ **Draw:** You can try designating a 2 to be a card that indicates a player must either draw two cards or play another 2 card of a different suit.

Give these variations a try. You'll find that they add a lot of life to the game.

The Least You Need to Know

➤ Hearts and Spades are good games for teenagers in the family, while Crazy Eights and Knockout Whist are better suited for those ages 7–12.

➤ In Hearts you want to do everything possible to ensure you do not get stuck with the Queen of Spades.

➤ Crazy Eights is a generic version of the commercial card game Uno, by Mattel.

➤ There are variations that can be played for all of these card games. Just make sure everyone playing is clear on the rules of the game before you begin.

Chapter 12

Classic Cards

In This Chapter

➤ Classic favorites

➤ Cribbage

➤ Rook

➤ Skip-Bo

➤ Tripoley

This chapter covers those classic card games your mother or Great Aunt Sally may have taught you. These timeless favorites are quirky and provide hours of fun for everyone—especially Cribbage, where keeping up with the language of the game is half the fun of playing. One for His Nob, indeed!

Cribbage

Cribbage is played with a standard 52-card deck—usually with two players. There are other versions that can be played by three or four players, but the standard game is just for two, so that's the version I'll cover.

The object of Cribbage is to be the first person to score 61 (or 121) over a series of matches. You accumulate points by forming card combinations during the game.

The Cribbage Board

You keep score by recording your points on a board that has holes where the pegs will be placed.

The cribbage board.

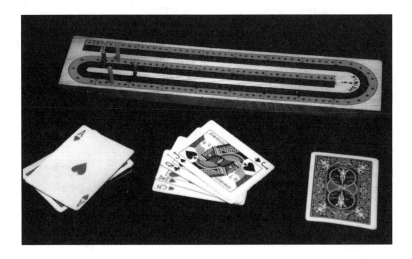

The cribbage board is placed between the two players. Each hole on the board is equivalent to one point. You have two pegs; one peg represents your current running score and the other peg marks your points from the last hand. In other words, each time you start a new game you'll alternate which pegs you use to move ahead. You'll always move the rear peg at the start of each new hand.

Playing Cribbage

There are two ways to play Cribbage. There's the five-card deal or the six-card deal. The only difference between the two games is in the scoring techniques. Basically, the six-card version has taken over the world of Cribbage while the five-card game is only played in parts of the United Kingdom. We will stick to the six-card version here.

Cut the cards to see who deals first; the person who cuts the lowest card will be the dealer. As compensation

Winning Plays

Cribbage has its roots in the United Kingdom and dates back to a seventeenth–century card and peg board game called "Noddy." However, some believe it actually dates back as far as Ancient Egypt! Cribbage remains particularly popular in the United Kingdom and the United States, and is still played with a board and pegs.

for not being the winner of the cut, the opposing player gets to peg ahead three points. You only cut cards in this manner on the first deal. After the first deal, you alternate for the deal. The dealer then shuffles the cards and the opposing player cuts them. Six cards are then dealt—one at a time—to each player. The undealt cards are placed face-down on the table.

At this point, each player must place down two cards from his or her hand to form the "crib." The crib is set aside until the end of the game. The nondealer should plan to discard nonvaluable cards (cards that will not form any combinations) because any card combinations in the crib will benefit the dealer only.

When the cards are dealt and the discards are set aside, it's time to choose a start card—this is done by both players. The nondealer cuts the cards and the dealer takes the top card from the bottom part of the cut and turns it face-up on top of the stack. This card is called the "start card."

If the start card is a Jack, then the dealer gets to peg ahead two points. The expression for this play is "two for his heels." You'll find a lot of expressions like this in Cribbage—probably originating from some centuries'-old pub card games.

Winning Plays

In some circles the crib is also known as the "box."

Let's Go! Play and Points

Now that the set-up is complete, it's time for the two players to get going. The nondealer starts by turning a card face-up in front of him- or herself. The dealer then does likewise. You alternate playing your cards, calling out the total point value of the cards with each card placed. You are playing to one pile. In other words, you are both adding cards to the same pile and adding the card to the total value as you play.

One person turns a card and says the total value, then the next person turns a card and says the new total value … and so on. For example: If the pile is at 10 points and you add a 3, then you say "13." This part of the game is not unlike Blackjack, only you try to score to 31 and not 21—and you're playing to one pile, not to individual piles.

You keep laying cards down in front of you until you reach 31. At this point of the game you cannot exceed 31 points. If you place the card that brings the total to exactly 31, you get to move your peg forward 2 points and the play is complete.

If you can't play without going over 31 points, you don't play a card, but instead say "go." If your opponent says "go" back to you, it means both players have either used all the cards in their respective hands or the players have cards that are too high to score 31. If neither one of you can score 31, the play ends and the last player to play a card gets to peg ahead 1 for the "last card." You continue playing until all the cards have been played—you start at zero again each time 31 has been reached or both players say "Go."

If you reach 61 points before your opponent reaches 31 points (or 121 points before your opponent reaches 91 points), you will be considered the winner of two games (this is called a "lurch").

Card Values/Points

This is another game for which you will need a pen and paper to keep score. Here's how you do it:

➤ Ace = 1 point

➤ 2 to 10 = Face Value

➤ Jack, Queen, King = 10 points each

If you score any of these points (see below), you must peg them immediately. In other words, if you place a card down and call out one of these totals, you automatically score points.

Points for combinations:

➤ 15 = 2 points

➤ 31 = 2 points

➤ Pair (two cards of same rank; i.e., you play one King, and then another King is placed down) = 2 points (scored by the person who lays down the second King in this example)

➤ Pair Royal (three successive face cards of same rank) = 6 points scored by the person who lays third card.

➤ Double Pair Royal (four cards of same rank) = 12 points scored by the person who lays fourth-ranking card.

➤ Run: three or more cards of consecutive rank (and they don't have to follow suit); 3-4-5 or Ace-2-3-4 (remember Aces are low). The point value of a run is equal to the number of cards placed.

Run Example 1: Let's say the run order is 4-2-3-5-6—the person who places the 3 scores 3 points; the player who places the 5 scores 4 points (because 5 is the fourth card placed in the run); and the player who places the 6 scores 5 points.

Three Strikes

Pay close attention! It's tricky during Cribbage to catch these runs in the beginning, and you very well may miss them. You'll be focusing on scoring 31 so you might not be thinking in terms of combinations. But, be alert—you want to score those points!

Run Example 2: Let's say the run order is 4-2-3-4-3. The player who puts down the first 3 scores 3 points for the run 4-2-3. The player who placed the second 4 scores 3 points for the run 2-3-4. The last 3 is not worth any points because it does not complete any kind of consecutive run.

The Show

At the end of the game, the players reveal the remaining cards in their hands—first the dealer, then the nondealer. The cards are scored. The start card also counts toward combinations at this point.

Let's look at some of the possible combinations:

➤ **15:** Any combination adding up to 15 points scores 2 points. So, if your hand at the end of the game contains a King, a Queen, and two 5s, you would score 8 points. (Look at the start card to see if you could possibly get more.) Here's why: you have four 15s because each face card can be paired with each 5. So you would say aloud "fifteen-two, fifteen-four, fifteen-six, fifteen-eight." Indicating how many 15s you have in your hand and their point value—ending with your final tally of 8.

➤ **Pairs:** A pair of cards of the same rank will give you 2 points. Three cards of the same rank will score 6 points. The reason for the 6 points is due to the fact that three matching cards consist of 3 different pairs—a "Pair Royal." Since four cards of one rank is actually 6 pairs, you score 12 points.

➤ **Run:** Scoring a run is a little complicated. Basically if you have an Ace-2-3, you score 3 points for the run of three cards. That's easy. But if you have a hand of 6-7-7-8, you score 12 points. Here's why: 6-7-7-8 contains two runs of 3, two 15s, and a pair—so the two runs of 3 = 6 + the two 15s = 4 + the pair = 2, which is a total of 12. Be careful not to miss the hidden points. If you have a 9-10-Jack-Queen, you will only score 4 points. You'd think you'd score 6 points, because there are clearly two runs of 3—but the rules say for this combination, you only get 4 points.

➤ **Flush:** There is no such thing as a flush when you're counting combinations during play. A flush only applies at the end of the game when you're showing your cards. A flush means you have four cards of the same suit in your hand and you score 4 points. If the start card is also of the same suit, you get an

Winning Plays

Did you know that Cribbage is the only gambling card game allowed in English pubs (gambling meaning it's the only card game allowed that can legally be played for money)?

extra point—so your total will come to 5 points. You do not score 4 points if you have three cards of one suit and the start card makes four. You have to have at least four of the same suit in order for the start card to count.

➤ **One for His Nob:** If you have a Jack in your hand that matches the suit of the start card, you score an extra point. There's another one of those old-fashioned British card-playing expressions!

High Score

Don't forget the start card: The start card can be very valuable when adding up your hand at the end of play. For example, if you have a 6-7-8-8 in your hand and the start card is a 9, you will score 16 points: There are three 15 totals (6 points), a pair (2 points), and two runs (8 points)!

The Crib

After the nondealer adds up his or her cards and pegs the appropriate number of points on the cribbage board, it's the dealer's turn to do some adding up. There should be four cards in the crib. So with those cards, the start card, and his or her own hand, points are added up and pegged.

The game is over when one person scores 61 points or more (or 121). This can happen at any point during the game: during play, during show, or when the dealer gets "two for his heels" (when the start card is a Jack) .

Rook

Rook has been in the United States for at least a century. A specially designed 57-card deck was officially introduced by Parker Brothers in 1906. There are four suits in this deck: red, green, black, and yellow, and the numbers on the cards range from 1 to 14. The Rook card, featuring the picture of a bird, is a high-point card that can be used as an extra trump.

Rook is a bidding and trick-taking game that should be played with a minimum of four people (two pairs). The object of the game is to score as many points as possible with the cards in your hand.

Cards are valued as follows:

➤ 5 = 5 points

➤ King, 10, and 14 = 10 points

➤ Ace = 15 points

➤ Rook = 20 points (counts as extra trump)

➤ Winning the last "trick" = 20 points

The number 14 card is high and 1 is low. There are 200 points that can be won in each hand. Decide beforehand how many points you would like to play to: It is common to play to 1,000 points.

Winning Plays

Did you know that Rook is very popular in the Mennonite communities of Pennsylvania, Ohio, and parts of Canada? It is believed that the game derived from fundamentalist religions that believed card-playing with a standard 52-card deck was evil. These fundamentalists may have gotten this idea from the bad rap that gamblers have given to various card games over the years, thus associating cards with drinking, gambling, and philandering. But clearly the need for such entertainment was great enough for Parker Brothers to fill the gap with the development of Rook. It is interesting that Rook has all the makings of a gambling game, and yet it is considered acceptable mainly because it is played with a special deck.

By Hook or by Rook

Partners should sit across from each other. Cut to see who deals first. The dealer shuffles and then deals all the cards and places the last card face-down on the table. Once the cards are dealt, the bidding can begin.

Each person bids, starting with the person to the left of the dealer, and continues bidding until everyone but one person has passed. That person, the winner of the bid, calls trumps.

The bidding starts at 70 and increases in increments of 5. You are bidding on the minimum value of points you think you and your partner will score by the end of the game (when the last trick is played).

The point of bidding is to win the right to call trumps. The trump suit beats all other suits. Remember when you are bidding that you can't see your partner's hand, and your bid is based on

Three Strikes

Be careful not to bid too high, because you will lose if you go over the total amount scored by you and your partner.

both your hands. As mentioned earlier, each hand is worth 200 points. You might be wondering why you would want to stop bidding before 200 since that's the highest you can go. Well, if you win the bid and you and your partner score fewer points than what you bid, you lose the number of points that you bid. So try for the minimum points you think you can get.

When the bidding is over, the winner of the bid takes the card from the center and returns a card from his hand face-down in front of him or her. The winner can return the original card that he or she pulled from the center if it is not useful to his or her hand. The winner and his or her partner keep any points that this dropped card is worth.

At this point in the game, passing begins. Each player passes three cards, face-down, to the right (or the left, but alternating right/left/right between hands). The winner of the bid must call trump before picking up the cards that have been passed to him or her. No one is allowed to pass cards that have been passed to him or her; you must pass cards from your original hand. When each player has passed cards and trump has been called, play begins.

Let's Rook

Play starts with the dealer or the person to the dealer's left (it's the dealer's choice). The goal is to try to play a card from your hand that matches the first card played. If you have no card in the suit of the first card played, you can play a trump card to beat the others playing in that suit (but follow suit first—you can only play a trump if you have none of the suit that was led).

If you don't have a card in the same suit and you also don't have a trump card, then you may play a card of any suit—but make sure it's a low card because it is likely you will not win the trick. The winner of the trick takes all the cards in the center, places the hand face-down in front of himself or herself, and then leads the next trick.

Whoever wins the trick gets to keep all the points associated with those cards. If you win the trick, you should keep the winning piles next to you or next to your partner. You then lead the next trick. Play continues until all cards have been played.

These are the rules for winning the trick:

➤ The winning card is the highest card played in the lead card's suit (with the exception of the trump card—trump cards beat all other suits).

➤ The highest card played in a trump suit wins (if other players play a card in the trump suit).

Winning Plays

Did you know that you can play Rook with a standard 52-card deck? Just use a Joker as the Rook and play the game according to the same rules as the special deck.

➤ In each suit, Ace is high and 2 is low.

➤ The Rook is always the lowest trump. It is always trump, but is lower than the 2 of trump. In other words, since it is a trump card it beats any other suit, but it is the lowest in its own suit.

Scoring

When all the tricks are played, it's time to count the points. There are 200 points in each game, and since you will likely play several games, running scores can go up to at least 1,000 points.

Here is where the bidding at the beginning of the game affects your total score. If the team who won the bid and called trumps at the beginning does have as many points as they bid, their points are considered "set." They cannot add the amount of their cards to their total, but have to subtract the amount that they bid from their total. The team that did not call trumps may add to their total with no restrictions.

For example, if you win the bid at 120 points and you win 120 points in the game, then you and your partner add 120 points to your total score and 80 points (the number of points your opponents won) are added to your opponents' total score.

But if you win the bid at 120 points and you only win 105 points, then 120 points are subtracted from your total score and 95 points (the number of points your opponents won) are added to your opponents' total score.

High Score

A rare bonus: If a team takes all the tricks, they get a 100-point bonus. This is a very rare occurrence—so rare that the other players might not be aware of it. So talk about it in advance and if it happens, be prepared to celebrate!

Skip-Bo

Skip-Bo is a great family game from Mattel. It can be played with two to six players, ages seven and up. The object of the game is to be the first to play all the cards in your "stock" pile (we'll get to that … don't worry!).

There are 144 cards in a deck plus 18 Skip-Bo cards. The numbered cards range from 1 to 12. The Skip-Bo cards are wild cards. You will have to make some room in the playing area for lots of card piles.

Miles of Piles

In the center of the table, or in the center of whatever play area you decide upon, place the "draw" pile. Next to the draw pile, set aside a spot for four "building" piles (which will be built during play and don't exist at the beginning of the game). Each player will have a "stock" pile in front of him or her and up to four discard piles (which will also be built during play and don't exist at the beginning of the game). Sound complicated? Well, it's really not—there are just a lot of piles to contend with.

Get Ready, Get Set, Skip-Bo!

Now that your playing area is set up and you have left plenty of space for all the piles you'll see accumulate in front of you, let's learn how to play the game.

To figure out who deals the deck, each player should draw a card—the highest card wins. If you pull a Skip-Bo card, you're out of the draw—those cards don't count. The play moves to the left of the dealer and that player draws the first card. How many cards each player is dealt depends on how many players are in the game.

When there are two to four players, the dealer hands out 30 cards to each player. When there are five or more players, each player is dealt 20 cards. The cards are dealt face-down and they automatically become your stock pile. Players must turn the top card of the stock pile over so that it faces up—but may not look at any other cards in that pile, which remains face-down. The remaining undealt cards become the draw pile and are placed face-down in the center.

To start the game, the player to the left of the dealer draws five cards from the draw pile. If this player has a number 1 card or a Skip-Bo card on top of his stock pile, or in his hand of newly pulled cards, he or she can use this card to start the building pile. Simply place your number 1 card or Skip-Bo card face-up and that will be the bottom of the first building pile. Then build consecutively from there (the number 2 card follows 1, and so on).

High Score

Don't forget that the only way to win the game is to play all the cards from your stock pile. So you want to make sure you've exhausted that pile before reaching into the others.

This player may then continue by playing another card from his or her stock pile. If the player is able to put down all five cards, then he or she may draw five more cards and continue playing. If you can't play any more cards, or choose not to, you must discard one of the cards from your hand onto one of your discard piles. When it is your turn again, you must first draw enough cards to bring your hand back up to five, then you may add to the building piles by playing the top card from your stock or discard piles, or from your hand.

When the draw pile is exhausted, you may shuffle the completed building piles and make those the new draw pile.

Keeping Score

The best way to play Skip-Bo is to play several rounds and keep a running tally after each game. The winner of each game scores 5 points for each card remaining in his opponents' stock piles. Additionally, if you're the winner, you get another 25 points just for winning the game. You win the game by using up all the cards from your stock pile. The first person to score 500 points is the winner. If you don't want to play several rounds, then the first person to use up his stock pile is the winner and you can just leave it at that.

Tripoley

Tripoley combines three card games in one: Hearts, Poker, and Michigan Rummy. It can be played by two to nine players (although it is best if played by four to seven people) and is a great game for teens and adults. The game is played using a standard deck of playing cards and chips. The object of the game is to make high-scoring card combinations by discarding and picking up new cards and making bids as you play. The first player to discard all his or her cards wins all the chips in the kitty.

The game is played with a standard 52-card deck, and Aces are high. You may also want to use chips for betting purposes. You should also have a chalkboard or a labeled piece of paper for writing down the stakes. You should separate the chalkboard, or piece of paper, into sections labeled: Ace of Hearts, King of Hearts, Queen of Hearts, Jack of Hearts, Ten of Hearts, King-Queen of Hearts, 8-9-10, Kitty, and Pot. This is your stakes board.

Winning Plays

Did you know that Tripoley is based on an old European card game called "Poch"?

Each player starts the game by placing nine chips on each of the labeled sections on the stakes board. Then the dealer deals out the deck, one card at a time, to each player, in a clockwise direction. The dealer also deals out a spare hand (as if there's an invisible player), which does not belong to anyone.

By the end of the deal, some players will have one more card than other players. After looking at his or her hand, the dealer can decide to swap his or her hand for the spare hand, but is not allowed to look at the spare hand before deciding to make the swap. When the swap is made, the dealer's hand is placed face-down and the dealer's old hand becomes the spare hand. The two hands cannot be combined.

Now here's a cool twist. If the dealer wants to, he can offer the *unseen* spare hand for sale to the highest bidder. The bidding is made in chips and the buyer of the hand must give the amount bid (in chips) to the dealer. The winner of the bid takes the spare hand and places his or her old hand face-down in the center. If the dealer offers the spare up to the auction block and no one bids, he or she can still choose to swap his or her hand for the spare hand.

Not only does the dealer have the right to swap his or her hand for the unseen hand, but even after he or she makes the swap, he or she can offer up his or her old hand on the auction block. However, when he or she makes the swap for the unseen hand, he or she has to keep that hand; he or she can't change it back for his or her old hand.

The Stakes Board

If you have any of the following cards in your hand, you take the chips from that corresponding spot on the stakes board:

Ace of Hearts, King of Hearts, Queen of Hearts, Jack of Hearts, 10 of Hearts.

If you have both the King and Queen of Hearts, you can take the chips from the King and Queen spaces as well as from the King-Queen space.

You can take the chips from the 8-9-10 space if you have 8, 9, and 10 cards in one suit. The suit does not have to be Hearts. If more than one player has an 8, 9, and 10 in one suit, you have to share the chips that are in the 8-9-10 space. However, the chips must be shared equally, so if there are two players who can take chips from that space and there are nine chips in the space, they each take four and leave the extra chip for the next winner of that sequence. It is not unusual to have leftover chips on the stakes board.

The Play

The play begins with a round of Poker. If you're not familiar with Poker, see Chapter 18, "Poker Face."

Each player picks five cards from their hand that they think will be suitable for a poker hand. The rest of the cards can be temporarily put aside. You don't have to play your best poker hand because you may have cards you want to hold on to until later in the game.

You place your poker bets in the space labeled "pots" on your stakes board and start the play to the left of the dealer. The player to place a bet, or to check (pass or bet nothing), should be the player to the left of the dealer. If this first player checks, then the next player can bet or check, and this continues in a clockwise direction. When all the players have checked, all the hands must be revealed and the person with the best hand (highest hand) wins the pot. If the first player bets and doesn't check, then the other players may do the following:

➤ **Pass** or **fold:** The player drops out of the betting and cannot win the pot. All chips placed in the pot by the player go to the winner.

➤ **Call** or **see:** The player puts an equal number of chips (bets an equal amount) as the player who placed the last bet.

➤ **Raise:** The player puts in the same number of chips that would be needed to "call" (in other words, matches the bet of the previous player) *plus* some additional chips.

➤ **Check:** The player may check if no one before him or her has bet. To check is to pass your turn or to bet nothing. If the player before you has placed a bet, you must either "see" (match) the bet or pass.

The betting continues until all the players (except one) fold. The player who doesn't fold wins the chips in the pot. No cards need to be exposed. The person who wins the pot could actually have a worse hand than the other players, but if he or she is the only one who doesn't fold, then he or she takes all the chips in the pot. In other words, in this case, it doesn't matter who has the best hand.

The betting can also continue until all the players who do not fold have equal stakes. So, after a bet or raise, and all other players either fold or call, a showdown occurs between the remaining players. Everyone reveals his or her hand, and the person with the best hand wins the pot. This means that the players who folded, even if they actually had a better hand, are out of luck. They cannot win the pot and they lose all the chips they contributed to the pot.

The players who folded do not have to reveal their hands. There's no point; they lost the round. If two players have an equal hand as revealed during the showdown, they must split the chips in the pot equally (even split—so if there are 21 chips in the pot, the two winning players get 10 each and the one remaining chip is left their for future rounds).

If you cannot lead after placing an Ace, or stop card (more on this later), because your cards are of the same suit previously played, then you will have to pass your turn to the player on your left. If that player can't play either, then he or she passes to the player on his or her left. If no one can play, then each player must place chips into the kitty. The chips placed into the kitty, in this situation, should be equal to the number of cards left in your hand. These chips will stay there until someone wins.

High Score

You should agree at the beginning of the game how high you will allow the betting to go. If you agree that the limit is 20, then no one may make an initial bet of more than 20. This means that they also may not raise the bet by more than 20 chips in order to match the previous bet or raise.

It is not unusual to have chips left over on the stakes board by the end of the game—usually in the King-Queen and 8-9-10 spaces. Most people prefer, rather than to divide up the chips amongst the players, to play an extra round of Poker for the chips. Just move the chips over to the pot and play your best hand. Don't add any more chips to the board, just play for what's left.

The Final Phase

Once the Poker hand is over and the winnings are collected, the players put their Poker cards back into their original hand. The winner of the Poker pot begins the next round of the game, which is similar to the game of Michigan Rummy. The Poker winner plays by putting down a card, face-up, in the center. (If there is a tie in the poker round, the person closest to the left of the dealer begins the next round.)

The card can be of any suit, but should be the lowest card that he or she holds in that suit. The player with the next-highest card in that same suit places a card down next, and so on. This continues until the Ace of that suit is placed down or until you reach a "stop card." A stop card is a card that is placed that no one can play to. In other words, if a 9 of Hearts is placed down and no one can place the 10 of Hearts because it is either in the spare hand or was previously played, then the 9 of Hearts is the stop card.

Whoever places that final Ace or the stop card makes the next play. They can put down any suit except the one just played. Again, they can play the lowest card they have in that suit. The play continues just like it did in the previous round until one person has used up his or her cards. The player to play all his or her cards wins all the chips in the "kitty." In addition to the kitty, the winner also collects chips from each player equal to the number of cards they have left in their hands.

The Least You Need to Know

➤ Cribbage is a complicated game for more sophisticated players. In addition to keeping track of combinations and point scores, there's a whole new vocabulary you can learn!

➤ Rook uses a specialty deck but can be fashioned from a standard 52-card deck if you prefer.

➤ Skip-Bo is a card game from Mattel for younger players. Make sure you allow lots of room for play with all those piles!

➤ In order to master Tripoley, brush up on your Poker hands first. Tripoley is a fun game for older family members—adults and teens—and involves bidding, bluffing, and high stakes!

Chapter 13

Fun for One: Games of Solitaire

In This Chapter

➤ Solitaire and Double Solitaire

➤ Forty Thieves and Pyramid

➤ Clocks, Calculation, and Russian

My earliest memories of card-playing begin with my parents playing solitaire. Sometimes my mother would sit at the kitchen table or on the living room floor and start idly playing a game. I used to watch her—wondering what she was doing as she flipped the cards, paused, and then flipped again. Eventually, when she thought I was old enough to understand, she showed me how to play.

She also used to play Clock. That was even more mesmerizing because the tableau is a circle. She taught me how to play that game, too, when I got a little older. In this chapter, you will learn how to play variations of standard Solitaire. So when the games are put away for the night and the kids are all tucked in, try a few rounds of Solitaire to wind down. Who knew that playing cards alone could be so much fun?

Solitaire's Not Always Just for One

My parents used to regularly challenge each other to a round of Double Solitaire. This was always entertaining and the outcome was almost always predictable. They'd be playing happily for a while, chatting about the game or other events in their lives when all of a sudden they'd both try to make the same play. My mother would hold her card down, trying to push my dad's hand off, and my father would tickle her to make her let go. My father usually won the battle and this would make my mother nuts. This kind of standoff happens a lot in Double Solitaire and a similar, faster game called Spit (see Chapter 14, "Cards for the Kids") and, although I wouldn't recommend my parent's way of solving these disputes, it certainly was entertaining to watch.

After a couple of standoffs, with my father always turning out the winner, my mother would get so fed up that she'd throw her cards down, lean into the foundation piles and with both hands mess up all the cards (this is similar behavior to some of her board-flipping techniques). This frustrated my father—who really liked to win—and he'd start grumbling something about her being a poor loser. While she laughed her way out of the room, my father was usually left to clean up the cards.

So, while Solitaire is designed to be a game for one person—with the exception of games like Double Solitaire and Spit—you can achieve hours of family laughter just watching people play the games.

So What's Solitaire All About?

The goal of Solitaire is to build piles with cards ascending or descending in some particular order. The piles may be square or they may be *fanned*. Sometimes the piles are empty—just waiting for you to build them.

The term "rank" in all card games refers to the face (or number) value of the card. For example, the rank of a 4 card is four, and so on. The Ace is the lowest-ranked card in Solitaire games—you can think of it as having a value of "one." The Jack, Queen, and King count as 11, 12, and 13 when building a pile.

It's in the Cards

A **fan** is a pile of cards fanned out and facing up. Only the top card of the fan will be fully visible—the rest will be partially covered. Fans may be spread out in any direction.

In a standard game of Solitaire, you build the tableaus down from the highest card (King) to the lowest card (2), alternating colors—black on red or red on black, but not according to suit.

Foundation piles are separate, and begin when you draw an Ace. You build up the foundation piles according to rank and suit—you will have four piles, one of each suit.

Other games allow you to build piles by rank alone—or by alternating colors (a red 4 goes on a black 5). In some games, you build the piles in a circular rotation—meaning you can build up and/or down according to rank (4 goes on a 5, you can put another 4 on that same 5, and so on). The rules of movement from one pile to another depend on the game you are playing.

In standard Solitaire (or Russian Solitaire), you build the piles by suit in ascending order according to rank.

The deal varies from game to game, but basically after you set up the *tableau,* you deal from the remaining cards left in the deck. Some games don't have any dealing at all because you use all the cards to build your tableau and foundation piles.

And finally, each Solitaire game has a different layout (the pattern of the game).

Now let's get started. There are hundreds of Solitaire games to learn, but I've picked some of the most popular.

It's in the Cards

A **tableau** consists of your working cards. You build and maneuver cards on your tableau in order to eventually move them to your foundation piles.

Clocks

Clocks is played with two decks for a total of 104 cards. It is predominantly a game of luck.

The object of the game is to move all the cards to the *foundation piles*, which in this case are laid out as a clock face.

Deal the cards in a circular pattern so that you have the specific number of cards in the pile that represents the number on the clock face. For example, one card goes in the 1 spot on the clock face, two cards on 2, three cards on 3, and so on, until you have twelve cards on 12. You should deal the cards one at a time as opposed to just counting cards and putting them on that spot.

It's in the Cards

The piles in Solitaire on which you are building are known as the **foundation piles.** The goal of most Solitaire games is to move the cards from the tableau to these foundation piles. Often the foundation piles are empty at the start—you build to them as the play continues.

There are 12 foundation piles. The piles are built in a circular pattern. The goal is to build these piles so that they correspond to their places on the face of a clock. For example, if you have a 5 card in the 2 o'clock space, you have to build that number down to a 2.

Use the following cards to complete the clock:

➤ Jack = 11 o'clock

➤ Queen = 12 o'clock

➤ Ace = 1 o'clock

It's in the Cards

Cards are said to be **available** when they can be moved. In other words, there's nothing blocking them from being moved from one place to another.

It's in the Cards

Your **stock pile** is the pile of cards from which you deal. Sometimes you draw three cards from the stock pile, sometimes two cards, and in yet other games, you draw one card. It all depends on what rules you decide to set for a particular game.

Aces are high or low, so you can put an Ace on a 2 or on a King.

There are 12 fans of three cards on the tableau. You build down in suit (a 10 can be played on a Jack, for example). The top card of each pile is considered *available* (playable) and can be moved from one tableau to another or to the foundation piles. You can only move one card at a time, and any card may be used to fill an empty spot on a foundation.

When you can't manipulate any more spaces on the clock, you start dealing from your *stock pile*. Deal three cards at a time; the top card dealt is the card you can play. You can use this top card to build on the foundation.

The game is over when the clock face is built with all ranking cards in their appropriate locations on the clock face.

Golf

This game is called Golf because people find this a difficult game to win. So instead of playing to win they play for "par." Each game represents a hole and the number of cards remaining in the tableau at the end of the game represents the number of strokes it took for you to play the hole. Each hole is par 4, so par for nine holes is 36. Hey, why not? It's better than flat out losing!

Lay out seven cards face-up in a row and deal four more cards face-up onto each row so that there are five visible cards per row. Above these rows of cards, place a card face-up—this card is the first card in your *waste pile*. Keep the rest of your deck in your hand.

The object of the game is to use your tableau to build on the waste pile. You can either build up or down according to the rank—but you can't do both. In other words, you can choose to build in ascending order or descending order, but you can't go back and forth. You can't build 2-3-4-3-2, but you can build 2-3-4-5 or 5-4-3-2. You cannot move cards between rows on the tableau. You can never build on a King. You can deal a single card from the deck in your hand onto the waste pile whenever you feel it's necessary.

It's in the Cards

The **waste pile** is the pile of cards that you cannot draw from to build either on your foundation or on your tableau. If the top card on the waste pile is playable, you can move it onto one of your layout piles. Once this card is played, the next card on the waste pile is considered the next available card. You can play it if there's a place for it to go—if not it just becomes part of the waste pile.

Forty Thieves

This game is played with two decks for a total of 104 cards. Mix the decks together by shuffling. (Have you ever tried shuffling two decks at once? It's not easy!) The goal of this game is to move all the cards from the tableau and discard pile to the foundations. You can only move one card at a time. Multicard moves are not permitted. Multicard move means to take a group of cards from a tableau and move it to the foundation.

Forty cards are laid out in 10 tableau piles. There are four cards to each pile and they are placed face up and fanned out. The remaining cards stay in the deck. The eight foundation piles and one discard pile start out empty. You will be building these as you go along. The top cards of the tableaus and the top card of the discard pile are considered available.

You build the tableaus down according to suit. Any available card may be played to an empty tableau.

Foundation piles are built up according to suit (starting with the Ace and ending with the King).

You may deal a new card any time you want to from the deck to the discard pile. You usually do this if there are no more moves available from the tableau.

Pyramid

Pyramid Solitaire is played with one deck of cards, and it's quite an interesting and challenging game. It's really hard to win, so similar to Golf, there is a point scoring system that allows you to play for par instead of the win.

The object of Pyramid is to discard all the cards from the pyramid and stock pile by eliminating pairs of cards that total 13.

Shuffle the deck and then use the cards to build a pyramid. Starting with one card at the top of the pyramid and adding cards to each row until you have a pyramid with seven cards on the bottom. There should be a total of 28 cards in your pyramid. At least two cards in each row should overlap a card on the row above. This applies to every row except the bottom row. This is your tableau.

After the pyramid is built, the remaining cards become your stock pile. There are two other piles, the waste pile and the discard pile—but at the beginning of the game, these piles are empty. The cards are turned up from the stock pile one at a time and then placed on the waste pile face-up. The top card of both the waste pile and stock pile are considered available for play. All cards on the pyramid are also available for play. The only cards not available for play are those that are overlapped by other cards.

Cards are gathered in pairs when they add up to 13.

The picture cards have the following values:

> ➤ Jack = 11 points
>
> ➤ Queen = 12 points
>
> ➤ King = 13 points
>
> ➤ Ace = 1 point

Other cards are equal to their face value.

So an Ace + a Queen = 13 and 5 + 8 = 13. Because a King is valued at 13, he can be discarded as a single card. You can redeal in this game by using the waste pile when you've exhausted the stock pile. Just turn over the waste pile and play it as the new stock pile. You may have a total of three deals. Once you've discarded all cards from the pyramid and stock pile, you win the game!

Because it is hard to win a game of Pyramid, there is a scoring system that allows you to play for par. Play the game as you normally would—if you discard all the cards in the pyramid, make a note of the deal on which you accomplished this (deal one, two, or three—remember you're only allowed three deals. When the game is over (meaning you've gone through three total deals and no other moves are possible), count the cards that were not discarded.

Winning Plays

Did you know that in England, Solitaire is called Patience?

Deduct the number from:

> ➤ 50—if you discarded the pyramid cards on the first deal.

> ➤ 35—if you discarded the pyramid cards on the second deal.

> ➤ 20—if you discarded the pyramid cards on the third deal.

You do not deduct anything if you did not discard the pyramid cards.

Winning the game by par: You win the game if you can play six games and finish with a total score of zero or more.

Calculation

One deck of cards is used in this game, and the odds of winning are slim. But, it is more a game of skill than luck; so if you do manage to win, consider yourself a worthy opponent.

The object of Calculation is to build four foundation piles in a specific sequence. Place an Ace, 2, 3, and 4 face-up in a row. It doesn't matter what suit they belong to. These cards form the base of the four foundation piles. You will build the waste piles underneath the foundation piles.

The foundation piles are built in the following sequence (regardless of suit):

> ➤ **Ace Foundation:** 2, 3, 4, 5, 6, 7, 8, 9, 10, Jack, Queen, King

> ➤ **2 Foundation:** 4, 6, 8, 10, Queen, Ace, 3, 5, 7, 9, Jack, King

> ➤ **3 Foundation:** 6, 9, Queen, 2, 5, 8, Jack, Ace, 4, 7, 10, King

> ➤ **4 Foundation:** 8, Queen, 3, 7, Jack, 2, 6, 10, Ace, 5, 9, King

With the remaining cards in the deck, deal one card at a time. Each card dealt is considered available and can be played on the foundations. If the card can't be played, place it on one of the four waste piles, which you will build beneath the four foundations.

The top card of each of the four waste piles is considered available for play. You'll want to build the waste piles with the Kings on the bottom so you don't block any cards from play.

You win the game if all the foundations are built to the King. If you can't make any more moves and the foundations are not completely built—you lose!

Russian

This is the Solitaire game that many of us are most familiar with. The object of Russian is to move all the cards to the four foundations. You build the piles in ascending order according to rank and suit (from Ace to King).

147

Winning Plays

Most people nowadays play Solitaire on their computers. There are several software pro-grams that let you take advantage of a multitude of games on your home computer. Chances are pretty good that on your train ride home from work every day, many of the commuters "working" on their laptops are actually playing a version of Solitaire. It's the perfect game for your computer because it is what it says it is: a game for one person.

In Russian (or standard Solitaire), after your cards are dealt, you should have a tableau of seven facing cards in front of you. You start to build the tableau by laying down seven cards—all face-down except for the first card (on the far left) which is placed face-up. The piles are numbered one through seven. After the first layer is dealt, you go back to the second pile and lay a card down face-up; on piles three through seven, lay down another layer of cards face-down. After that layer, again go back to pile three and lay a card face-up, then continue to piles four through seven and lay the next layer down face-down. Go back to pile four and continue to lay cards in the same fashion. Continue on until you have all top cards facing up. You are now ready to play.

You play the tableau fan in descending rank from King to 2. You alternate the place-ment of cards according to color. For example, you can place a red 10 on a black Jack and so on.

There are eight foundation piles, starting with Aces. You build up in ascending order according to suit, starting with an Ace as your base card.

The top card of each column is available for play. You can play to another tableau or you can play to the foundations. You don't have to move just one card at a time—you can move groups of cards. So, if you have a 5 buried in a pile that you need to put on a founda-tion, you can move a whole group of cards off that card as long as you have a place to move the group. Empty spaces can be filled with a King.

You can take one card at a time from the stock pile for play on the tableau or on the foundation piles.

Winning Plays

There are also many different games of Solitaire to be found for the computer. You can find free downloads on the Internet and can also purchase many dif-ferent game versions.

If you manage to build all four foundation piles from Ace through King, you win and you can give yourself a big pat on the back! The odds are often against you in this game, so pay careful attention to how you move your cards—one wrong move and you could get stuck—meaning you won't be able to move any more cards. That means you lose!

Double Solitaire

Double Solitaire is the exception to the solo-game rule that we've come to learn. I had to include it, though, because it is how I learned to play Solitaire (not to mention the antics of my Solitaire-crazed parents).

The object is to build eight foundation piles starting with Ace and building up in ascending order to King. The game is played with two decks—by two people. You each get a deck and you each lay out your own tableau.

You lay out the cards in the standard (Russian) Solitaire way and begin to play in the exact same way as Russian Solitaire.

You deal three cards at a time from your stock pile. The top card of the cards dealt is the available card and can be played either to the foundation or to your tableau. You cannot play to your opponent's tableau. You can assist your opponent if you want. Believe it or not, if you help your opponent, you may keep the play going. He or she might think there are no more moves left in his or her hand, but if you see one, feel free to point it out in order to keep the game in motion.

You play the game as though playing Russian (standard) Solitaire—playing cards to your own tableau. Your opponent will be playing his or her tableau and you'll be playing yours. You don't have to take turns, you just play at whatever pace you want. But keep your eye on those foundation piles and make sure you're putting down at least as many cards on the foundation as your opponent. The difference between Russian Solitaire and Double Solitaire is that in Double Solitaire you can put any card on any foundation pile whether it was started by you or your opponent. This is where the fun begins!

You win the game when you're the first one to use all your cards to build the foundations. In order to win, you cannot have any cards in your stock pile or in your tableau.

In Russian and Double Solitaire, I like to play all the cards from my tableau to my foundation before dealing any cards from the remaining stock pile. I like to know that all the visible cards have been played before laying down any more cards in front of me.

In Double Solitaire, remember you're playing with two decks and two people. Be sure to have identifiable decks because you are going to mix up the cards (hopefully not by way of a tantrum or tickle fight) and you need to know which deck is which at the end of the game. If the game is a stalemate, you can always count the cards on the foundation piles to determine a winner. The person who laid the most cards on the foundations wins the game.

The rule in Solitaire regarding "group" moves is really up to you. But in Double Solitaire be sure that you and your opponent are on the same page about the rule. A "group" move means that if there's a card you need buried in the middle of the fan of your tableau, and you have a place to move the group, then you can do so to free up that buried card. For example, let's say you have a 5 of Diamonds buried in a fan on your tableau and you need that 5 to put on the 4 of Diamonds on one of the foundation piles. If you have a 5 of Hearts open and available on one of your tableau fans, you can lift the group of cards starting with the black 4, move it to the open 5 of Hearts, and you've officially freed your 5 of Diamonds to play on your foundation. My parents never agreed on the issue of "group" moves, and that was the cause of many card-flipping moments. It was quite amusing to watch, but if you want to avoid any family conflicts, make sure all players agree on that maneuver.

The Least You Need to Know

➤ Solitaire is a game designed for one player, but there are games for two players and it's also a fun game to watch others play.

➤ There are hundreds of different games of Solitaire.

➤ The goal of Solitaire is to build piles with cards ascending or descending in some particular order.

➤ Some games of Solitaire involve more than one deck of cards.

Chapter 14

Cards for the Kids

In This Chapter

➤ War

➤ Concentration

➤ Spit

➤ Old Maid

➤ Go Fish

I remember learning my first card game while staying at my grandmother's beach-house near the Long Island Sound in New York. My sisters and I spent every day on the rocky beaches running away from jellyfish, throwing seaweed at each other, collecting shells, and paddling around the shoreline in my grandfather's blue, plastic rowboat.

On the rainy days, my poor grandparents had to figure out a way to entertain three little girls. Sometimes we made things out of seashells, other times we painted with watercolors. Most times we pinched and teased each other and wound up running to my grandmother crying, "She hit me." On one such rainy day, my grandmother pulled out a deck of cards, sat us in a circle, and said, "Let's play cards."

Well, that certainly shut us up. She dealt the entire deck and taught us our very first trick-taking card game—War. War is a wonderful game for small children, as are any of the games covered in this chapter.

War

War was a great way for my grandmother to distract us from our own daily battles with each other. It was also a great way to help us learn the art of cooperation through game-playing. We played this game tirelessly through the rest of that summer, and continued to play even when we were back home in our daily routines of school and homework.

Our parents used to engage in a few games, but mostly we played against each other. I wouldn't want to kid anyone and say this was the miracle that solved our childish bickering—I'm sure we accused each other of cheating and wound up in a few hair-pulling war-games ourselves, but mostly I remember really enjoying the game.

When my siblings weren't around, sometimes I'd play by myself. I used to split the deck and play against an invisible opponent. I just played my mystery friend's hand as though someone else was actually sitting there playing against me. It didn't take me very long, however, to realize that this game required no brain power and ceased to be a challenge altogether. Then I moved on to bigger and better card games. But War sure was a great place to start.

How to Play

The object of War is to win all the cards in the deck through a series of tricks.

You use a standard 52-card deck. Aces are high. The tricks are played according to rank; suits are ignored. All 52 cards are dealt to each player (if you have two players, each player has a total of 26 cards). You do not look at your cards—you hold them in a stack face-down.

It's in the Cards

In the game of War, a **war** is a means to break a tie. When two cards of the same rank are played, you break the tie by playing new cards. The player with the highest-ranking new card wins the tie breaker and all the played cards.

Holding the stack of cards face-down in one hand, you use the other hand to flip the card face-up on the table in front of you. Each player flips a card, so if you have two players, you will have two cards facing up in front of you. The highest card wins the trick.

The person who wins the trick takes the cards from the center of the table and places them at the bottom of his or her stack of face-down cards. You continue play like this until one of you has accumulated all the cards. Believe me, this can feel like the never-ending game—your very own 100 Years War!

If you both play a card of the same rank—let's say you both play an Ace—you have to have a *war*. You leave the Aces face-up on the table and put one card on top of your Ace—face-down—and then another card face-up on top of the face-down card. So you'll have the following configuration of cards in front of you: the tied Ace, a face-down card, and a face-up card. The person with the highest face-up card takes all the cards on the table and places them face-down at the bottom of their stack.

If the top card is another tie, you place another face-down card, then a face-up card—basically, you keep going until someone wins the war. This is the best and fastest way to accumulate cards. If one of you runs out of cards in the middle of a war, the other player wins.

War for More

War can be played with more than two players (a relief to my grandmother, I'm sure). It is pretty much the same game for more than two, but, obviously, each player starts with fewer cards.

Each player should have an equal number of cards. If you have three players, deal out 17 cards each. If you have four players, deal out 13 cards each.

All players turn over a card and the highest card in the trick wins all the face-up cards on the table. A war is performed in the same way. If two or more players place down the same highest card (a tie), then everyone must participate in the war, including the lowest cardholders. If there is still a tie, you keep going until someone wins the war. To win the war, you must place down the highest card.

If a player runs out of cards at any point during the game, that player is out. The game continues until one person has managed to accumulate all 52 cards.

To make things a little more interesting, my sisters and I used to play Double War. That means that instead of placing just one card face-down during a war, you place two cards face-down. That way, you accumulate even more cards after a war and you speed up the game a little bit.

We also used to play with two decks and force our little brothers to join in the game. That was a very long game and keeping our brothers' attention on it was a bit of a challenge. But who knew that one simple little card game could keep five rambunctious kids occupied—on their own much of the time—for hours on end? The novelty did wear off when we realized it was solely a game of luck. That's when we graduated to other card games like Go Fish, for example.

High Score

Games such as War and Go Fish are great distractions for little ones on the go. Always keep a deck of cards on you for emergency measures. You never know when you'll be stuck in an airport or in traffic or just need a little break (while the kids are busy competing at cards). You won't regret lugging them around with you.

Old Maid

Despite the fact that the term old maid is not very nice in modern times, there are some really amusing Old Maid commercial card games out there. I know that many people play Old Maid with a standard 52-card deck, but honestly, to really entertain the kids, go buy one of the commercial versions of the game. The cards are often hysterical; kids will get a good laugh at some of the character face cards. There's something really fun about the visual image of the Old Maid—it makes receiving her 10 times more interesting than using a standard Queen.

But, in order to give you the basic understanding of the game, I will describe it here in its standard 52-card deck format. You'll need to know this version anyway—just in case the commercial deck gets lost on a rainy day. Don't get left stranded without that Old Maid!

Winning Plays

"Old maid" is an old-fashioned, and certainly outdated, reference for an older woman who has never been married. In modern times, this is a very rude way to refer to a woman who may have chosen to remain contentedly single—but since this is an old game, the term is not intended to offend women of independent means. In other words, it is not politically correct to refer to an unmarried woman as an "old maid"—it is insulting and derogatory. Try this: Instead of making the Old Maid card a Queen, make it a King and call the game "Depose the Monarch"—whoever gets stuck with the King is the loser.

Getting Started

This children's game can be played by two or more players. From a standard 52-card deck, remove one Queen, leaving 51 cards. (This way there is an odd Queen left in the deck, which will become the Old Maid.) Deal and play moving clockwise.

After all the cards are dealt, players should look at their cards and remove any pairs from their hand and put them over to the side. Cards are paired according to rank—suits are ignored in this game. Once all players have eliminated any pairs from their hands, the dealer starts the game.

Where's That Old Maid?

If you are the dealer, you must offer your hand to the player to your left. You do so by turning to your left and fanning out your cards face-down in front of the player next to you. The player must pull one card from your hand—without seeing it—and add it to his or her own hand. If this card makes a pair, the player who pulled the card removes the pair from his or her hand and places the cards to the side. If the card does not complete a pair, then the card remains in the hand of the player who pulled the card.

Play then continues to that player's left. In other words, the person who just pulled a card from the dealer's hand offers his or her hand, face-down, to the player on his or her left. That player pulls a card and either discards a pair the card completes, or keeps the pulled card in his or her hand.

The idea is to get rid of all your cards. Once you do, you're safe and out of the game.

What about the Old Maid, you're asking? Well, the play continues until everyone is safe (rid of his or her cards)—the one person left will be holding the Old Maid card. That player is the loser.

Concentration

This is a game that kids can probably beat most adults at hands down because it requires a good memory. (My memory was excellent as a kid and seems to have diminished with age and exhaustion!) The game is simple and a lot of fun. If you play it with kids, you'll find that they can spend a long time focusing on it and will show real determination to beat you at what they have to do a lot, thanks to school—memorize.

Take a deck of 52 cards and shuffle them well. Lay all 52 cards face-down on the floor or table in a square, grid-like pattern. Turning over one card at a time, you take turns trying to make a match. A match is two cards of equal rank—for example, two Aces, two Kings, and so on. You flip over two cards per turn. The object of the game is to memorize where the cards are on the floor. If you make a match, remove the matching cards from the grid. If you don't make a match, turn the cards back to their original face-down position and try again on your next turn. You keep turning over the cards trying to make a match until all the cards have been removed from the grid. Obviously, you will be trying to match rank and not suit.

The winner of the game is the player who has taken the most pairs.

Winning Plays

Did you know that concentration games are so popular that there are countless computerized versions sold in toy stores?

This game is definitely worth playing with your kids. You'll be amazed at how good their memories are.

Spit

When I was about 12 years old, I spent an entire summer in the country playing Spit with my best friend. I'm not exaggerating. Every day for two and a half months my friend and I played Spit while watching TV on rainy days or hanging out at the lake when the weather was nice. We were excellent opponents. We knew the game cold; we knew each other's tricks and maneuvers. We had rules established to avoid the whole card-messing scenario that my parents used to indulge in, and we even made up several of our own rules as we went along.

I considered myself a highly skilled player. I could move those cards so quickly—it became quite an art. I'd like to say I was a great painter or mathematician—it would be a much more interesting way to portray myself to the general public—but I was a talented Spit player. I'd also like to say I was better than my friend, but in truth, it's a tough call. We were both so good at it that taking on any other opponent was rather dull—and besides, another opponent would have thrown off my momentum.

Double Solitaire Gone Mad

Spit is basically "speed" Double Solitaire with a twist. You may want to teach your kids how to play Solitaire before teaching them this fast-paced version. It is played with two people, and the object is to move quickly and be the first one to eliminate cards from both your tableau (see Chapter 13, "Fun for One: Games of Solitaire") and your stock pile. You don't take turns—you play at the same time. The idea is to be faster than your opponent; you have to have a quick eye to see your moves before they happen, and an even quicker hand to get your cards onto the foundation piles.

High Score

Try to find an old beat-up deck for Spit. There are two reasons for playing with an old deck: First of all, your cards are going to get damaged in the craziness. And second, you'll be able to get a better grip on the cards if the deck is a little used. If it's a new deck, the cards will slide all over the place and you won't be able to move them around as quickly.

You set the game up in the same way as Double Solitaire, but with five piles in your tableau instead of seven (see Chapter 13) using a 52-card deck.

Split the deck so that you each have 26 cards. You each then set up your own tableau by dealing out five piles in front of you—cards face-down. On the first pile you will have one card, on the second pile two cards, on the third pile three cards, and so on. When you are done, turn up the top card on each of these piles. You will have 11 cards left in your hand (stock pile).

Begin to play as though you're playing Solitaire. The cards on the tableau are played by rank in descending order—alternating between red and black cards. Suit is not relevant on the tableau.

The foundation piles, referred to as "spit piles," are set up in the center space between you and your opponent. After the cards are dealt and your tableau is built, you may make any necessary moves on your tableau before turning a spit card. When you play a face-up card on your tableau (meaning you move it elsewhere), you then turn over the face-down card underneath it. If there is no card underneath it, you will be left with an empty space on your tableau. You can put any card in that space, it doesn't have to be a King (as it does in Russian Solitaire). You can never have more than five piles on your tableau.

Don't turn any cards from your stock pile until you and your opponent are finished making changes to your respective tableaus and you're both ready to "spit."

Sit opposite your opponent and set up your tableau.

1-2-3, Spit!

You will have 11 cards remaining after you lay out your tableau. These cards should be held in one hand, face-down. You will use your other hand to turn the cards one at a time. The cards you turn over are your "spit cards."

Here's the "spit" part: Before you turn the spit card over (face up), you and your opponent must say "spit" at the same time. What my friend and I used to do—just to be sure that we were both ready—was say "One, two, three, spit!" turning the card over on the word "spit." "Spit" basically means "go" (but isn't it way more fun to say "spit" than "go"?). By saying "One, two, three" before the word "spit," there is no question about one person turning a card before the other player was completely ready.

You cannot look at your stockpile until the top card is turned after saying "spit."

Making Your Moves

The card you turn over is considered available and can either be played to your tableau or to the spit piles. While you don't play to each other's tableau, you do play to each other's spit piles.

So after you "spit," the action begins. The object is to build on these two spit cards. You can play your stock pile and tableau cards to either of these spit cards. Suit does not matter; you play by rank of the card and you can play in ascending or descending order—this is called "circular" play. In other words, you can put a red 6 on a red 7 and your opponent can then put a black 6 on that red 7. You can also put an Ace on a King or a King on an Ace.

High Score

By the way, you can only use one hand to move cards to the spit piles. You can play the cards on your tableau with two hands, but any cards moved to the spit piles must be one-handed moves. (My friend and I used to play that you could only play with one hand, period.) So don't use two, or you may have to forfeit.

Let the Spit Fly

The art of Spit is to play quickly and beat your opponent to the spit piles. You are in a race to build the spit piles, using up all your cards in your stock pile and on your tableau before your opponent uses up his or hers. Not only will you have to keep your eye on your tableau and on the spit piles, but you'll have to keep one eye on your opponent's tableau to anticipate future moves. That's the tricky part!

Don't forget, you play to both spit piles; but when you spit again, you spit on top of your original spit pile. You can only spit again when you both cannot make any further moves. If you see a move your opponent can make that he or she isn't seeing, you can point it out ... but don't do that unless you think it will benefit you—otherwise, your opponent might wind up on a roll and you might be stuck.

The funny part is that sometimes your opponent will be completely stuck, unable to make any move, and you'll be flying around, moving cards on your tableau and to the spit piles. The good thing for your opponent is the more cards you add to the spit piles, the greater his or her chances of becoming unstuck. If you put down a 5 of Clubs on a spit pile, your opponent might have a 6 of Clubs to play on top of your 5. This could put your opponent back on the fast track, opening doors for other plays on his or her own tableau or to the spit pile.

Spitting Tips

Spit play is so fast that it's sure to cause a lot of laughter and even a couple arguments. My friend and I were such pros that we had our rules well memorized. We stuck to the rules, and rifts were almost always avoided. Here are some tips to make your Spitting match fast and fun:

➤ If neither one of you can make a move after turning a spit card, then you have to spit again.

➤ If one player runs out of stock pile cards before the other, the one player spits alone onto one pile. The player with the remaining stock pile can choose which spit pile he or she wants to spit onto—but must stick to that one pile.

➤ When both players run out of spit cards, both players get to pick a spit pile to add to their hand. But in this game, nothing is as casual as just picking a pile. You have to watch each other very carefully to see which one of you is running out of cards, because the second it happens, you both slap your hand on a spit pile and shout ... of course ... "Spit!" You want to try and slap your hand on the pile with the least cards—because the object is to be the first one to get rid of all your cards.

You may find yourself slapping your opponent's hand if you both attempt to slap the same pile. If you feel skin rather than cards, you lose and your opponent takes the desired pile (and you take the other), but if you land your hand on the pile first, you take the pile. However, if you accidentally slap the bigger pile (which will happen sometimes) you have to take the pile you slap, whether you like it or not.

Try playing Spit with only one hand. Your stock pile should be held in one hand while you play with the other. If your stock pile is exhausted, you are still obligated to play with only one hand.

You continue to play by shuffling the spit pile you took—and it becomes your new stock pile.

New Tableau Layout

After you've shuffled your "chosen" spit pile, you each lay out a new tableau. One player will probably have more spit cards in his or her stock pile than the other player. That's okay; you'd be surprised how quickly the tables will turn throughout the game.

If one player has less than 15 cards, he or she will not be able to build a complete tableau. In this case, the player should build the tableau as far as it will go, using up all of his or her cards, and turns over the top card of each pile. This means the player won't have any cards left in his or her stock pile with which to spit. So the opponent will spit onto one spit pile and the other player continues to play as normal—both players building onto one spit pile this time.

The first person to get rid of his or her spit cards does not take a spit pile. The person with cards remaining takes the spit pile and the unplayed cards from his or her tableau. If you get rid of all your spit cards *and* the cards from your tableau—congratulations—you've won the Spitting match!

Go Fish

So, going back to my days at my grandmother's house by the Long Island Sound. It might have been the next summer, but she also taught me and my siblings how to play Go Fish. It was necessary to teach us a game that involved a little bit more skill and concentration—there's only so far War will go before kids start catching on that it's basically a losing battle.

The object of Go Fish is to collect *books*. You gather the cards by simply asking for them. If you suspect a player has a certain card that you want, you simply say, "Joe, do you have any 7s?" If Joe has a 7, he gives you the card; if not, he tells you to Go Fish. Whoever collects the most books, wins the game.

The game requires a 52-card deck and is best played by three to six players. (You can play with two, but it's not really as much fun. Each player is dealt five cards. The remaining cards are placed face-down in the center of the playing area.

The player to the left of the dealer goes first by asking any player if he or she has a specific card. The strategy, of course, is to look at your own hand and try to ask for cards that will allow you to make a book as fast as possible. For example, if you have two 7s in your hand, you're going to want to ask someone if they have any 7s. In other words, build on your pairs.

If the player has the card you ask for, then he or she just hands it to you and you get to go again. If that

It's in the Cards

A **book** consists of four of a kind (four cards of matching rank).

player has two 7s, then he or she must give you both cards. You have to have at least one of the cards you're asking for in your own hand.

If Joe does not have any 7s, he says "Go Fish!" That means you have to take a card from the stock pile and add it to your hand. If the card you pull is the card you requested (a 7 in this situation with Joe), then you show it to the other players and you get another turn. If the card is not the rank you asked for, then you keep the card in your hand and the play continues with the person on your left.

When you collect four cards of one rank, you have a book. You show the cards to the other players by laying them down next to you, face-up. The game continues in this way until you have no cards left in your hand or until the stock pile is used up. When one player is out of cards and there are no cards left in the stock pile, the game is over. The person with the most books wins.

You can also play so that each player must make books of pairs of cards rather than four cards.

Winning Plays

When we were kids, we used to enjoy dragging out the word "any" when making a request for a card. For example "Joe, do you have aaannnnyyyyyy ... 7s?" It became part of the game. It was silly, but hey ... we were kids! We thought that dragging out the word added to the suspense of the moment.

Fishing Commercially

There are some very unique and unusual versions of Old Maid and Go Fish. Some of the images on the decks of commercial card games will have your kids in stitches. For example, the "Old Maid" deck I played with depicted the Old Maid with a large mound of gray hair with all sort of things hidden in it, like twigs and flowers, and even a little spider.

There is a commercial version of Go Fish, popular in the United Kingdom, called "Happy Families." The deck consists of 44 cards featuring pictures of a mother, father, son, and daughter of 11 different families. The object of the game is to build families of cards by asking another player for a specific family member. If that player doesn't have the card you asked for, he or she replies, "Sorry, not at home."

There is no skill whatsoever in these games—it's the luck of the draw. Mostly it's just a great way to teach kids to play cards. Kids learn to recognize the cards, and in some games they learn the standard rules of rank and suit. Play cards with the wee ones and open up their eyes to the wonderful world of cards.

The Least You Need to Know

➤ There is no skill needed for any of the games in this chapter—they're all luck of the draw.

➤ Games like these are a great way to teach kids how to play cards. Kids learn to recognize the cards and in some games they learn the standard rules of rank and suit.

➤ Concentration is good for exercising the kids' memories as well as the adults'.

➤ Games like Spit can be a good way to liven things up. Whoever thought you'd get exercise playing cards?

Chapter 15

Casino Games

In This Chapter

➤ Casino games you can play at home

➤ Blackjack (21) for fun

➤ Baccarat for everyone

One snowy afternoon in the Laurentian Mountains of Quebec, my grandfather pulled out a deck of cards and taught my siblings and me how to play two games—Poker and Blackjack. I was young, so I found Poker a little harder to grasp, but I took to Blackjack right away, and my passion for the game is with me still.

In this chapter, we will take a look at some of the casino games you can play at home (or at the casino)! All-time favorites such as Blackjack and Baccarat are explained for hours of family gambling. From pennies to candy to family chores—bet away!

Blackjack!

It is believed that the game of Blackjack has its roots in France. It was originally known as "21." The goal of the game is to beat the dealer's hand by scoring 21 or as close to 21 as you can get without going over. If the dealer scores closest to 21, you lose.

Winning Plays

Although Blackjack goes way back to the early American gambling houses, it was never as popular a game as Poker, so gaming houses had to spice it up a bit in order to give it a little more mass appeal. Some gambling houses offered bigger payouts for Blackjack hands, while others gave bonuses for certain card combinations—namely an Ace of Spades with a Jack of Clubs. That's how "Blackjack" gets its name—from the combination of those two cards.

In modern versions of the game, any 10-value card with any Ace is considered Blackjack, but wouldn't it be fun to mix it up a bit when playing at home and give an extra chip or two to the player who gets the Jack of Clubs/Ace of Spades combination?

A very interesting event occurred in the 1960s that changed the way people think of Blackjack and caused casinos to enact protective measures to minimize losses. A mathematician named Edward Thorpe took it upon himself to prove that the dealer's edge over the game could be eliminated. He used computers to calculate every card combination that would give a player an advantageous lead over a dealer's hand. His calculations helped define a set of moves known as "basic strategy." Basic strategy has been modified over the years, and because of it, casinos have had to modify their own rules as a protective measure.

High Score

The really good Blackjack players know the ins and outs of basic strategy, so you may want to steer clear of some of these savvy players when you sit down to play in the casino. Better yet, learn the rules and get in there with the best of them.

Let's Play

Blackjack is played with a standard 52-card deck and is a very simple game that requires a certain amount of skill based on a certain amount of luck. The luck part has to do with the cards you are dealt and the skill has to do with learning some basic strategies—mainly knowing when to *hit*, stand, split, or double-down. The goal is not to beat the other players at the table—whether that's the casino table or the kitchen table—the goal is to beat the dealer's hand.

The dealer begins by shuffling the cards. Some casinos play with up to as many as six decks, but at home one deck will do just fine. The dealer will then deal the cards to each player and to him- or herself. The dealer should be standing or sitting across from the other players and always starts the deal with the person on his or her left.

On the first deal, each player is dealt two cards, face-down. The dealer deals him- or herself one card face-down (the *hole card*) and the other card face-up. Each player is basically playing a separate game based on the cards he or she is dealt and in relation to what the player thinks the dealer has. The dealer begins with the first player on his or her left. That player looks at his or her cards and determines if he or she can take another card without going over 21. It's important to get a good look at the dealer's face-up card because that could determine what strategy you decide to use in playing your own hand.

The cards are valued as follows:

➤ Ace = Either 1 point or 11 points

➤ Face cards = 10 points

➤ Number cards = Face value of card

➤ Blackjack: One Ace and any card with a 10-point value

It's in the Cards

When you request a **hit** in Blackjack you are asking the dealer to give you another card.

It's in the Cards

The **hole card** is the dealer's face-down card.

Technically, scoring 21 with more than two cards is not considered Blackjack, but you can still win this way. If you total 21 before the dealer or any other player, you win the pot.

When your cards are dealt, add them up and figure out whether you want to "stand" with what you have or take another card. In home games, you will say to the dealer, "hit me" or "stay," while at the casino you will use hand motions to tell the dealer what you want to do.

There are many strategies for standing or hitting, but basically, you just have to figure out your odds. If your cards total nine, chances are pretty good that you'll be able to take another card without going over 21. If your cards total 18, your chances of going over 21 are much greater, and you will likely want to stay. Remember that you are not only trying to score as close to 21 as possible, but you are trying to beat the dealer—so you have to check out the dealer's cards too. The problem is, you can only see one of his or her cards at this time and you have to do some guessing to figure out if you can beat him or her.

Hitting and Standing

When you have your cards, you have to decide whether to hit or stand. As I mentioned earlier, sometimes your choice will be obvious. The tricky cards are the ones that add up to between 12 and 16.

The dealer works with one player at a time, starting with the first player on his or her left. The dealer stays with that player until he or she stands or busts (goes over 21). When that first player is finished with his or her turn, the dealer moves on to the next player and continues around the table until each person has played his or her hand.

If you decide to take the hit, the dealer will toss down a card face-up in front of you. You can either indicate that you want another hit or that you want to stand. If your hand is blackjack, turn your cards face-up to show the dealer what you have. If you're playing for chips, you will immediately receive a payout at this point and the game continues with the other players. If the dealer also has a blackjack, the play is called a push. You keep your original bet, but you don't win anything more.

The Dealer's Hand

After the deal, the dealer will have one face-up and one face-down card in front of him or her. If the face-up card has a value of 10, the dealer will look at the face-down card to check for a blackjack. If he or she has blackjack, he or she will turn over the cards and take your bet and your hand away. If you have blackjack, the dealer will take your cards, but you keep your bet. If you are not playing for money, you and the dealer are considered tied if you both have blackjack. If the dealer does not have blackjack, he or she will continue the play around the table. If the dealer's face-up card is an Ace, he or she will go around the table and ask the players if they want "insurance."

High Score

You can keep score according to wins, and determine the winning player by the number of games won. If you don't want to play for money, play for chips or for chores around the house. My grandfather used the packing peanuts to teach us how to play. We used all sorts of things when playing Blackjack, including real nuts, candy, and loose change.

Insurance

If you are playing for money, or in the casino, the dealer will ask you if you want insurance if his or her face-up card is an Ace. The Ace is, of course, the card that determines a blackjack. If the dealer's face-down card is a 10-value card (and there are 16 of these cards) he or she has blackjack.

If you decide to take insurance, you can bet up to half of your original bet by placing your chips (or peanuts) below your original bet. If the dealer has a 10-value card, then he will pay off the insurance bets at two to one, but you lose your original bet. If the dealer does not have blackjack, the players lose their insurance bets and play continues with the original bets. This is why you're no better off taking insurance.

Let's say you bet $10 and you decide to take insurance because the dealer's face-up card is an Ace. You place another $5 under your original bid. If the dealer does not have blackjack, you lose your $5, but keep your original bet of $10. You're out $5. If the dealer does have blackjack, you lose your original bet of $10, but the dealer pays out two to one, thus giving you back $10. You haven't made a penny. Why is insurance even an option then? Beats me. You neither gain nor lose from it—only the casino turns a profit from insurance.

Three Strikes

Casinos will use the insurance rules, but don't be fooled—it's just a sneaky way for casinos to try and make some extra cash. The odds are against you in taking insurance, so beware.

Splitting and Doubling-Down

The abilities to *split* or double-down are the strategies that make the game interesting. If you are dealt two cards of the same value—let's say two 8s—you can split the hand.

If you are dealt another 8, you can resplit and play three hands by moving that 8 alongside the other two cards, or just place another bet on the table, equal to your two previous bets.

Casino rules will vary, but some have strict rules about resplitting. If you are unsure of the rules, just ask the dealer. Also, some casinos will not allow you to touch your cards, so in this case, just place another bet over your cards and the dealer will know that you are splitting. At home, make sure you establish the rules before you start the game. It might be fun to adopt some of the strict casino rules just to liven things up a little.

Experts advise that you should always split Aces, and it is highly recommended to split 8s.

Doubling-down refers to doubling your bet, so if you're playing for money or chips at home, you can certainly employ this strategy. It is a strategy that is definitely used in the casinos—so you should know about it if you're heading to a blackjack table near you.

It's in the Cards

When you **split** your hand in Blackjack, what you do is turn your two cards face-up side-by-side, and if you're betting, place another bet of identical value to your original bet. You are now playing two hands. The dealer will deal to the hand on your right first—until you stand or bust—and then the dealer will play to your other hand.

Doubling-down means that you can double the size of your original bet. You do this by turning your cards face-up and placing another bet on the table that is equal to your original bet. When you double-down, you are dealt one more card—meaning you do not have the option to stand on your original hand or take any more hits after you are dealt the one extra card.

High Score

The best time to double-down is when the two cards in your hand total 11. That means you are banking that the next card you are dealt will be a 10-value card. It's a real gamble, but the odds are pretty good that you will get a 10-value card because there are so many of them in a deck.

High Score

There are strategy tables on the Internet that you may find very helpful to figure out when you should hit, stand, split, or double-down. Some experts suggest you memorize these tables in order to play the best hands.

Basic Strategy

Blackjack is not just a game of chance. While a lot depends on the luck of the draw, there are many strategies to better your odds of winning. Here are some basic strategies to help you play a better hand:

➤ Always hit any hand that totals 11 or under.

➤ Stand on 17 and over. (The only exception to this rule is when you have a soft 17—meaning the hand contains an Ace. And even here, be careful of the dealer hand—check out his or her cards before asking for a hit.)

➤ For cards totaling 12 to 16, whether to hit or stand depends on the dealer's face-up cards: Hit if the dealer has a 7 or higher; stand if the dealer has 2 or 3 points.

➤ Never take insurance.

➤ Always split Aces and 8s.

➤ Never split 4s, 5s, and 10-value cards. The odds will be against you.

➤ Never double-down below 8 points.

➤ Always double-down on 11 points.

➤ When you have 10 points, double-down when the dealer shows 2 and 9.

Baccarat

Baccarat is the Rolls Royce of the casino world. Legendary movie hero James Bond was known to play a few hands on some of his extraordinary missions. It is a simple game that is very popular in Europe. It's the ambiance surrounding the game that makes it so unique. In most Las Vegas casinos, the game is played in a roped-off area with dealers dressed in tuxedos. The roping-off is nothing more than a means to attract the more sophisticated high-rollers (the players who make the big-money bets).

Anyone can play Baccarat, but you might want to have your fanciest duds on hand if you're looking for a night of serious Baccarat. If that's not your style, then just play at home with the kids. It's a pretty easy game to follow. I'll give you the casino rules here and you can modify them if you want to give the game a whirl on family game night.

The game does not require any particular skill. The object is to assemble a hand of two or three cards with a point value as close to 9 as possible. In the casino, the tables seat 15 people and there are three dealers per table. The *caller* stands between seats 1 and 15. He or she controls the game as he or she deals the cards from the "shoe," a box filled with the cards used to play.

Players wager before the deal. Each player bets either on the bank or on the players. Then the cards are dealt.

Winning Plays

The word baccarat derives from the Italian word *baccara* meaning zero. The term refers to the zero value of cards in the game of Baccarat.

It's in the Cards

The **caller** is the main dealer in Baccarat.

The Play

The rules of Baccarat are clear and rigid. In other words, there is not the same kind of flexibility with your hand as there is in Blackjack. The object of the game is to score a two-card total of nine (otherwise known as "a natural"). It's the best hand you can have—it cannot lose. The second-best hand is a two-card hand that totals eight (also called "a natural").

You are, like in Blackjack, playing against the dealer (or the bank). If a player and the dealer have the same hand, there is a tie and neither the player nor the dealer wins. If you have a two-card hand of six or seven, no more cards can be drawn to your hand.

If you have any other two-card totals, you can draw another card at the direction of the dealer. The dealer determines the draws. The only thing the player has to worry about is how much he or she bets.

The Payout

As mentioned earlier, bets may be made on either the player or on the bank. When the winner is declared, the dealers at the table pay out to the winners and collect from the losers. If you win, you must pay a five percent commission to the house. So if you bet $100, you must pay $5 to the house. That doesn't seem fair, but the advantage in Baccarat is almost always on the winner—so this is a way that the casino can ensure it doesn't lose too much money. You don't have to pay the five percent after each win; one of the dealers will keep track and will expect you to pay up when you're ready to leave the table. Bets can range from as low as $20 to as high as $2,000.

Card Combinations and Rules

In order to play with the best of them, or just to practice at home, here are some basic rules to guide you along:

The player:

➤ If the first two cards total 1, 2, 3, 4, 5, or 10, the player draws a card.

➤ If the first two cards total 6 or 7, the player stands.

➤ If the first two cards total 8 or 9, the player stands (this is a natural).

The bank:

➤ If a player's hand totals 3, the banker draws when the player's third card is 1, 2, 3, 4, 5, 6, 7, 9, or 10. The banker stands if the third card is an 8.

➤ If a player's hand totals 4, the banker draws when the third card is 2, 3, 4, 5, 6, or 7. The banker stands if the third card is any other number.

➤ If a player's hand totals 5, the banker draws when the third card is 4, 5, 6, or 7. The banker stands if the third card is any other number.

➤ If a player's hand totals 6, the banker draws when the third card is 6 or 7. The banker stands if the third card is any other number.

➤ The banker always stands if the player's first two cards total 7, 8, or 9.

Hand Values

All cards Ace through 9 are valued at face value. Tens and face cards are worth 0 points. If cards add up to more than 10, the 10 must be subtracted. So if you have an 8 and a 6, the value is 4 (14 minus 10 = 4). If you have a 10 and a Queen, the value is 0.

The Least You Need to Know

➤ You can play any of the casino games at home—just modify the casino rules to suit your household!

➤ Blackjack is also called 21, since the object of the game is to get as close to 21, or to get 21, without going over.

➤ Blackjack is made up of both skill and luck. The luck part has to do with the cards you are dealt and the skill has to do with learning some basic strategies—mainly knowing when to hit, stand, split, or double-down.

➤ The goal in Baccarat is to score as close to nine points as possible. Getting nine points with the first cards dealt is called a "natural."

Part 4

Let's Make a Deal

The games in Chapters 16 through 19 are card games best suited for the older crowd—some of the games can get very involved and complicated. You can certainly play them at home with your teenagers—especially Poker and Rummy—but you might want to save Bridge and Pinochle for a night out with friends, unless the family is up for a challenge.

You can use some of these card games as a means to get to know your neighbors— or even better—get to know the parents of your kids' friends by organizing a Bridge or Rummy night. Card games played in teams are a great way to get out there and socialize!

Chapter 16

Rummy Noses

In This Chapter

➤ Basic Rummy rules

➤ Gin Rummy

➤ Knock Rummy

➤ Rummy 500

➤ Contract Rummy

Rummy games go back to at least the late nineteenth century in North America, but probably have their earliest origins in China where playing cards was invented. A Bridge tutor named Elwood Baker is credited with restructuring the scoring system of basic Rummy to make it easier for gambling purposes.

The popularity of Rummy games, especially Gin Rummy, skyrocketed in the 1930s when it became a hit within celebrity circles and made several appearances in Hollywood movies and Broadway plays. In this chapter, you'll learn how to play all kinds of Rummy games—from basic Rummy to Rummy 500 to Contract Rummy and more!

Rummy Go!

Rummy games are draw-and-discard games, and the object of most of these games is to improve your hand by forming groups of cards of either the same rank or sequence.

The "draw" in "draw and discard" means that after your hand is dealt you will have a face-down pile of stock cards (stock pile) from which to draw new cards for your hand, and a stack of face-up cards (discard pile) also from which to draw. "Discard" refers to the discard pile, where you drop unnecessary cards from your hand after drawing a card. For every card drawn, you must always discard. When you have built your groups of cards, you lay them face-up on the table in what is known as a *meld*.

The varieties of Rummy games are so diverse and widespread that you should want to make sure you're clear on exactly what game you're playing before you sit down to play. You'll find that some people play with different rules in different parts of the world. The variants can be very confusing. The best way to start playing Rummy is to learn the basics with Basic Rummy. You can try the more complicated games once you get these easy rules under your belt.

Basic Rummy

Basic Rummy uses a standard 52-card deck and can be played with two to six players. The general object of Rummy is to form the cards that are drawn from either the stock pile or the discard pile into sets of rank or suit (groups and sequences), otherwise called melds.

These sets may consist of three or four cards of the same rank, or three or more cards of the same suit. When your melds are formed, you remove them from your hand and place them on the table, face-up, which is called "melding."

Cards are dealt starting on the dealer's left. The dealer can be picked at random. The deal rotates to the left when more than two players are involved in the game, but if there are only two players, the winner deals the next hand.

The cards are dealt in the following manner:

➤ Two players: Each player gets 10 cards.

➤ Three to four players: Each player gets 7 cards.

➤ Five to six players: Each player gets 6 cards.

After the cards are dealt, the remaining cards should be placed face-down in a stack to form the stock pile. The first card of the stock pile is turned face-up and placed next to the stock pile to form the discard pile.

Let's Play!

Because the object of the game is to form *sequences* and *groups*, the goal is to pull from the stock or discard piles in order to get the necessary cards to form these sequences or groups. The player to the dealer's left goes first by taking a card from the stock or discard pile and then returning a card from his or her hand to the discard pile.

A player's turn is complete when he or she places a card on the discard pile.

It's in the Cards

A **sequence** (or run) is three cards of the same suit in sequence (such as Ace, 2, 3 of Spades). A **group** (or set) is three cards of the same rank (such as three 3s).

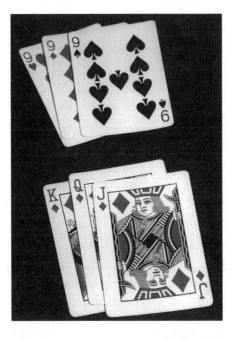

Groups and sequences in Rummy.

Aces are low, but can be melded either before a 2 or before a King—in other words, suit sequences can be circular (otherwise known as "an around-the-corner game"). For example, in the suit of Hearts you can meld Ace, 2, 3 or Ace, King, Queen or King, Ace, 2.

You can meld (lay down groups) as you go along or keep them in your hand—you are not obligated to meld once you have a group in your hand.

You can also add cards to your melds, or to the melds of another player, as the game goes along—this is called "laying off." You can meld and lay off on the same turn—but your turn is not complete until you discard.

You win the game when you get rid of all your cards. If you draw a card that allows you to meld all your remaining cards, then you don't have to discard. You can also win if you meld your remaining cards except for one—that remaining card can then be discarded and you win the game.

If you discard a card that could have been laid off on an existing meld and another player spots this, that player may call out "rummy," and then pick up the discard and make the meld. Any player can do this out of turn, but when picking up the card, must discard another card from his or her hand.

If the stock pile is exhausted before a player goes out, then play ends and the player with the lowest points in hand wins the game.

Note: You can borrow from one of your own melds in order to form another meld as long you maintain a minimum of three cards per meld.

Keeping Score

You score points according to the cards remaining in your opponents' hands—not on their melded cards. Face cards are worth 10 points, Aces are worth one point, and all other cards are worth their face value (4 = four points, 3 = three points, and so on). So if one of your opponents has a King, an Ace, and a 3 left in his or her hand, you would score a total of 14 points. If you have more than one opponent, you score points according to what's left in all other players' hands.

Gin Rummy

Gin Rummy is credited to a member of the Knicker-bocker Whist Club of New York. He apparently called the game "Gin" after the alcoholic drink, as a kind of analogy to the original game of Rum—although there is no indication that "Rummy" is named after any alcoholic beverage at all. The game is usually played by just two people, but there are variations of the game that allow for more players. A standard 52-card deck is used, and Aces are low.

High Score

If you are able to meld all your cards without having any previous melds, you collect double-points. This is referred to as "going rummy."

High Score

Remember for all games of Rummy: A group is three or more cards of equal rank (same card of different suits, like three 4s or four 6s) and a sequence is a series of three or more cards of the same suit in order.

Gin Rummy is actually just like "Knock Rummy," but it is played by only two people. There are other versions of Gin that can be played with more than two, but the basic game is two-handed. Like all versions of Rummy, it is a draw-and-discard game.

Luck of the Draw

Cards are drawn from the deck to determine who deals first. The person who drew the highest card can choose to deal or not to deal. After the initial drawing of cards, the winner of each hand gets to deal in subsequent games. The dealer has the option of shuffling the cards last before the next deal, and the nondealer usually cuts the cards before the deal.

After these fine-tuned preliminaries, the cards are dealt one at a time—10 cards to each player. The remaining cards are placed face-down on the table to form the stock pile, and the first card of the stock pile is turned face-up to form the discard pile.

How to Play

Like in other Rummy games, the object is to form your cards into sets, or melds. Sets are comprised of a sequence of cards according to suit or rank. You must have a minimum of three cards in rank or suit to start a meld. Cards that do not form part of a meld are called "unmatched cards."

Play begins with the nondealer. The nondealer has the option to draw a card from the stock pile or from the discard pile. The nondealer can also opt to pass his or her turn to the dealer. If the nondealer passes the first turn to the dealer, the dealer has the same option to pass, and, as a result, the nondealer has to draw the first card anyway.

If the nondealer chooses to draw the first card, the play continues with the players alternating drawing and discarding. When you draw a card from either pile, you must discard another card to the discard pile. You cannot discard the card you draw on the same turn.

Who's There?

A player can choose to "knock" at any point during the game as long as his or her unmatched cards (after discarding) total less than 10 points. Knocking means you lay down all 10 of your cards in sets, with any unmatched cards separated into another pile. If you can make all 10 cards into sets, it means you "go gin" and your total count is zero. When you "go gin," you score the total value of your opponent's unmatched cards plus an extra bonus of 25 points (in some versions of the game, you score a 20-point bonus).

The goal is to score 100 points, which you accumulate over a series of games.

The cards are valued as follows:

➤ Face cards = 10 points

➤ Ace = 1 point

➤ All other cards = face value

Three Strikes

Try to keep very low cards in your hand (like Aces, 2s, and 3s), even if these cards have low prospects of forming any matched sets. Otherwise, if your opponent wins, you could get stuck with a large number of points at the end of the round!

If the knocker's unmatched cards have the lesser value, he or she wins the difference of the counts. So if the knocker has 5 points in unmatched cards and the opponent has 10 points in unmatched cards, the knocker scores 5 points. If the opponent has a lesser (or equal) value in unmatched card points, he or she "undercuts" the knocker and scores the difference plus a bonus (10, 20, or 25 points—depending on whom you are playing with). If the knocker and opponent have an equal value of unmatched card points, then the opponent gets the bonus. A knocker cannot be undercut by the opponent if he or she has "gone gin."

If no one has knocked by the time the fiftieth card is drawn, the game is over and no one scores any points.

If one player knocks, the opponent may lay off any unmatched cards to the knocker's matched sets. That way, as the opponent, you can reduce the point value of your unmatched cards.

Winning the Game

You keep playing rounds of Gin until one of you scores a total of 100 points. The first person to score 100 is the winner.

Knock-Knock: Knock Rummy

Knock Rummy is basically Gin Rummy with more than two players. You play with a standard 52-card deck and the cards rank the same as they do in Rummy—Aces are low. If you decide to play with two people, you each get 10 cards. If you play with more than two players, you deal out seven cards to each player.

In Knock Rummy, you draw and discard the same way you would in Gin Rummy. When a player knocks, points are added up and play is over. A player may knock at any time during the game.

Scoring

Scoring is the same as in Gin Rummy. Face cards and 10s count as 10 points, Aces are worth 1 point, and all other cards are worth their face value. After one player knocks, the other players add up the value of their unmatched cards remaining in their respective hands. The player with the lowest total of unmatched cards collects—from all the other hands—the difference between his or her hand and each opponent's hand.

The player also takes an extra 10 points away from the knocker (in some versions of the game, the knocker relinquishes 20 points if another player has the lowest total of unmatched cards).

If the knocker has the lowest value of unmatched cards, then no points are scored. If someone has an equal value of unmatched cards as the knocker, then that player still collects from the other players, but the knocker neither relinquishes nor collects any points in relation to the unmatched cards. If two or more players (other than the knocker) tie for low score, all players divide the winnings.

Going Rum

A player "goes rum" when he knocks with all his or her cards formed into sets (with no unmatched cards remaining). When this happens, the knocker scores 25 points from each player in addition to the points in his or her hand. A hand that goes rum cannot be tied. If a player notices he or she has "gone rum" after someone knocks, then that player must pay the knocker an additional 25 points.

Rummy 500

Rummy 500 is played with a standard 52-card deck with two to eight players. If you have four players, you can play in teams of two. Players find that the best number of players is between three and five.

The point value of the cards is the same as other Rummy games with the exception of the Aces (which are played low). Face cards and 10s are worth 10 points and other cards score their face value. Aces carry a value of 15 points if left in the hand or melded as a group of Aces. Aces equal 1 point when they are melded in a sequence of Ace, 2, 3. Cards are dealt from left to right—one card at a time. You can draw from the pile of cards to see who deals first. Subsequent deals will go to the winner of each hand. When there are two players, each player receives 13 cards. With three or more players, each player is dealt seven cards. The remaining cards are placed face-down to form the stock pile, and the first card of the stack is turned face-up beside the stock pile to form the discard pile.

The discard pile is handled differently than in other Rummy games. The cards are fanned and any card can be removed from the pile, but it's not that simple—there are restrictions on when you can draw from the discard pile:

181

➤ The drawn card can be immediately melded.

➤ All cards above the drawn card must be taken as well. (These cards must be left on the table face-up until the player's next turn, so that other players may inspect and memorize what you've taken from the discard pile).

After drawing a card, players can meld as many sets as they want. Play is completed when a card is discarded on the discard pile.

Players may lay off cards to any players' sets. So if you have a 4 of Diamonds that can be added to a Diamond set of Ace, 2, 3, you may do so. However, you keep the card near your own sets and do not place them directly on the other player's melds.

Play ends when one player has melded all his or her sets and discarded his or her last card, *or* when the stock pile has been exhausted—whichever comes first. Play can continue after one player melds all his or her cards, as long as cards can still be drawn and players can still meld. The minute one player passes, the round is over.

At the end of play, each player adds the value of his or her melded cards. Each player then adds the value of the cards remaining in his or her hand and subtracts that number from the value of the melded cards. If the value of the unmatched cards exceeds the value of the melded cards, a negative value is scored. Unlike other Rummy games, all cards left in the hand are valued whether or not they can be made into melds.

A running score is kept for each player. The first player to reach 500 points is the winner.

Three Strikes

Make sure that when you are adding to a meld, you indicate to which meld you are adding so that the other players are aware of what you're doing!

It's in the Cards

A **contract** refers to the required combination of cards (sequences and groups in Contract Rummy) a player must obtain before laying down his cards.

Contract Rummy

Contract Rummy also has its variants in games like Liverpool Rum, Joker Rummy, Progressive Rum, and King Rummy. The difference between other Rummy games and Contract Rummy is that there are a set number of deals and a *contract* by which groups and sequences are formed per deal.

When playing with three or four players, shuffle together two 52-card decks including one Joker. This will give you a total of 105 cards. With five to eight players, you will deal together three decks of cards including two Jokers for a total of 158 cards. The Ace can either rank high or low. It can be laid off on a meld either before a 2 or after a King, but sets do not wrap "around the corner" or in a circular pattern (meaning if you lay off an Ace after a King, you cannot then lay off a 2 on that Ace and so on—the meld ends with the Ace). Aces and wild cards count as 15 points.

Contract Rummy consists of a total of seven deals. You can draw cards to see who deals first. After the first deal, all subsequent deals rotate to the left. Each player is dealt 10 cards one at a time in the first four deals. In the last three deals, each player receives 12 cards.

The game is very similar to other Rummy games, but you have a "basic contract" in terms of what melds can be made in each deal. The first meld made by a player must be according to the basic contract. After this, players can lay off to existing sets but cannot build any new suits outside of the contract. Play ends when one player has laid off, or melded, all of his or her cards.

The basic contracts are as follows:

➤ Deal #1: Two groups.

➤ Deal #2: One group and one sequence.

➤ Deal #3: Two sequences.

➤ Deal #4: Three groups.

➤ Deal #5: Two groups and one sequence.

➤ Deal #6: One group and two sequences.

➤ Deal #7: Three sequences, but with no unmatched cards. The first meld of this deal terminates play.

Each group must consist of no more than three cards (with the exception of the last deal). If you have four or more cards in your hand that could be melded to a three-card group or sequence, you must hold on to those additional cards—you can meld them to the three-card sets later. Each player plays his or her own basic contract according to the number of the deal.

If a player chooses not to take from the discard pile, anyone may claim it. If more than one player wants the card, it automatically goes to the player nearest the left of the player currently on his or her turn. This player must take the discard and one card from the top of the stock pile and does

Winning Plays

The first Contract Rummy game is believed to be a game called Zioncheck developed by a woman named Ruth Armson.

Three Strikes

Be careful! When a contract calls for two sequences, the sequences must consist of two different suits. (Some people play that they can be of the same suit but must be disconnected—in other words, you can have a sequence of Spades 2-3-4, but your other Spades sequence must have a break after the 4 of Spades. So your next Spades sequence could be 6-7-8, but not 5-6-7).

not discard anything. Play then returns to the player who passed on drawing the discard. The "in-turn" player must draw from the top of the stock pile—but cannot draw a card from the discard pile because he or she refused the discard at the outset of his or her turn.

Jokers are wild cards and may be used to complete any set. You can move a wild card in a sequence to either end if you need to build on a sequence. Just remember—no sequence may consist of more than 14 cards. The holder of the joker may also replace the wild card with the natural card in the sequence, provided that this player has already melded his or her basic contract.

As in other Rummy games, the play ends when the deals end. Each player adds up the points remaining in his or her hand. The winner is the player who scores the least points after Deal #7.

The Least You Need to Know

➤ Rummy games are draw-and-discard games. The object of most Rummy games is to improve your hand by forming groups and sequences (sets and runs).

➤ Sequences are three cards of the same suit in sequence. They are also known as runs. Groups are three cards of the same rank, regardless of suit. They are sometimes called sets.

➤ When you obtain all the sequences and groups you need to fulfill your hand requirement, you can meld your cards—lay them down on the table for other players to see.

➤ "Going rum" means to meld all your cards in one turn and dispose of all the cards in your hand.

Chapter 17

Building Bridges

In This Chapter

➤ Bridge origins and basics

➤ Tricks and bids

➤ Trumps and no trumps

➤ Declarers, dummies, and contracts

There are many celebrity Bridge players and enthusiasts, one of the most famous being Omar Sharif. He has written books on his love of Bridge and writes a newspaper column on the game that includes tips, trends, and just general thoughts. Sharif wrote of the game: "Bridge grips you. It exercises your mind. Your mind can rust, you know, but Bridge prevents the rust from forming." Others also have positive words on Bridge. The great author Somerset Maugham said that "Bridge is the most entertaining and intelligent card game the wit of man has so far devised."

Bridge is a card game that you may have heard about throughout your life but may never have bothered to learn. It sounds complicated, and it is—but only a little. It is less complicated in its basic form than in its strategies. There are entire books written on strategy alone.

Bridge America

My mother and her friends recently decided to get together and attempt to learn the Bridge. It's not because they were fascinated by the science of strategizing, but because they wanted to find a unique way to spend more time together. I hear that when Bridge becomes part of your life, there's no turning away from it. Because the game is played in teams of two, it is a very popular adult social activity. Many couples learn to play Bridge just for that purpose. We've all seen movies and television shows where couples get together for a weekly "Bridge night."

It's quite a complicated game, and learning the strategies can take years. It's not really a game for the entire family, but it's definitely a game that parents can play together. (What a great way to get to know the parents of your kids' friends.) It seems like an old-fashioned way of socializing, but sometimes I think the older generations had the right idea. Adults are as bad as kids when it comes to zoning out in front of the boob tube. Why not try something different? There's only so many ways couples can hang out and what better way than over coffee, cake, and a couple hands of Bridge?

The word "bridge" is believed to come from the Russian game of Whist called "biritch," which means "announcer" or "herald." In the modern game of Bridge, players announce their contract bids.

Winning Plays

Bridge was such a popular game in the 1950s that it became a favorite American pastime. President Dwight D. Eisenhower was known to play the game with experts on a Saturday night whenever possible. He was considered an excellent player and attended tournaments frequently.

High Score

If you're just learning the game and you meet a couple that already knows how to play and is willing to teach you, you're in luck. But it also might be fun to learn the game as a group. You'll definitely have to read up on the game and its strategies. There are also many good Web sites that will help you. Check out some of the books on Bridge in Appendix B, "Resources."

Winning Plays

Bridge is most likely derived from an old English card game called Whist. Whist goes back as far as the sixteenth century, and Bridge can really only trace its roots back at far as the late nineteenth century. In 1925, the famous American multimillionaire Harold S. Vanderbilt perfected a new form of Bridge, with revised rules and the introduction of a scoring table; and the game soon became known as Contract Bridge.

There are several different versions of Bridge but Contract is the most popular. Rubber Bridge is the basic form of Contract Bridge and is played by four players in partners. Duplicate Bridge is the game that is normally played in tournaments and clubs and requires eight players.

Let's Play Bridge

It is traditional for players to sit across from each other at the bridge table—with partners sitting directly across from one another. The players' positions at the table are referred to as "North," "South," "East," and "West." North and South would be partners as would East and West. Players should take their places at the table in their proper seating positions.

A standard 52-card deck is used and Aces are high.

In this game, the suits have a rank in terms of how powerful they are when trick-taking starts. The order of rank is Spades, Hearts, Diamonds, Clubs. This is easy to remember if you notice that the rank of the suits is in reverse alphabetical order: S, H, D, C. The most powerful cards (highest ranking) in a suit are King, Queen, Jack, and 10. These cards are called the "honor" cards—the rest are referred to as "spot" cards.

Winning Plays

A man named Ely Culbertson wrote a top-selling book on the game of Bridge in 1931, which popularized Bridge in the United States.

The dealer is chosen by drawing cards from the deck. The players that draw the two highest cards become partners as do the players drawing the lowest cards. If two players draw the same card—let's say they each draw a Queen—the tie is broken by the highest suit.

The dealer shuffles the cards and the person to the dealer's right cuts the cards. The dealer then deals out all the cards one by one to each player. With each hand the deal rotates in a clockwise direction.

It is tradition to use two decks of cards, but there is only one deck in play at a time. The second deck is shuffled by the dealer's partner and set aside for the next hand. This is just a way to save a little time from hand-to-hand.

Winning Plays

Bridge is still very popular in the United States and the United Kingdom. There are over 1,000 annual American Bridge tournaments and well over 4,000 Bridge clubs.

Tricks and Bids

Bridge is a trick-taking game, meaning that when the cards are dealt and the bidding completed, players lay down one card at a time in an effort to take other players' cards. You do this by taking one card from your hand and placing it face-up in the center of the table—there are a total of 13 tricks in a game as there are 13 cards in each player's hand. The player who lays down the most powerful card in terms of rank and suit wins the trick. When playing a trick, players are required to follow the suit of the lead card. The lead card is the first card put on the table by a player.

When the cards are dealt the bidding begins. Bidding is the most important part of the game because it "writes" the contract for the game. The bidding identifies the number of tricks and whether or not there will be a trump suit. You bid according to how many tricks you will try to win during the course of each hand. You score based on whether or not you meet the bid you won (or "the contract you made"). The team that wins the bid is responsible for fulfilling their bid commitment (contract).

Players look at their hands after the cards are dealt and the bidding begins starting with the dealer and rotating to the left. You may call to pass, bid, double, or re-double.

If you don't wish to bid, you say "pass." If everyone passes, the cards are tossed in and the player on the dealer's left deals a new hand.

In bidding you have to be careful not to overbid or underbid. You are basically guessing based on the cards in your hand (and in the hand of your partner) how many tricks you think you will take during the course of a game. If you guess correctly, you score points. If you don't win as many tricks as you thought, or you go over the amount of tricks you thought you could take, you lose and your opponent scores points.

To win the bid, you have to say that you will take more tricks than the opposing team. In bidding you also decide whether or not there will be a trump suit. You do so by naming the suit and the number of tricks you think you can take during the bidding process. Because there are 13 hands, you must take at least seven tricks to win the game. You are bidding for anything over six. *Books* are not counted in the bidding process.

So, if you call "one-Spade," you are saying that you will take seven tricks with Spades as trumps (a book of six tricks plus one additional trick). Likewise, if you call "three-Clubs," you are expected to win nine tricks with Clubs as trumps (one book or six tricks and an additional three tricks). You can also bid "no trumps"; you do so by saying "three no trump." This bid means you are expected to take nine tricks and no trump suit. The maximum you can bid is seven. If you bid seven, it means you are actually winning 13 tricks (all the tricks you can play in one hand).

It's in the Cards

A **book** is the number of tricks a player must win before any trick can have scoring value.

Bidding Rules

Bidding starts with the dealer. Partners may not directly speak to each other regarding how they think they should bid, but you'll know what's going on with your partner by how he or she bids. For example: The dealer goes first. If the dealer says "pass," he or she is basically communicating a bad hand. If you bid one Heart, you are telling your opponent that you have a decent hand and enough Hearts to want to make Hearts the trump suit. The first bid is called the "opening bid."

High Score

Only one suit can be trump in a given hand. The existence (or lack thereof) of a trump suit in each deal is determined by the player who wins the bid.

If everyone else at the table passes, you have just made the contract and you must win seven tricks with Hearts as trumps. If another player decides to enter the bidding (also called an auction), he or she may bid to take a higher number of tricks, or bid that he or she will take the same number of tricks, but with a higher-ranking "strain." The strains are "no trumps" and "trumps." "No trumps" ranks the highest and the suits follow according to their rank (remember reverse alphabetical order: Spades, Hearts, Diamonds, Clubs).

So, the next player to bid might say "one Spade" and outbid you because Spades rank higher than Hearts. Or the player can bid "one no trump" and because "no trump" is the highest strain, that call would still outbid the one-Heart call. It's okay to outbid your partner.

You must always make a higher bid than the previous one, so pay careful attention to the card-suit combinations and learn which suit beats which. A player may rejoin the auction after passing as long as he or she re-enters with a higher bid than the previous bid. The bidding continues until there are three consecutive passes—the last highest bid wins and play begins. The player that wins the bid is called the "declarer." The declarer's partner is called the "dummy." The final winning bid is the "contract."

Three Strikes

Make sure you're paying attention to each other's bids to ensure you are working together to get the most successful contract. Watch your partner carefully and study his or her bids or you may miss some clues as to the best way to play your hands.

Doubles and Redoubles

There are two other options in the bidding process. You can double and redouble. To double means you are doubling the bid of the last caller (bidder). So if one of your opponents calls "two-Diamonds" and you think you can double it, then you call doubles. If the following bids are three passes, the final contract is two-Diamonds doubled. This means that the declarer is saying he can take eight tricks during the game.

If the declarer, and his or her partner, fails to meet the contract, they will pay an additional penalty for bidding the double. The point of doubling is to increase the scoring value of tricks. Doubles can be outbid. For example, if a three-Clubs bid is made and then doubled, it can still be outbid by a three-Hearts bid. You can only double an opponent's bid—not a partner's bid.

High Score

The only time the three-consecutive pass rule would not apply is when it happens on the first round of bidding. If three players pass, then one player would not have had an opportunity to bid, and all Bridge players agree that that would not be fair. In this case, bidding would end after four consecutive passes and a new hand would be dealt.

You can also choose to redouble. You can redouble the last bid if it was made by you or your partner, if it was doubled by an opponent, and if it has not been redoubled before. Redoubling is another means to increase the scoring value and is not the final word in bidding. Like with doubling, you can outbid a redouble with normal bidding methods.

The Play

When the bidding is complete, play begins with the player to the dealer's left, who leads the first trick. After the opening card is laid face-up in the center of the table, the dummy exposes his or her cards arranged neatly according to suit. The cards should be placed on the dummy's right (declarer's left). Play then proceeds to the left (clockwise).

Each player must try to lay down a card that follows the suit of the lead card. If the declarer lays down a Diamond, you must lay down a Diamond as well. If you don't have a Diamond, you may lay down a card of another suit. The goal is to try to win the tricks away from the declarer so that he or she cannot meet the contract. The trick is won by the highest trump, or if this is a no-trumps game, the winner of the trick is the person who lays down the highest card of the suit led. The winner of one trick leads the next trick.

The dummy does not take an active part in the play of the hand. The declarer plays the card exposed by the dummy by telling the dummy, and the opponents, which card is to be played by the dummy's hand. The dummy then plays the card announced by the declarer. The dummy may not comment during play. If a dummy card wins the trick, the declarer will tell the dummy what card to lead to the next trick. If the declarer fails to say the name of the suit or rank of the card to be played, the dummy must play the lowest-ranking card in his or her hand.

Contract Bridge is often referred to as Rubber Bridge. A rubber is the best two out of three games. The game is won when a team scores 100 (or more) points over a series of hands.

Scoring

Divide the paper into two columns headed "We" and "They." Then draw a horizontal line halfway down the page, across the two columns. Scores for successfully won contracts are recorded below the line and count toward winning the game. Bonuses and penalties (overtricks and undertricks) are recorded above the line—but these points do not count toward winning the game.

A side that has won a game is said to be "vulnerable." Vulnerability will get you some additional bonus points if you succeed again—but you will also get increased penalties if you don't meet a contract.

If you successfully complete the contract (meet the bid you made at the beginning of the game), you score points for your team. The points are based on the bid you made above six tricks.

For example:

➤ If trumps, Clubs or Diamonds—you win 20 points per trick.

➤ If trumps, Hearts or Spades—you win 30 points per trick.

➤ If no trumps—you win 40 points for the first trick and 30 for each additional trick.

➤ If the contract was doubled—the points are doubled.

➤ If the contract was doubled and redoubled—the points are multiplied by four.

➤ If you succeed in doubling a contract—you score 50 bonus points above the line. This is referred to as "50 for the insult."

➤ If you succeed in redoubling a contract—you score 100 bonus points above the line.

If the declarer goes over the number of tricks bid (without doubles), he or she will score extra points according to the regular scoring rules (20 points per trick if minor suit is trumps and 30 points per trick if major suit is trumps or if there are no trumps). Overtrick points are scored above the line. If the contract is doubled or re-doubled, overtrick points are scored above the line according to vulnerability. If a team is not vulnerable and declared doubles, the above-the-line score is 100. If a team is vulnerable, the score is 200. If the bid is redoubled and the team is not vulnerable, they score 200 points and if vulnerable—400 points.

Penalties are recorded if fewer tricks are won than you actually bid. Neither side scores anything below the line, but the declarer's opponents score above the line. The opposing team's score depends on the vulnerability of the team and whether or not the points were doubled or redoubled:

➤ If not vulnerable and not doubled: 50 points to opponents.

➤ If vulnerable and not doubled: 100 points to opponents.

➤ If not vulnerable and doubled, the first undertrick scores 100 points.

➤ If vulnerable and doubled, the first undertrick scores 200 points.

➤ If not vulnerable and doubled, the second and third undertricks score 200 points each.

➤ If vulnerable and doubled, the second and third undertricks score 300 points each.

➤ Whether vulnerable or not vulnerable and doubled, each subsequent under-tricks (over three) scores 300 points each.

➤ Redoubled undertricks cost twice as much as doubled undertricks.

If you win 12 contracted tricks, it's called a "small slam." If you win all 13 contracted tricks, it's called a "grand slam." A small slam will get you 500 extra points if you are not vulnerable and 750 points if you are vulnerable. A grand slam will score 1,000 points if you are not vulnerable and 1,500 if you are.

When either side wins two out of three games, the round is over. The side that wins two games in a row is said to "win the *rubber*."

It's in the Cards

A **rubber** is the odd game that determines the winner in a tie.

The winner of the rubber scores 500 points if their opponents have won a game, and 700 points if their opponents have not won a game. All above- and below-the-line points are added up and the side that scores the most points wins the difference between its score and its opponents' score. If you're playing for money, you can transfer the difference in points to the difference in coins!

The Least You Need to Know

➤ Bridge is an advanced game, so either save it for the adults or teach older children. It is too complicated for younger kids.

➤ Bridge is a trick-taking game.

➤ The four players' positions at the table are North, South, East, and West.

➤ The rank of suits is Spades, Hearts, Diamonds, Clubs, with Spades being the highest-ranked suit.

➤ You must be careful not to over- or underbid in Bridge. The player who wins the bid is called the "declarer." The declarer's partner is called the "dummy." The final winning bid is the "contract."

Chapter 18

Poker Face

In This Chapter

➤ The history of Poker

➤ Straight Poker and Draw Poker

➤ Poker hands and placing your bets

➤ Five-Card and Seven-Card Stud

Poker is as much a part of American culture as baseball and the American flag. Even though it's played all over the world, it has been called America's national card game. I don't think there's a single American Western film made that doesn't have some aspect of Poker featured in it.

In this chapter, we'll take a look at this popular card game. From the history of Poker to some of the different games of Poker to standard Poker hands, I'll give you some insight into the joys and frustrations of this game of skill and strategy, and a bit of luck.

What Is Poker?

No one really knows how Poker came to be. Most people have concluded that it is made up of a variety of earlier games. In its earliest recorded history, Jonathan H. Green (believed to have first attached the word "Poker" to the "cheating game") saw the game being played on a Mississippi riverboat and was intrigued. He described the game as being played by two to four people, with 20 cards—only the Aces, Kings, Queens, Jacks, and 10s were used—and each player was dealt five cards.

Why did he call it Poker? Researchers looked into games of other countries to see if there was any game whose name sounded anything like "poker." They came up with an eighteenth-century French game called *poque*, a German game that involves a certain amount of bluffing called *Pochspiel*, and there's even a suggestion that the word derived from a Hindu word: *pukka*.

Well, more realistically, the word "poker" probably finds its origins in the underworld of thieves. Some of the card hustlers may have already been using the expression since "poke" was a slang word used by pickpockets. It is believed that card hustlers, who emerged from that same underworld to cheat unsuspecting opponents, used the word in relation to their card-playing victims. The "r" might have been added to throw off players who were wise to the underworld slang. The reason Poker has such seedy origins has mainly to do with the fact that it is a simple game (sometimes even a quick game, depending on the version you're playing), it involves an element of cheating, and it's played for money.

The Wild West period is the famous Poker-playing era in the United States history—many infamous characters came out of that time, including figures like gun-slinger Wild Bill Hickok. Doc Holliday, the dentist turned killer and outlaw, was also known for his propensity for Poker.

Winning Plays

Wild Bill Hickok used to sit with his back to the wall and his face to the door of any saloon. He drank with his left hand, so he could save the right hand to draw his gun from his holster should he need it. Wild Bill had a lot of enemies. He made a fatal error one day in a crowded saloon—he couldn't get his preferred seat, so he sat with his back to the door. He was shot in the back of the head by a man seeking revenge for Hickok killing his brother. When Hickok's body slumped over, he dropped his hand to reveal pairs of black Aces and 8s. This hand is still known today as the "deadman's hand."

Poker evolved over the years to include the other 32 cards in the deck. Jokers are used only when playing with wild cards. It is widely played in casinos and is a very popular home game. Poker night is often associated with cigars, potato chips, and beer-swilling men, but it can also be played by families and friends while seated around a living room coffee table. You'll find the experts playing in tournaments, clubs, and casinos.

It's a game of skill, strategy, and luck—but mostly, it's just really fun. There are several variants on the basic rules and sometimes the best way to play is to switch the version of the game from deal to deal. There are even silly versions of the game, like Strip Poker (that's for you and your loved one on a quiet, child-free night), and a version where you hold the cards behind your head for your opponents to see and bet on. The variations are endless and you may find yourself making up your own rules as you go along.

Straight Poker

Straight Poker is played with a standard 52-card deck with anywhere from 2 to 14 players; the ideal number of players is 7 or 8. Aces are high and there are no high or low ranking suits. Jokers are often used as wild cards.

The object of Poker is to form the cards into "structures." The structures consist of card combinations of two or more cards of one rank or sequences of cards of the same suit. (For more detail about rank and sequence, see Chapter 16, "Rummy Noses.")

In Straight Poker each player is dealt five cards. (Five cards are also dealt in Five-Card Stud and Draw Poker while seven cards are dealt in Seven-Card Stud.) The object of any Poker game is to take the cards you are dealt and make them into the best possible card combination in an effort to beat the other players.

In Straight Poker you must make the best of the cards you are dealt with no chance of improving them. (Draw Poker allows you to exchange cards and therefore make the betting a little more interesting.) Straight Poker is a game of luck and—if you're clever enough—a game that involves a good deal of bluffing, in the hope of fooling the other players into thinking you have a better hand than you actually do.

Succeeding at a good bluff can depend on the quality of your *poker face*. If your hand is a Royal Flush, you don't want your opponents to know that. If

High Score

Jokers, as wild cards, can also be designated "the bug." This means that the Joker is wild, but with limitations. It can be used as an Ace or it can be used as a card of any suit or rank needed to make a Flush or a Straight.

It's in the Cards

Poker face refers to keeping a straight face no matter what cards you hold in your hand. You don't want to tip off your opponents to either a good hand or a bad hand.

your hand is atrocious, but you want to stay in the game, you can try smirking a little throughout the betting process to fool other players into thinking you have a
good hand. Bluffing relies heavily on your poker face.

Rank and File

Here are the ranking orders of card combinations:

➤ **Five of a Kind:** Four cards of same rank plus a wild card—the highest possible
hand. Example: four Kings plus a Joker.

➤ **Straight Flush:** Five cards in a sequence in the same suit. This is the best hand
you can have without a wild card (the best "natural" hand). Example: 7-8-9-10-J
in the same suit. Note: Aces can be high or low, but do not wrap around—
meaning you can have A-K-Q-J-10, or A-2-3-4-5, but you cannot have K-A-2-3-4.
An Ace high straight (A-K-Q-J-10) is called Royal Flush and it is the highest natural hand you can have.

*A Straight Flush is the
best "natural" hand.*

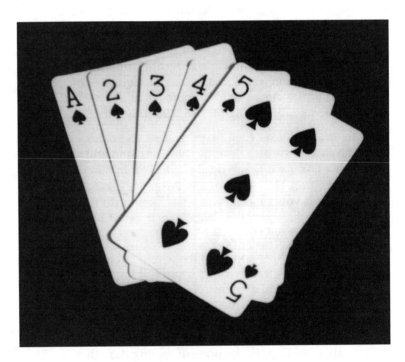

➤ **Four of a Kind:** Four cards of one rank, plus any fifth card of any rank or suit.
Example: 4-4-4-4-8.

➤ **Full House:** Three of a Kind and a Pair. Example: Q-Q-Q-3-3. If there are two
Full Houses on the table, you have to look at the cards as three of a kind. So if
you have Q-Q-Q-3-3 and your opponent has J-J-J-2-2, your hand wins because

your Three of a Kind (the three Queens) is higher than you opponent's Three of a Kind (the three Jacks). If you both have three Queens, you have to look at the Pairs to determine the winner. In the example I've given, if your hands both had three Queens, you would still win because a pair of 3s is higher than a pair of 2s.

➤ **Flush:** All cards of the same suit. Example: K-A-7-J-2 of one suit. In the case of a tie, you would have to use the rule for High Card to determine the winner.

➤ **Straight:** Five cards in ranking order, but not of the same suit. Example: 2-3-4-5-6 of different suits. Aces can be high or low, but cannot wrap around (K-A-2-3-4). In a tie, the Straight with the highest cards wins. If the cards are the same, you would split the winnings.

➤ **Three of a Kind:** Three cards of equal rank plus any other two cards of different ranks. Example: Q-Q-Q-4-5. (If the last two cards were the same, it would count as a Full House.) In a tie, the highest ranking Three of a Kind wins. So if you have Q-Q-Q-4-5 and your opponent has J-J-J-2-3, you win. If the cards are of equal value (this would only apply in wild card situations), use the High Card rules to determine the winner.

➤ **Two Pair:** Two pairs of equal rank plus any fifth card. Example: 2-2-4-4-6. In a tie situation, the highest ranking pairs win. If the cards have the same value, use the High Card rule to determine the winner.

➤ **One Pair:** Two cards of the same rank plus any other three cards that do not combine with the other two to form any other hands listed here. Example: Q-Q-7-6-4 (you would refer to this hand as a "Pair of Queens").

➤ **High Card** (also called "No Pair"): This is the lowest ranking hand, but is used as a tie-breaker. It consists of five cards that do not make up any particular combination of cards listed here.

The cards are shuffled by any player and cut by the player to the shuffler's right. The person who shuffles the cards then deals the cards face-up (starting with the person on his or her left). This preliminary dealer keeps dealing until a Jack turns up. The person who receives the Jack becomes the first game dealer. The cards are then reshuffled—by any player—and should be shuffled at least three times. The player on the dealer's right cuts the cards. The cards are then dealt, face-down, one at a time to each player, starting on the dealer's left. Each player is dealt five cards.

The Bets Are On!

You bet against other players to determine who has the best hand of cards. Each new deal is a separate game, so you are betting on your current hand—there are no points to be added up at the end. You win if you keep betting and your hand beats every other hand. When the cards are redealt, you start a fresh game with fresh bets. The object of the game is to win the pot!

The amount of betting intervals depends on the game you are playing. One betting interval consists of every active player having had a chance to bid.

Some people will start a hand of Poker with an *ante* before the cards are even dealt. Antes are used in hands of Draw Poker—less so in Straight Poker.

High Score

Antes are a good idea if you are just playing at home with friends or with the kids and you want to set a limit on the amount you can bet. Each player tosses in an equal amount of money before the cards are dealt. The ante establishes the opening bet, and at home, you can use it to establish the limit on bets allowed. If you are playing at home, you may want to make the ante a nickel or a dime (or one or two chips). You toss your coins (or chips) into the center of the table to start the "pot."

Betting and folding must be done in turn. Betting goes around the table in a clockwise direction, starting with the player to the left of the dealer. There are three options when it comes to betting:

It's in the Cards

An **ante** is a Poker stake usually put up before the deal to build the pot. Before the cards are dealt, players toss in a minimum amount of change or chips to start the pot. In home games, a nickel is recommended. In the casinos, the ante will be a low-valued chip.

➤ **Call:** This means that you have to contribute to the pot (your bet) as much as—but no more than—any other player per betting interval. So if the betting starts with two chips—you must match the two-chip bet by tossing two chips into the pot. This is called the "call." You must "call" to stay in the game. If you don't think your hand is worth the chips, you can fold (give up your hand).

➤ **Raise:** This means that not only do you call, but you may throw in a few more chips to emphasize that you have confidence in your hand. The next person to bet must call by matching the total amount of chips contributed by the previous player—but is not obligated to raise. So if the last player called with two chips and raised another two chips, you must put in four chips to call. If that player wants to raise, he or she would put in the four chips plus one or more chips to raise. That means the next player would have to put in five or more chips.

➤ **Fold** (or drop): If you don't want to participate in the betting, you lay your cards facedown on the table and say, "I fold." This means the betting skips over you and moves to the next player in turn. Once you fold, you cannot return to that round and you lose the chips you contributed to the pot.

If you are playing Straight Poker with one betting round, all players must contribute what they owe the pot before revealing their cards. When all the bets are in, everyone reveals their cards and the highest hand wins the pot. You do not need to announce your hand when you lay it down—as often seen in the movies or on TV—the cards will speak for themselves. However, if you are using a wild card, you must announce what card the wild card is representing.

The people who folded during the game are not included in this final phase.

Three Strikes

Most Poker games will have a cap on the amount of money you can bet. This is a good idea, or you could lose your shirt. A word of wisdom—no one makes a fortune on small-stakes games, so try to play for fun, not money. If you are playing for higher stakes, remember—this is gambling—never bet the farm!

High Score

If you are playing with more than one betting round, when the betting returns to the first bettor, he or she must pay the pot what he or she owes. For example: If the bet is up to five chips, and the first bettor has only contributed a total of two chips, he or she must put in three extra chips to make up the difference of what he or she owes the pot. In this case, the first bettor must put in the three chips owed, plus his or her next bet and the next betting round continues.

High Score

Some Poker variations allow players to check rather than bet. To check means you don't bet anything, but you want to stay in the game. The only way you can check is if no one else has bet anything yet in the game. So if the first player checks, and your turn is next, you can check also. You can keep checking until someone bets, then you either have to bet or fold. If all players check, the hand is over and the cards must be redealt.

Draw Poker

Draw Poker makes the game of Poker much more interesting because you are not stuck with one hand. Near the beginning of the game, you are entitled to take cards out of your initial hand and exchange them with cards from the deck.

Draw Poker is played with a standard 52-card deck and the ideal amount of players is seven. You can play with as many as eight or more, but you may find that's just too many people for a good game.

To establish who deals first, follow the same guidelines as outlined in Straight Poker. When you have a dealer, he or she deals five cards face-down to each player starting with the player to his or her left. The person to the left of the dealer starts the betting.

Winning Plays

Did you know that the term "jackpot" originated from Poker? In an effort to liven up the game, some versions of Poker pots were designated "jack" pots. This meant the stakes could be "jacked" up by raising the limit and increasing the ante—thus a bigger pot and a more interesting game. Later, this rule was taken a step further to say that players could not start betting unless they had a Jack (or better) in their hand—thus play rested in the hand of the Jack, making the pot a "jackpot." This is still the rule in Draw Poker today.

Ready, Set, Bet

When the cards are dealt and each player looks at his or her hand, the betting commences. Betting begins with the player to the dealer's left. This player may open, check, or fold:

➤ The first player may open with a bet as long as he or she has a Jack or higher card in his or her hand. If the player bets, then the play moves to the next player and that player must bet or fold.

➤ The first player may check, which means that he or she does not make a bet but reserves the right to do so later. If the first player checks, the second player may also check. Checking can continue until someone finally opens. Once someone places a bet, no more checks are allowed—each player must then fold, call, or raise.

➤ If all players check on the first round, the deal is said to be "passed out." At this time, each player antes another chip (or coin) and the cards are redealt. The player to the left of the first dealer deals the next hand.

Three Strikes

You can check even if you have a Jack or better in your hand, but be careful, because if everyone checks, then the cards must be redealt and a new hand played.

Return Policy

After the first betting round (which works the same way as in Straight Poker), and all the bets have been equalized (meaning everyone pays what they owe to the pot based on the previous bet), you are entitled to swap cards from your hand with the cards remaining in the deck. The exchange starts with the player to the left of the dealer. Let's say you want to exchange three cards—take the three cards from your hand and place them face-down on the table and announce how many cards you want to exchange. The dealer takes an equivalent amount of cards from the top of the deck and places them face-down in front of you. The dealer discards and draws last. Players who have folded are not permitted back in this hand, so they cannot exchange any cards.

High Score

Just like you need to know what version of Poker you are going to be playing, you should also be aware of the various nuances of the version you are playing. In other words, be sure players are aware that "to stand" means "to knock," otherwise others might think you're a little weird to be knocking on the table for no apparent reason.

To "stand pat" means you decide not to exchange any cards. You can either say "I stand" or you can knock on the table when your turn comes.

The player who opens may discard to the pot the specific card (or cards) that allowed him to open in the first place. This card is still considered part of your hand but it is laid down as a kind of proof that you actually had the right to open the betting (remember—you had to have a Jack or higher). This is done at the time of the open and may be referred to later if anyone questions your right to open.

You may find when the exchange of cards (the draw) is underway that there are not enough cards remaining in the deck to handle all the players' needs. In this case, the dealer will have to shuffle the discards. The discard of the opening card and the discards of the player next in line for the draw are not included in the shuffle.

When the draw is complete, the player who opens must bet or check—if this player folds, the next person to the left must bet or check. Each player must then bet or check in order of his or her turn. The betting process works the same as in Straight Poker—you may call, raise, or fold. You must equalize the pot after the betting interval (pay the pot what you owe according to the preceding bet). When all players have checked, or when the pot has been equalized after the betting interval, you show your cards in the showdown. The highest-ranking hand wins the pot.

As I mentioned above, the opener must be able to prove on demand that he or she had the card that allowed him or her to open the betting—this is usually done by discarding that card to the pot after the open is made. If you can't prove that you had the right card, then your hand is considered foul. All active players (ones that have not folded) may withdraw all their chips from the pot (except their ante). The ante contributions stay in the pot for the next hand.

Stud Poker: Five-Card Stud and Seven-Card Stud

Stud Poker can be played with seven to nine people, but is best played with two or four. A standard 52-card deck is used.

In Five-Card Stud the dealer can be chosen in the same way you choose a dealer in Straight Poker. After you have established who will deal, the dealer gives each player one card face-down (the "hole" card) and one card face-up. The rest of the deck is laid aside and the betting begins.

After the bets have been equalized in the first betting interval, the dealer gives each player another face-up card (excluding any player that folded in the first interval). There is another betting round after the second deal. The bets are equalized and a third card is dealt to any remaining, active players. This continues for a fourth deal until each player has five cards in front of him or her. There is one more betting round, after which the showdown takes place. Each player turns up his or her hole card. The highest hand wins.

Betting

There is no ante in Stud Poker unless all players agree to one. In the first betting interval, the player with the highest face-up card must place a bet. If two players have the same high card, then the player closest to the dealer's left must bet first. In each subsequent betting interval, the person with the highest-ranking poker hand showing chooses the first player to bet. You do not have to bet after the first interval.

There is usually a betting limit in the first three betting intervals of Stud Poker. In the final interval, the stakes are usually raised. It is also customary to raise the limit in an earlier interval if one player is showing a pair.

Checking is permitted as long as no one has placed a bet before you.

When you fold, you should place your face-up cards down and do not reveal your hole card.

High Score

It is the dealer's responsibility to point out the first bettor by saying (if the highest card is a King, for example): "First King bets." The dealer should also point out a player's ranking combinations. For example if a player is showing three Spades, the dealer should point to that hand and say "possible flush."

Seven-Card Stud

In Seven-Card Stud, each player is dealt three cards before the first betting interval: two face-down and one face-up. You then have your first betting interval. After the first betting interval is complete and the pot is equalized, one card is dealt to each player face-up.

There are three more rounds after the first deal (of one card face-up), each round is followed by a betting interval. After the fourth interval of betting is over and the pot equalized, one more card is dealt face-down to each player that has not yet folded—and one more betting interval takes place. This time, after the pot is equalized, the showdown takes place. At this point, each player turns over the three face-down cards and selects five cards from his or her hand to make the highest possible Poker combination. The highest-ranking hand wins the pot.

So, now you're ready to play Poker. Ready, set, bet!

The Least You Need to Know

➤ The object of Poker is to form cards into combinations of two or more—either of one rank or sequence of cards in the same suit.

➤ An important part of Poker is the ability to bluff—a good poker face is an asset.

➤ Some of the combinations you can shoot for in Poker are: Five of a Kind, Straight Flush, Four of a Kind, Full House, Flush, Straight, Three of a Kind, a Pair, and High Card. Five of a Kind is the best Poker hand.

➤ Some of the types of Poker you can play are Straight Poker, Draw Poker, Five-Card Stud, and Seven-Card Stud. No matter which you choose, you're sure to have a great time!

Chapter 19

A Royal Marriage: Pinochle for Everyone

In This Chapter

➤ Basics of Pinochle

➤ Two-Handed Pinochle

➤ Three-Handed Pinochle

➤ Double-Deck Pinochle

There are so many different versions of Pinochle that in talking to people and looking through various publications, I discovered that no two games are alike. There are general rules for Two-Handed, Three-Handed, and Four-Handed (or Auction) Pinochle, but everyone seems to have a variation that he or she learned as a kid or plays now as an adult. It's a great game for the family and even better for teams of couples.

My grandparents and my great-grandparents used to play Pinochle. I remember picking up the unusual deck they used, wondering where the rest of the cards were. How could you play a game of cards without any cards below 9—and why were there so many face cards? I always thought it was funny that my grandparents never taught me how to play. They taught me almost every other card came in this book—why not Pinochle?

Like Bridge, Pinochle is popularly played by four people in teams of two, but there are many other versions you can play. Like Bridge and Rummy, it can get a little complicated and might not be interesting to kids under the age of 13 or so.

In this chapter, we will look at the rules for Basic Pinochle, Two-Handed Pinochle, Three-Handed Pinochle, and Double-Deck Pinochle.

Back to Basics

Basic Pinochle requires at least four players, arranged in partners. The deck is a special one, made up of 48 cards that you can either buy in any game store, or you can make your own deck from a couple standard 52-card decks. The special Pinochle deck contains doubles of the following cards: Ace, King, Queen, Jack, 10, and 9 in all suits. Cards less than 9 are not included in the deck. So if you don't want to go out and buy a special deck, but you have at least two standard 52-card decks already at home, it's easy to make up the cards. Just take the two 52-card decks and isolate all the cards 9 through Ace—and voilà … Pinochle!

The more unusual Pinochle games are covered in this chapter. Basic Pinochle is similar to Double-Deck Pinochle, but only one deck is used and Jacks and 9s are worth no points. Triple and quadruple point systems do not apply.

Winning Plays

Pinochle shares many of the attributes associated with Rummy, Bridge, and Poker—combined. It's the fourth most popular game in the United States behind Rummy, Bridge, and Poker. It derived from the French game Bezique and the German game called Sixty-Six.

Two-Handed Pinochle

Two-Handed Pinochle is the original version of the game. It is—like the name suggests—played by two people. The card ranking is different than in other card games: Ace (high), 10, King, Queen, Jack, and 9.

This game is a trick-taking, meld-making, draw game. This means that you score your points by winning tricks and by laying your cards down in sets (melds).

Here's the Deal

Pick the dealer by cutting cards. You each draw a card from the deck and the highest card deals first. The nondealer shuffles and cuts the cards; the dealer may give the deck one last shuffle before the deal. The winner of each hand gets to deal the next game. When playing to 1,000, the deal alternates between players.

The dealer deals 12 cards to each player—three at a time and face-down. When the cards are dealt, the dealer turns up the next card on the top of the deck and that card becomes the "trump" card. The trump card is a card whose suit must be followed in trick-taking during the game. The trump card is face-up on the table and the remaining deck is placed on the table, partly covering the trump card. This stack of undealt cards becomes the stock pile.

A Pinochle deck.

Melds and Tricks

The object of the game is to score points by melding cards or winning tricks. You meld your cards in sequences or groups immediately after winning a trick and before drawing from the stock pile. Melds are still considered part of your hand, but as you construct them, you lay the cards face-up on the table for all other players to see.

Here are the point values of different types of melds:

➤ **Run:** A-10-K-Q-J of trump suit = 150 points.

➤ **Marriage:** K-Q of the same suit = 20 points.

➤ **Royal Marriage:** K-Q of trump suit = 40 points.

➤ **Aces Around:** One Ace of each suit = 100 points.

➤ **Kings Around:** One King of each suit = 80 points.

➤ **Queens Around:** One Queen of each suit = 60 points.

➤ **Jacks Around:** One Jack of each suit = 40 points.

➤ **Pinochle:** Jack of Diamonds and Queen of Spades = 40 points.

➤ **Double Pinochle:** Two Pinochles = 300 points (This is the only meld that gives you a bonus for having more than one. All other "double" melds simply count twice. For example: Double Kings Around = 160 points.)

➤ *Dix:* 10 of trumps = 10 points.

It's in the Cards

The **dix** in Pinochle is the 10. Dix (pronounced "deece") is French for the number 10.

A run in Pinochle.

Double Pinochle.

The Rules of Melding

Here are some tips to better explain the rules of melding:

➤ You can only meld after winning a trick.

➤ You can use a card in more than one meld as long as it is used to make a different kind of meld. For example: If a player melds a marriage in Hearts, he can later add three Kings for Kings Around; or three Queens for Queens Around. You cannot, however, add another King of Hearts to make a second Marriage.

➤ You don't score the same number of points for adding to a meld to create a new meld as you would if the original meld was made to begin with. For example, if you meld a Royal Marriage and later add the Ace, 10, and Jack or trumps for a Run, you only score an additional 110 points instead of 150.

➤ If a player melds a Pinochle and later adds on to make a Double Pinochle, they only score an additional 260 points instead of 300. If the first Pinochle has been broken to use the cards for tricks, then the second Pinochle only scores 40 points.

Tricks and Play

In Two-Handed Pinochle, there are basically two phases of the game. The game is in the first phase as long as there are still cards in the stock pile. When the stock pile is exhausted the game moves into its second phase.

Phase 1: After the cards are dealt, the game begins. There is no bidding in Two-Handed Pinochle. The nondealer leads the first trick and the dealer lays down a card to the trick. The dealer is not required to follow suit or trump. The winner of the trick is the person who lays down the highest-ranking card. The trump suit beats every other suit.

The person who wins the trick takes the top card from the stock pile and places it in his or her hand. The loser of the trick takes the next card from the stock pile and places it in his or her hand. The winner of the trick may now meld if he or she chooses. The winner of the trick leads the next trick. The person who leads the trick can either take a card from his or her hand or use a card from his or her melds on the table. Phase 1 continues until there are no cards remaining in the stock pile.

High Score

There is a special rule concerning the dix. The first dix to be melded must be done so by exchanging it for the face-up trump card (the card the dealer turns up at the beginning of the game). Even if the card is the other dix, it must still be exchanged. The dix may immediately be used in the meld after the exchange.

Three Strikes

Remember there are two identical cards of each rank and suit. If one of them has been used in a meld, the other one may be used in an identical meld—but it must be composed of cards not used in the first meld.

When there is just one card left in the stock pile, plus the face-up trump card that was placed on the table at the beginning of the game, the winner of the trick may choose to take either card. After these last two cards are picked up, the winner of that trick may also meld. When you meld in phase 1, you score points and you should write the points down immediately on a score sheet.

Phase 2 begins at this point. There are no cards left in the stock pile and now the rules have to change a little bit. Each player picks up any meld they've made and places it in his or her hand. The winner of the last trick from phase 1 leads the next trick. The second player must follow suit if possible. If not, he or she must play a trump card if possible. If the player doesn't have a trump card, he or she may play any card. The winner of this trick leads the next trick and players keep playing until all the cards have been played.

Here is a trick taking example: If hearts is trumps, and the lead card is a Queen of Hearts and you lay down a King of Hearts, you win the trick and lead the next trick.

Card Values

You must mark down your scores on a score sheet as you go along in order to keep track. Both melds and tricks score points right away. Here are the values for the tricks:

➤ Each Ace taken = 11 points

➤ Each 10 taken = 10 points

➤ Each King taken = 4 points

➤ Each Queen taken = 3 points

➤ Each Jack taken = 2 points

The winner of the last trick scores another 10 points.

If the dealer turns up the dix as the first trump card, he or she immediately scores 10 points.

Point-Scoring Rules

Here are some basic scoring rules you'll need to know:

➤ You can play the game to 1,000, 1,200, or even 1,500 points.

➤ You can try a simplified scoring method by counting every Ace, 10, and King as 10 points. This way all your scores will end in a zero.

➤ Points for taking tricks are added after the last trick is won.

Declaring Out

Let's say you're playing for 1,000 points. If you feel you have scored 1,000 points at any point in the game, you can "declare yourself out." This includes melded cards as well as tricks taken. When you declare yourself out, play stops and cards are counted. The new count is added to your previous score. If you have 1,000 points, you win the game. If you don't have 1,000 points, you lose.

If no one declares him or herself out, you count up your totals after the last trick is taken. If you both score 1,000 then the game is undecided and play continues until either one of you reaches 1,250 points. You can declare yourself out at 1,250 as per the rules previously indicated. You can keep going like this by raising the amount of points. The next score would be 1,500 and then 1,750. In other words, you just keep adding 250 points to the total until you have a winner.

Three-Handed Pinochle

Three-Handed Pinochle follows the same rules as Two-Handed Pinochle with a few exceptions to accommodate the extra player. In Three-Handed Pinochle, the 64-card deck is used (with 7s and 8s added to the normal 48-card deck). The deal rotates to the left as does play. Each player plays to each trick. If two players put down the same card, the card that is played first outranks the other. The winner of the trick is the only player that gets to meld on a given turn. After the trick is won, each player, in turn, draws one card from the stock pile.

The first player to reach 1,000 points wins the game.

Double-Deck Pinochle

Double-Deck Pinochle requires at least four players in teams of two. You use a deck of 80 cards, made up of 4 cards of each rank in every suit in the following order: A, 10, K, Q, and J. You can make this deck by combining two Pinochle decks and removing all the nines. This game involves bidding, drawing, trick-taking, and melding.

Winning Plays

You can play Two-Handed Pinochle with a 64-card deck with only these slight differences. This version is called Goulash and the deck includes 7s and 8s.

If you're playing with 64 cards, you deal 16 cards to each player—four at a time face-down.

High Score

When your partner leads a winning card (such as an Ace of trumps) throw off a high card—such as a 10—to ensure your team the most points!

All cards are dealt out to each player—at least four cards at a time. Each player should wind up with 20 cards. After the deal the bidding begins.

Let's Bid

The bidding begins to the dealer's left. Players bid the number of points that their team will attempt to win. Whoever wins the bid gets to choose the trump suit and leads the first trick. You score points by declaring and melding, and by winning Aces, 10s, and Kings during tricks. The goal is to achieve a score of 500 or more points.

You can make a bid, announce a meld, or pass. If you pass, you may not re-enter the bidding.

Here's a sample bidding hand:

If you had a Royal Marriage and a Run, you have a meld of eight points. Because you have a strong trump suit you are likely to win many of the points on the play. There are 50 points available during play so you can take many of those points into account when you bid. Also remember: your partner will most likely have something to meld to add to your points system!

The minimum bid is 50 (some people start the bidding at 500), so the first bidder must bid that amount or higher. Each subsequent bid—until you reach 60 (or in 10s until you reach 600)—can be made in increments of one. Bids over 60 should be made in multiples of 5. Each bid must be higher than the previous bid. If you don't wish to bid, you can pass. If the first three players pass, the dealer must bid 50. When you pass you cannot re-enter the bidding on a later turn. The bidding continues until three players have passed. The winner of the bid gets to call the trump suit and lead the first trick.

Trumps and Melding

The winner of the bid announces the trump suit. The bidder must hold at least a Marriage in his or her hand in order to call that particular suit. If the bidder does not have a Marriage, the hand cannot be played and the bidder loses the amount of his or her bid.

Once the trump suit is called, players lay their melds face-up on the table.

You can count the same card in melds of different types. For example, a Queen of Spades can be used in a Marriage, a Pinochle, and a Set of Queens. However, the same card cannot be used in more than one meld of the same type. For example, a King and two Queens do not count as two Marriages. Partners should add the total of their melds and mark them on a score sheet.

Play Day

The person who won the bid leads the first trick. Then the play rotates to the left. Each player lays down a card. Trumps beats every other suit. If there is no trump, then the highest card of the lead suit wins the trick. If there are two or more identical cards played to the trick, the first card played to the trick wins. The winner of the trick leads the next trick.

Any card may be played when leading a trick. Each player may follow suit if possible and must attempt to play a card that is higher in rank than the last highest card played. If you cannot *crawl* (you don't have a high enough card) you must still attempt to follow suit—even if the card will not win the trick.

If you don't have a card in the suit that was led, you must play a trump card if you have one. If someone has already placed a trump card, you must try and beat that trump card with a higher trump card. A player who cannot follow suit or play the highest trump must still play a trump even if it means losing the trick. If you have no lead suit card and no trump card, you may play any card—but you'll most likely lose the trick.

It's in the Cards

Crawling is a term used in Pinochle. It means to play a card higher in rank than the highest card played so far.

1, 2, 3, Score!

When all the cards have been played, each team adds up the tricks it has won. If the original bidding team meets its bid then both teams add up their points and add the new score to the cumulative score.

If the bidding partnership does not meet their bid then they are considered *set*. The nonbidding partners get to keep their points.

If the bidding partner knows that the team will not meet its bid before play begins, he or she may throw in the hand. No points are scored and the bid is subtracted from their total score. The nonbidding partners get to keep whatever points they've accumulated so far and add the points to their total score. This allows the bidding team to avoid losing trick-taking points to the opposing team.

It's in the Cards

To be **set** means to fail to make your bid on the meld. Your entire bid is subtracted from your total score and you score none of your points in that hand.

Points for Tricks

The cards rank in the following order: Ace, 10, King, Queen, Jack. At the end of play, the teams total the points they have won in trick-taking. Each Ace, 10, and King is worth one point. The team that wins the last trick scores two additional points. There are a total of 50 points available for tricks.

Points for Melds

Like in many card games, there are some terms you will need to know in order to build melds and score points. You should memorize these terms and what they mean before playing the game.

➤ **Run:** A-10-K-Q-J of trump suit = 15 for single

150 for double

225 for triple

300 for quadruple

➤ **Royal Marriage:** K-Q of trump suit = 4 for single

8 for double

12 for triple

16 for quadruple

➤ **Marriage:** Kings and Queen of same suit = 2 for single

(NOT trump suit) 4 for double

6 for triple

8 for quadruple

➤ **Pinochle:** Jack of Diamonds and Queen of Spades = 4 for single

30 for double

60 for triple

90 for quadruple

➤ **Aces Around:** An Ace in each suit = 10 for single

100 for double

150 for triple

200 for quadruple

➤ **Kings Around:** A King in each suit = 8 for single

80 for double

120 for triple

160 for quadruple

➤ **Queens Around:** A Queen in each suit = 6 for single

60 for double

90 for triple

120 for quadruple

➤ **Jacks Around:** A Jack in each suit = 4 for single

40 for double

60 for triple

80 for quadruple

Note: A set of 10s is not worth anything in a meld.

No matter which game of Pinochle you choose to play, you're sure to have some great family fun!

The Least You Need to Know

➤ The standard Pinochle deck is made up of 48 cards: doubles of Aces, 10s, Kings, Queens, Jacks, and 9s.

➤ You can make your own Pinochle deck from two standard playing card decks.

➤ There are many different versions of Pinochle: Basic, Two-Handed, Three-Handed, and Double-Deck, to name just a few. Rules vary widely from region to region and family to family.

➤ Basic Pinochle requires at least four players but there are games you can play with two or three players as well.

➤ In most Pinochle games there are two stages: the trick-taking stage and the melding stage.

Part 5

Everywhere Games

"How many more miles?" "Are we there yet?" "I'm bored." "She hit me." "He's look-ing at me." Oh … the good intentions of loving parents to take that family road trip! What a nightmare it could be if you don't have a means to stimulate your kids.

There are so many great games you can play that require little more than imagina-tion! You can use these games in a doctor's office or in line in the grocery store. From word games to visual games, learning some of these could be a lifesaver on your next family outing!

You'll also find some classic birthday party games in this section that may bring back some memories for you. Try these old-time favorites at your child's next party.

Chapter 20

Road Trip: Car Games

In This Chapter

➤ Car game supplies

➤ I Spy games and License Plate Bingo

➤ Camping Trip and Who Am I?

➤ Desperation moves

Kids love games and it's amazing how the games we played as kids are now being played by our own kids. The games just keep getting passed down from generation to generation by virtue of experience. The games our parents taught us on long car rides are now being taught to the next generation of kids … and the cycle continues.

This chapter is all about car games—filling those hours in the car while you travel with the kids, on vacation, to Grandma's, wherever you need to go. Stave off the inevitable "Are we there yet?" with one of these memorable travel games for kids.

Things You May Need in the Car

For some car games you will need to have some tools on hand to make game-playing easier. Here are just some of the things you'll need:

➤ Pen

➤ Pencil

➤ Pencil sharpener

➤ Paper

➤ Crayons

➤ Coloring books

➤ Tray table (please make sure this is safe, first)

➤ Back seat storage

➤ Map

Three Strikes

You should always be careful when allowing a child to use a pen or a pencil in the car. These tools should only be used with children of a certain age and always under supervision. Remember, you're in a moving vehicle and any pointed object can be dangerous.

High Score

A map will not only be useful for navigation purposes, but you can use it to show the kids where you are at any given time, and help them plot the course of travel.

Let's Go!

It would not be possible to take long trips with children without the use of games such as the ones discussed here. Nowadays, kids have electronic hand-held games, and cars come equipped with TVs and VCRs, but every so often the kids will even get bored of these things and start to get fidgety and whiney.

Little kids will do anything to get their parents' attention and, frankly, all the TVs and videos in the world will not keep them happy for the next few hundred miles. It would be nice if the kids could just get into a good book and not want to put it down; this might happen if your kids are old enough to read—but it's that word "might" that could cause you big problems down the road if you don't have a plan B.

When the books are put away, the attention spans wane, the batteries wear out, and the videos become repetitive, it's time to pull out the good old standbys. Anyone born before 1985 knows these games very well because we *had* to play them in the car. The only other electronic gadgets we had to distract ourselves with were portable cassette players or radios—if we were lucky enough to have owned them.

When you decide to take family car rides, you're taking your kids away from their friends, their bedrooms, and their regular playgrounds. It means that they are out of their element—and we all know that most kids require consistent stimulation or boredom sets in very quickly. So, if you're planning a long trip, you should also plan to bring along many forms of entertainment—the best of which are the games that don't require batteries. They are the games that were made up out of moments of desperation by parents and teachers—games that keep the peace for as long as everyone can keep playing. You'll want to know a few of these games because even *they* will lose their interest from hour to hour.

Well, I can't guarantee these games will be the cure-all, but the more games you know the more chances you will have of hour-free fidgetiness, crankiness, and general chaos. As the Boy Scouts and Girl Scouts say: "Be Prepared." It's your best defense!

The history of these "car games" is virtually unknown. They are probably as ancient as procreation itself. They have been played in various ways, in various countries, in multitudes of languages for ages. There was a time, before kids had so much electronic stimuli, that parents had to be more interactive with the kids just to manage their own levels of chaos. Now, rather than let the kids zone out, this is a great opportunity to work with them—let them use their minds, their imaginations, and their creativity, rather than just passively absorb all that information technology.

Little kids will be thrilled to get your undivided attention, but you might have a bigger struggle with the teenagers. Rather than resort to plug-pulling to get them to zone in, maybe they'll see the younger kids having so much fun that they'll tune in for a few minutes to see what all the laughing is about. Their level of interest will depend on the level of the game, however. Maybe the games for little kids will spark some of their own memories and they'll want to teach their younger siblings a thing or two.

Three Strikes

Coloring books and crayons should be stored in a compartment in the back seat for safety purposes. Don't leave stuff out so it can fly around the car and hurt someone.

High Score

You'll need some kind of storage to keep the back seat safe, neat, and organized. You can buy the storage pouch that attaches to the back of the front seat. This way the kids will have easy access to what they need and you can keep everything tidy and safe in the process.

The I Spy Games

I Spy is one of the first car games your kids will probably ever learn. It's the kind of game you start playing with kids long before the first car trip. You may have played it for the first time with your little one in the doctor's office—when you were waiting ... and waiting ... for your name to be called. It might be one of the first games that pops into your head to keep your child from getting bored. It's a great game to play one-on-one or in a group.

Three Strikes

Never remove a seat belt from a child to play a game.

I Spy with One Child

If you're playing with one child, you start by saying "I spy with my little eye, something that is …" and fill in with a color. The child is then required to guess what it is you're looking at. You can pick any color, of course. It's a great way to help your child build an understanding of colors.

When the child guesses the object, it is then the child's turn to "spy" something. You keep going back and forth, alternating turns.

If the child is a little bit older, you can use letters. "I spy with my little eye, something starting with the letter B." If the child knows some basic reading skills, you can easily play this game with him or her.

If one of you never guesses the object and "gives up," the person who did the spying gets to take another turn.

High Score

You can play I Spy with more than one child very easily. One person goes first and the first person to guess the object gets to spy the next object.

Three Strikes

If you find that all chaos breaks loose with kids shouting out their answers, you can do one of two things: Let them shout out the answers and let an adult be the referee. If two people say it at the same time, the referee has to pick the winner. If you don't want to have that kind of chaos, tell the kids that they have to take turns guessing the answer. The child who guesses it correctly is, of course, the winner.

License Plate Bingo

This game works best in traffic jams because you can get a good, long look at the license plates. For License Plate Bingo you'll need a pen and paper. Give each child a piece of paper and a pen. The kids should write the letters of the alphabet on the piece of paper. They then need to look out the window and see what letters of the alphabet they can spot on the license plates of other cars. The kids cross off each letter on their piece of paper as they see that letter on a license plate. The object of the game is to cross off all the letters and shout "Bingo" by the time the traffic starts moving again.

To liven things up a little, you might want to give the kids different windows, on different sides of the car, to ensure that they are looking at different license plates.

To liven things up even more, tell the kids that they have to find the letters in alphabetical order. In other words, they can't just cross off the letters in any old order. You might want to resort to this if the cars haven't moved and you need a round two!

You can try playing License Plate Bingo without paper and pencil also. Just have the kids shout out the letters in alphabetical order as they see them. You can do the same thing with billboards along the highway. Try reverse alphabetical order for a change of pace. Have the kids start with the letter "z" and go backward to "a."

What If

All you need for What If is some imagination and maybe a map. Some of the best games you'll ever play with your kids are games that involve creativity and imagination.

In this game, you pose a "what if" scenario to your child and he or she has to describe the conditions and possibilities.

For example: Ask your child, "What if the car trip we're taking was actually in a covered wagon?" The questions the child should consider answering are things like:

➤ How long would the trip take?

➤ How many times would you have to stop to feed and water the horses?

➤ What would you eat?

➤ How much water would you need to bring?

You can look at the map with the child and try to imagine what the country looked like with single lane dirt roads. What kind of obstacles would you encounter on these roads?

A map is an excellent prop for this game. Use some of your own historical knowledge to liven up the discussion. If you have time before the trip, study up on the history a little bit and offer information to the children to liven up their imaginations and knowledge that much more. You can even bring along a couple of books on the topic. If someone else is driving, you can always look at the

Winning Plays

Who knew that the Studebaker company—the famous manufacturer of automobiles started by Henry and Clement Studebaker in 1852—began as a blacksmith shop building covered wagons? The road trip 150 years ago was probably not a whole lot different than the road trips we take today. Just bumpier!

pictures in the book with the child and talk about what life in the "olden days" was like. If you are the only one driving, brush up on the geography before the trip with the kids, circle highlights on the map, and have the kids spot them as you continue the journey.

You can also set up an even more imaginative scenario: What would the trip be like if you did it a thousand years from now? Would you be traveling to other planets? What kind of vehicle would you be traveling in? What kind of fuel would it take? What would you be eating and drinking? What obstacles could you encounter? Kids will love this game. There's no history lesson to teach, just a lot of creative energy to indulge.

Camping Trip

Camping Trip is a game my friends and I used to play when we couldn't sleep at night. It can be a memory or guessing game, and for some reason, stretching my memory always made me sleepy.

There are a couple ways to play the game. You can play it as strictly a memory game or you can play so that the other players have to guess the rules of play as you go along:

The first person starts off by saying:

"I'm going on a camping trip and I'm going to bring ..."

At this point the person says something he or she would want to bring on the camping trip. Let's say it's a "toothbrush." The next person would then say:

"I'm going on a camping trip and I'm going to bring a toothbrush and ..." This person would then have to add something else that they would bring on the trip. But this time, the object must start with the last letter of the pervious object. In the case of "toothbrush," the last letter is "h," so the person would have to think of an object that starts with an "h." Let's say the person chooses "horse."

The third person would then have to say, "I'm going on a camping trip and I'm going to bring a toothbrush, a horse, and an electric guitar." The game continues until someone forgets an object on the list. That person is out and the game continues until there is only one person left.

You can simplify this version of the game by taking away the memory element. The children don't have to repeat the other objects on the list; they just have to add another item to the list that starts with the last letter of the previous item.

High Score

If you play Camping Trip as a memory and guessing game, you might want to have an adult keep track of all the things on the camping trip list. That way, you can have a referee to guide the game along.

Alphabetical Version

You can also play Camping Trip using objects in alphabetical order. For example: "I'm going on a camping trip and I'm going to bring an asteroid." Then "I'm going on a camping trip and I'm going to bring an asteroid, and a baseball ...."

The game continues the same way until there's only one person left who didn't forget an item on the list.

Who Am I?

When I was a kid, we called "Who Am I?" 20 Questions. One person thinks of something—person, place, or thing—and asks, "Who am I?" To figure it out, the other players have to ask questions like:

➤ Are you an animal?

➤ Are you blue?

➤ Do you swim in the ocean?

The person answering should only give "yes" or "no" answers to make the game a little trickier. With little kids, you might want to allow full answers so they don't get too frustrated with the game.

What's Next?

If you're on a really long car ride and you've exhausted all other games, here are some games for the desperate parent or child.

Thumb Wrestling

When all else fails, don't give up. Do not pull your hair out or resort to threats—there's always the good old thumb wrestle.

Tell the kids to put out their hands. Each kid puts out his or her right hand (or you can have each child put out his or her left hand) as though to shake hands. Instead of locking hands, though, they make their fingers into a "c" shape and lock fingers. Each child's thumb should be resting on the top of the "handshake." You move the thumbs back and forth over each other saying "one, two, three" and let the wrestling begin.

Winning Plays

ParentCenter.com recommends thumb wrestling for children ages two to four. Who knew?

Another way to begin the game is for the kids to chant: "One, two, three, four—we will have a thumb war; five, six, seven, eight—try to keep your thumb straight." Then the wrestling begins.

The object is to use your thumbs in an effort to trap the other person's thumb—meaning that one person should be pressing down on the other person's thumb so that that person can't lift their thumb. The "challenge" of the game is that you cannot unclasp your fingers to maneuver your thumbs, and you cannot move your whole hand—only the thumb.

Kids are very funny people. I hear they've made up a variation since my thumb wrestling days. It's called "Snake in the Grass." It's basically just a way to cheat. One person uses their index finger to trap the thumb saying it's a snake in the grass.

The Purse Game

This is the ultimate game of desperation. A mom can play with the kids by emptying her purse and letting the kids go through her stuff. With little kids, you have to be careful that they don't get their hands on anything they shouldn't! You can have the kids categorize the objects they see. They can group together things that are round or square. Or they can group together things that are made of paper. You can even have them categorize things that are of a certain color. This game will work with kids around the ages of four through six.

I wish my mom had played that game with us. She always carried such a huge purse full of interesting stuff. Dads may not be able to play this game with the kids unless they have a mighty interesting wallet or briefcase.

The Least You Need to Know

➤ You should pack the following items in case you need them on your car trip: pen, pencil, sharpener, paper, crayons, coloring books, tray table, a map, and some kind of backseat storage.

➤ Today, kids have video games and electronic toys to busy hands and minds, but family interaction and car games can entertain them just as well—if not better. And also build family closeness!

➤ I Spy, What If, Camping Trip, and Who Am I? are great car games that need no props or supplies.

➤ When you get desperate to entertain those cranky little kids, break out the purse and see what happens!

Chapter 21

They Say It's Your Birthday!

In This Chapter

➤ Supplies you will need to play the games

➤ Birthday rhymes

➤ Indoor and outdoor games

➤ Games for little children

Birthday parties take a lot of energy, and any parent who undertakes a big party for little kids deserves a lot of credit—and aspirin. It really is great fun to plan a kid's party, but when you do it for the first time, you'll find it requires a lot of creativity and patience.

Nowadays, there are all sorts of theme restaurants that offer party space for kids, and that's not a bad idea if you want to keep the chaos and mess out of your house. But if you've never planned a kid's party at home, give it a try. You'll be surprised how much fun it can actually be if you're prepared.

This chapter covers children's party games of all kinds. From what you'll need to what to say to how to play those silly childhood games, this chapter has it all. The memories will probably start to fly as you read about Red Rover, Red Light/Green Light, Hot Potato, and Telephone. Let the games begin!

Party Games

I attended many fun birthday parties as a kid, and my parents were great at organizing our own parties. Almost every party I attended was chock-full of the best games, cake, ice cream, goodie bags, hats, and balloons. My parents put the same kind of energy into our parties as well.

Winning Plays

There are so many wonderful rhymes associated with children's games. Does anybody remember this one?

"The wonder ball goes round and round

To pass it quickly you are bound

If you're the one to hold it last

The game is past

And you are out!

O-U-T—out!"

—Rhyme for a version of Hot Potato

The best party I remember was my sister's sixth birthday. Her entire class plus the neighbor kids were invited. The house was packed with little girls in patent-leather shoes and boys in bow ties. After a few rounds of musical chairs, my mother laid out huge pieces of newsprint and watercolor paints and we painted while listening to tunes from Broadway musicals. We painted and painted: faces, houses, clowns, cats, dogs, cars, trees … whatever we wanted. When we were done my mother taped the paintings all around the basement walls so everyone could admire each other's work. It was magical to walk around and look at all the beautiful colors.

Each child was given a prize for creating a masterpiece and was allowed to take his or her picture home at the end of the party. I remember wishing we could keep all the pictures on the walls, so our gray basement would always be colorful.

The worst party I ever attended was one where the parents served watermelon for dessert. It was a large group of kids seated at several tables scattered throughout the living room, and we made a horrible mess. The party ended in a watermelon-spitting contest, and we were all sent home early. The little birthday girl was crying when we were shuffled out, and I don't think we ever got to the present-opening. Stick to the cake and ice cream—watermelon, and other messy foods, might not be such a good idea for an indoor party. That kind of food is just fodder for trouble-making minds!

What You'll Need

You will need the following supplies for your child's party:

➤ Chairs for Musical Chairs.

➤ Stereo and CDs (or radio) for Musical Chairs and Hot Potato.

➤ Beanbag or ball for Hot Potato.

➤ Sneakers (for outdoor games).

➤ Space (both for inside games and outdoor games).

➤ Prizes for winners and losers alike!

➤ Hat, pen, and paper: You'll need these things to pick players at random. Some games require someone to be "It," in which case you will have to do some selecting. (More on being "It" below.) The best way is to write each child's name on a piece of paper and place the names in a hat. When a child's name has been picked, remove the name from the hat and don't return it. This way, you won't pick the name again and other children will have a chance to be it. It's all about fairness!

If your child's party is in the summertime, you can play most of these games outside in a backyard or even at the park. For some of the games you'll need a good amount of space, while for others you should be able to get by with moving some furniture out of the way.

Three Strikes

If you plan to allow the children to engage in any potential clothes-staining crafts, tell the parents in advance that casual clothes and smocks may be in order for the occasion. You wouldn't want to send a child home in a paint-smeared party dress.

High Score

You should have prizes on hand for the winning team members or players. Prizes can be small, inexpensive toys or even candy. Kids just like to know that there's some sort of reward at the end of the game. It makes playing even more exciting. But I also believe in consolation prizes for the kids that don't win. We don't want anyone to go home empty handed.

Choosing "It"

I used to hate it when my parents and teachers would say, "life isn't fair." I agree in most cases … however, my retort was always "It can be." Whenever there's a way to make things fair for kids, you should try. The fairness issue has been around a long time in the arena of children's games especially in reference to choosing "It." "It" is the person who does the chasing, replying, winking, questioning—whatever the game requires of "It." Sometimes being "It" is a position of power, while other times you want to be anything but "It"—that all depends on the game.

There are several rhyming games that work particularly well for choosing "It." When the rhyme is done you either have your "It" or eventually get to the "It" by process of elimination.

For all the rhymes, each child puts out a fist in front of him or herself. The person who recites the line (an adult at a party, or the bossiest kid if an unsupervised game) taps each child on the fist with his or her own fist (they include themselves in this by tapping themselves on the chin). With each word, a child is tapped.

Here are some of the rhymes:

Engine Engine

> Engine, engine, number nine,
>
> Going down Chicago line,
>
> If the train falls off the track,
>
> Do you want your money back?

The child who is tapped on the word "back" says "yes" or "no."

If the answer is "yes," the tapping child continues the rhyme and the taps by tapping "y-e-s, spells yes, and you shall have your money back." If the answer is "no," the tapping child continues the rhyming and tapping by saying, "n-o spells no, you don't get your money back."

The person who is tapped on the last word is "It."

One Potato

> One potato, two potato, three potato, four.
>
> Five potato, six potato, seven potato, more.

The child tapped on "more" removes their fist and the rhyming and tapping starts again with the other children. The last child to be holding out a fist is "It."

Icka Bicka

> Icka bicka soda cracker
>
> Icka bicka boo;

Icka bicka soda cracker

Out goes you.

This one is pretty self-explanatory. The last child remaining is "It."

Eenie, Meenie, Meinie, Moe

Eenie, Meenie, Meinie, Moe,

Catch a tiger by the toe,

If he hollers, let him go,

Eenie, Meenie, Meinie, Moe.

The person who is tapped on "Moe" is "It."

You can use any of these rhymes to establish who is "It" in your party games; you can also pull names from a hat, as mentioned earlier.

Three Strikes

I am greatly opposed to letting kids pick the teams. If you were the uncoordinated athlete in your childhood and have any recollection of your days in school gym class, you'll understand why. Kids (although they don't mean any harm) pick their friends or the best players to be on a team. This does nothing for the self-esteem of the less popular or less coordinated kids, and I think the practice is wrong. Picking teams at random is the best way to go.

Everybody Outside!

Take the fun outdoors! There are many memorable outdoor games to play at a child's party. Here are just a few.

Red Rover

Red Rover is best played outside for a summertime party. It requires a lot of space and room to run.

The game begins by picking two opposing teams, which should be done by an adult or by picking names from a hat. Then give each team a name. You can call them the "A" and "B" teams or the "Jets" and the "Sharks"—whatever you prefer. You can pick silly names, too: Try the Weebles and the Wobbles for little kids.

The two teams should form opposing lines—facing each other—with a large space between them. Each child holds the hand of the child next to him or her to form a chain.

The team that goes first (and you can choose by the "Eenie, Meenie, Meinie, Moe" method or one of the other rhymes) forms a huddle to decide which member of the opposing team they want to "call over." When they make the decision, they rejoin hands and say "Red Rover, Red Rover, we call Joey over." Joey then high-fives his teammates and prepares for the run, while the opposing team clasps hands as hard as they can.

High Score

You can have a really good time just picking the names for your various teams. Let the kids get really creative. The sillier the name, the more they will giggle—the more fun for everyone!

It's Joey's job to try to run as fast and hard as he can to breakthrough the opposing team's chain. If he breaks through, he gets to go back to his team. If he doesn't, then he joins the opposition and must call over, and hold back, other members of his original team.

If Joey breaks through the line and returns to his team, his team then gets to call someone over. If Joey doesn't break through, then not only does he join the opposing team, but they get to call someone over again!

High Score

I always liked the idea of a prize "grab bag." Buy several little toys, games, or books, wrap them in birthday party paper, and put all the prizes in an oversized trash bag. When a child or team wins, let them dig into the bag and pull out one wrapped item. But never let any child feel like a loser. Every child should have a chance to dip into the bag at some point in the party. This is supposed to be fun for everyone! Try to take note of which children didn't win anything during the party and let them dig into the bag before they go home. Make sure you get enough gifts to go around.

You keep playing until one team has "captured" all the players from the opposing team. When the game is over, you divvy out the prizes to everyone—because you'll note here—all the children wind up on the winning team in the end. In Red Rover, everybody wins!

Red Light/Green Light

Red Light/Green Light is another great game for the outdoors. You can also play it inside, in a basement for example, if you have enough room (at least 15 to 20 feet).

In this game, one person is the "stoplight." You can choose the person by drawing the name from a hat or using one of the rhyming methods. The person acting as the stoplight stands at one end of the yard with his or her back to the rest of the players. There should be about 15 feet between the stoplight and the players.

With his or her back to the others, the stoplight says "green light" which give the go-ahead for players to start walking toward the stoplight. At any time, the stoplight may say "red light" and turn around quickly to spot anyone who doesn't stop in time. If the stoplight catches anyone still moving, that person is out. The stoplight points to each player who was caught moving and calls out his or her names one at a time. For example: pointing to each player one at a time, he or she says: "Tara, I saw you" and "Matthew, I saw you, too." Those children have to sit on the sidelines and watch the rest of the game.

Play resumes when the stoplight again turns his or her back to the others and says "green light." The play keeps going like this until either everyone is out or someone touches the stoplight.

If all players are caught, the stoplight wins. If someone touches the stoplight before he or she turns around, that player is the winner.

What's the Time, Mr. Wolf?

For this game, one child is chosen to be the wolf. The wolf stands about 10 feet away with his or her back to the rest of the children. The children call out in unison: "Mr./Ms. Wolf, what time is it?" The wolf returns the call with a response of 1 through 12 o'clock—turning around to face the other children as he or she does so.

The children will then take as many steps as the time announced. For example: Let's say the wolf says it's 10 o'clock—the children can take 10 steps forward. There is no limit on the size step the kids can take—they can take huge steps or little steps.

When everyone has taken a step, the wolf turns his or her back to the other children again and the children cry out the same question. It keeps going this way until the wolf finally says "dinner time!" The wolf turns around and chases the children. The children have to run back to the start line. If they make it to the start line, they are safe. The wolf has to try and catch at least one person to become the next wolf.

Indoor/Outdoor Games

There's one thing you can't predict: the weather. The following games are suitable for either inside or out, making planning your party a lot less stressful.

Musical Chairs

For this game you will need several chairs. If you plan to play the game, you may need to borrow chairs from your neighbors or rent some from a local party rental supply. You'll need one less chair than children. For example, if there are 10 children at the party, you will need nine chairs.

The chairs should be set up in a circle with the seats facing into the circle. The children should also be inside the circle. The chairs should be set up far enough apart so that the children can parade in front of them.

You will need a CD player or radio to play this game. The children start to parade in front of the chairs when the music starts. When you stop the music, the children have to scramble quickly onto the seat of a chair—only one child per chair. One child will be out because there won't be enough chairs.

Each time a child goes out, you have to remove a chair to equalize the child-chair ratio. There should always be one less chair than child. Eventually you will have two children and just one chair. Those last two kids will have to parade around the one chair until the music is stopped. The first one to make it onto the seat of the chair is the winner. This child should be given a dig in the grab bag or handed a slightly larger toy than you give to the kids who go out.

The one thing I remember about this game is that an argument almost always broke out when two kids tried to squeeze onto one chair. Rather than pick one child over another as the victorious seated party, you should just play the music again and make them go around a second time. The odds of the same two kids fighting over the same chair again are pretty slim. You will have to use your best conflict-solving abilities if you want to include this game in your party. If the same kids do keep fighting over the same chair, change their position in the parade of children.

Mother May I?

This is a game that can be played indoors or outdoors. There is no running involved.

One child stands with his or her back to the others. This person is called "Mother." (If the child is a boy,

Three Strikes

I never liked Musical Chairs because it made me anxious if I knew I wasn't going to make it to a chair in time. It gave me the same kind of anxiety as getting stuck with the hot potato. To soften the blow for more sensitive children, you might want to give them a parting gift, like a lollipop or a little toy. You may have an upset child on your hands—be prepared!

you can change it to "Father.") The children ask: "Mother/Father, may I take a step?" Each child must make the request one by one.

In response to each question, the Mother may respond in one of the following ways: "no" or "yes, you may take [number and size] steps." The Mother fills the blanks with the number and size step he or she wants each child to take.

For example, the Mother can say: "Yes, you may take three giant steps," or "Yes, you make two baby steps," or "Yes, you may take four medium steps." If the Mother senses someone is just a little too close, she can say "no."

If the child forgets to say "Mother, may I?" he or she has to go all the way back to the starting line.

The goal is for the players to try and sneak up on the Mother and touch her.

Use one of the "It" choosing methods to start the game. The person who goes first might be placed on the far left and the turns can then move to the right. It's up to you how you want to organize it, but the key is to be as fair as possible.

High Score

In some versions of Mother May I? people make up their own steps. You can try "ballet steps," for example, where the child will have to try and do some fancy turn or "pee wee steps" where the child can only move the tiniest possible step.

Hot Potato

This game, like Musical Chairs, is one that builds anticipation as the music starts and stops. You'll see such concentration on the faces of the kids as they pass that potato from one to another. Wait for the shrieks when the music stops. This game is fun for the kids to play and sometimes even more fun for the adults to watch. Here's how to play.

All the children either stand or sit in a circle. You can use any object as the potato. Some people really use a potato while others use a beanbag. You will need a CD player, tape deck, or radio for this game.

Turn on the music and hand the hot potato to one of the children. This child must pass the hot potato either to his or her left or right. Each child must continue to pass the potato until the music stops. When you stop the music the child left holding the potato is out and must leave the circle. Again I recommend some sort of "booby prizes" so that the children don't feel bad. The children will shriek with laughter and fear when the music stops. The anticipation on their faces during this game is worth the noise.

I was at a party where the family used a store-bought hot potato that looked like one of those cartoon canon balls with a built-in ticker. It was quite intimidating to hear that ticker just humming away as the black plastic ball was passed quickly from child to child. If you can't find such a manufactured hot potato, you can try using an egg timer and place it in a soft black sock. The kids will hear the timer but they won't be able to see how much time is left.

Party Games for Little Kids

Here are some games that may be appropriate for pre-schoolers. Not only are these games fun, but they have also proven to be educational. You'll find that kids already know some of these games from school.

For the really wee tots, try some of the following games.

Simon Says

This game is very simple and children really love it. You'll never see them concentrate so hard!

Have the children stand facing you or another child who is deemed to be "Simon." The person playing Simon gives the other children an instruction that almost always begins with "Simon Says."

If Simon says "Simon says touch your nose," all the children must touch their noses. Then Simon might say: "Simon says hop on one foot." All the children should then hop on one foot. Then Simon might say: "Hold up two fingers." If any of the children holds up two fingers, they are out. Why? Because Simon didn't say so. If the instruction doesn't start with "Simon says" and a child follows the instruction, he or she is out and must sit down. The last child standing gets to be the next Simon.

Winning Plays

Simon Says is one of the first group games I learned to play. It was actually used as a teaching method in my nursery school class. The teachers taught children the names of their physical features by using this game.

Duck Duck Goose

This is another game you might have learned in the classroom. My kindergarten teachers used to let us play just before the end of the school day. We used to look forward to it everyday.

All the kids sit in a circle facing each other. One child is picked to be "It." The child who is "It" walks around the outside of the circle (the backs of the children) and touches each child on the head saying, "duck … duck … duck …." Each head touched gets a "duck." When a child is touched on the head and "It" says "goose," the child who is the "goose" must stand up and chase "It" around the outside of the circle. "It" has to try and sit in the empty spot vacated by the goose. The goose has to try and tag "It" before "It" can sit in his or her spot. If the goose cannot tag "It," he or she becomes "It" and the duck-duck-goosing starts again.

If "It" is tagged by the goose, he or she must sit in the center of the circle. The goose then becomes "It" for the next round. The person in the center cannot move until another player is tagged—then they can take that person's spot in the circle.

Telephone or Grapevine

Telephone is a great party game for kids of all ages. I've even played it with my adult friends. It's always good for a laugh.

Everyone sits in a circle about arm's-length from each other. Someone in the circle starts by whispering a message to the person to his or her left or right. The message should only be one short sentence. The person who receives the message must then pass the message onto the person next to him or her. The last person to receive the message must deliver it aloud to the entire room. The kids will really have a good giggle when they realize just how misconstrued the message became as it traveled from child to child.

By the time the message reaches the last person it is rarely in its original form and can even be completely misconstrued. It just goes to show the damage that gossip can do! By the time a story travels around a room, it's seldom in its original form, so imagine what can happen to a story if it travels around an entire school! This is a way to teach kids about gossip and even proper telephone message-taking skills.

High Score

Telephone is a great game to play when all the kids are seated around the table in their party hats, munching on cake. Keep those little minds busy!

The Least You Need to Know

➤ Make sure you have chairs, music, ball or beanbag, sneakers, space, prizes, and pen, paper, and a hat on hand.

➤ Choose who will be "It" by reciting one of the rhyme games to ensure fairness and fun.

➤ Red Rover, Red Light/Green Light, and What's the Time, Mr. Wolf? are good games to play outdoors.

➤ Some fun indoor games are Musical Chairs, Mother May I? and Hot Potato—although they can be played outside as well.

➤ Little kids will like to play Simon Says and Duck Duck Goose.

Chapter 22

Giggle Games

In This Chapter

➤ Names of ... and Follow the Leader

➤ Alphabets and Honey, Do You Love Me?

➤ Sausage and Forbidden Letter

➤ Never Ending Words and Password

➤ Story Line and Why and Because

The whole point of kids' parties is to entertain the kids, but there's nothing better for an adult than watching the kids laugh. I've done some of my best giggling when I'm hanging out with kids. They know how to have a good time, and the games in this chapter are sure to evoke some side-splitting silliness.

Most of these giggle games can be played by adults, too. They are perfect games for rainy days and snow days. Get the whole family together and be prepared for some good laughs.

Names of ...

Names of ... is a game you may have played at camp or in Girl or Boy Scouts when you were a kid. Your kids are probably well versed in the game and could teach you a thing or two. It's a clapping game that requires a certain amount of hand and brain coordination. I was always terrible at the game because I have no rhythm. It does take a little bit of practice and skill.

All the players sit in a circle with their legs crossed. The more players you have the better. One person is picked to be the leader and is responsible for getting the rhythm in motion. The rhythm is a slap on thighs, a clap, and two snaps of the fingers (first with the right then with the left). So the rhythm sounds like this: slap, clap, snap, snap. When everyone is slap-clap-snapping at the same time, the leader thinks of a category and starts when he or she has an idea. Players can speak, one at a time, in turn, on the rhythmic snap of the fingers. Play can go counterclockwise or clockwise—it's up to you.

The play goes like this:

> Player 1: Slap, clap ... then on the snap, snap: "Names of."
>
> Slap, clap ... then on the snap, snap: "Ani-mals" (the word "animals" said to the snapping beat).
>
> Player 2: Slap, clap ... then on the snap, snap: "Mon-keys."
>
> Player 3: Slap, clap ... then on the snap, snap: "Ele-phants."
>
> Player 4: Slap, clap ... then on the snap, snap: "Birds" (note the one syllable...as long as it's said in rhythm, on the snap, you're okay).

High Score

You may want to have a few practice rounds of Names of ... before the game officially begins because it takes a little while to get everyone up to speed.

As people make mistakes and say a word out of rhythm, or miss a beat and don't say something quickly enough, they are out, and the next person in line picks up the rhythm again.

Names of ... is a concentration game, so it's really easy to mess up! I used to mess up because I'd be anticipating my turn and then find myself speechless and laughing when it finally came to me. You have to pick your word, and then focus on the rhythm as best you can. The people who go out can stay in the circle and not slap, clap, and snap—or they can leave the circle and the remaining players tighten up the circle.

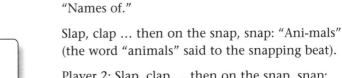

High Score

Other fun categories for Names of ... are bathroom objects, Chinese food dishes, car parts, types of dogs, countries, and girls' names.

You can make your own rules as you go. You can either change the category whenever a player wants to, or you can make the rule that only the leader is allowed to change the category.

Follow the Leader

Two people are selected at the beginning of Follow the Leader—one person to be the leader and another to be the guesser. The guesser must leave the room before the leader is selected. You obviously don't want the guesser to know who the leader is. It's his or her job to figure it out when the game is in motion.

When the guesser is safely outside the room, the leader starts doing goofy things, like scratching an ear, or rubbing his or her nose, or ringing his or her hands. The idea is to do it as surreptitiously as possible so as not to be noticed by the guesser when he or she is called back into the room. The other players must follow the leader. Each time the leader switches an action, the other players must switch to the new action. The players should be as subtle as possible in their transitions also. They want it to be tough for the guesser to figure out who is the leader!

When the play is underway, the guesser is allowed back in the room—someone can stop and let the guesser back in or you can all just shout "Come in guesser!"

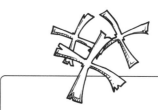

It is now the guesser's game! He or she must watch carefully to figure out who the leader is. It might take a few minutes, so you may find a bad case of the giggles beginning as the players wink, wave, and bow around the room. You want to do your best to keep a straight face, but it could be tough! A good leader should be able to graduate to more extreme movements without getting caught—and good players should be able to make the transitions without making the leader an obvious target.

Three Strikes

When playing Follow the Leader, don't stand around staring at the leader waiting for the next move—just try to watch him or her out of the corner of your eye somehow. Otherwise, you'll give it away!

Honey, Do You Love Me?

Have the kids form a circle with one child in the center. The child in the center must go up to one of the children in the circle and say, "Honey, do you love me?" The child being addressed must respond, "Honey, I love you, but I just can't smile." If the child being addressed cracks a smile, he or she must go into the center and the child in the center takes his or her place in the circle.

Well, that sounds easy enough—but the trick is that it is the goal of the person in the center to make the person in the circle laugh. The child in the center cannot touch the child in the circle, but can make as many funny faces as he or she wants. You may have to time how long it takes the child to laugh. Usually 30 seconds is more than enough time.

If the child doesn't laugh, the child in the center must do it again to another child in the circle.

There are no winners in this game, just a lot of giggles.

Sausage

The children sit in a circle with one child standing in the center. The children in the circle may ask the child in the center one question at a time. The questions can be anything the children want to ask. But the child in the circle may only respond by saying "sausage." The first child to make the child in the center laugh, wins—and gets to take his or her place as the sausage-sayer.

Example:

Q: What color is your shirt?

A: Sausage.

Q: What time is it?

A: Sausage.

Q: What is on your head?

A: Sausage.

You can use any word in Sausage—though "sausage" is kind of an amusing one and often gets a few giggles. You can try "rutabaga," "rhubarb," or "pickle." You can even try changing the word from game to game.

Three Strikes

Small children are not good candidates for Never Ending Word. Their limited vocabularies will frustrate them and turn fun into frowns. Save this game for older kids and you'll have a much nicer time.

Never Ending Words

The goal of Never Ending Words is to make one long word as a group. Each person takes a turn calling out a letter to add to the previous letter in an effort to make a word. The goal is *not* to be the one to finish the word. Keep adding a letter to try to keep the word going. Eventually it will have to end, but that's the fun part—to see who finally has to put on that closing letter.

For example: Player 1 calls out a letter—let's say "c." The player seated either on his right or left (whichever way you decide to rotate play) calls out a second letter (with the intention of building a word—so the second letter should work with the first one). Let's say player 2 calls out: "u." Now the word is in the hands of player 3. Let's say he or she calls out "s." As player 4, I might think of the word "custom" and add a "t." However player 5 might be thinking of the word "custard" and will add an "a." The play continues until each player has contributed a letter toward the creation of the word while trying to avoid completing the word.

If you can't think of another letter, you're out and the play continues with the player next to you. You can also try to bluff—add on any letter without a word in mind. Players are allowed to challenge your bluff, however. Only the next person in line to add a letter may challenge the previous player's letter. If you are correct in your challenge, you win the game. If you are incorrect, you're out and the play continues with the next person in line—and the start of a new word!

Three Strikes

Be careful! If a word is formed along the way in Never Ending Word, the person who forms the word is out.

For instance, if you said D, E, and someone adds N, thinking of DENT, they are out. They formed a word: DEN!

Story Line

This is my favorite imagination game. You can play with as many people as you want, but a good number of people is about 10. Divide into two teams. You will need to do a little preparation in advance of the game—you need a couple of index cards that have a crazy sentence written on each one. For example: "The cherry-colored rabbits hopped along the riverbank until they approached the bearded turtle." The goal is to incorporate this crazy sentence into a story line and see if the other team can guess what the crazy sentence was in the body of the story.

Each team must appoint a spokesperson. The spokesperson reads the card to him or herself and then shows it to his or her other team members. He or she then begins telling a story.

The spokesperson starts the story and can, at any time, point to another team member to have that person continue the story where he or she left off. The next person can either point to someone else to continue or you can time each person's story telling (give each person about a minute). Depending on how many people are on your team, the story can be about 10 minutes long. Each person on the team should get a chance to add a portion. You should try to get the crazy sentence in before the last person has added to the story line.

The object is to work the crazy sentence into the story line at some point. It can be at the beginning, the middle, or the end. When you're done with the story telling the other team has to figure out what the crazy sentence was.

You score points for correct guesses:

➤ Three points for guessing what the sentence was

➤ Two points for getting the sentence in

➤ One point for guessing whether the sentence got in or not

You can also play with both teams contributing to the story. Both teams get a crazy sentence and they both have to fit it into the same story. So, you're all telling the same story, but working in a different sentence—you then guess and score in the same way. You can play to 20 points or whatever you choose.

The Least You Need to Know

➤ There's nothing quite as fun as watching little kids get into giggles—it's contagious!

➤ You may want to practice the clapping rounds in Names of ... before beginning—it's harder than it looks!

➤ Honey, Do You Love Me? is a game where you try *not* to laugh.

➤ Never Ending Words is a great vocabulary and memory game.

➤ A good imagination game is Story Line.

Chapter 23

Say the Word: Word Games

In This Chapter

➤ Anagrams and Word Bluff

➤ Quick on the Draw

➤ Hangman

➤ Match Game

➤ Sentence by Sentence

There's nothing like word games for getting a group of people riled up. And there's nothing like word games for getting your kids to learn different ways of seeing and using words. Imagination and knowledge mean power in these games you'll find in this chapter!

Anagrams

You can play Anagrams with as many players as you want. It's very easy and can even be educational. Pick a word that has a lot of letters in it and try to make as many words (anagrams) out of that one word as possible. For example:

The word: ESTIMATE

Other words you can make:

time

mate

test

state

meat

meet

… and so on

You should set a time limit on the game, and when the time is up, players score points for legitimate anagrams. In other words, the anagrams have to be real words that exist in the dictionary—you can't just make up words. You can change the rules from age group to age group. If little kids are involved, let them make two- and three-letter words while older kids have to come up with four or more letter words.

You only score points if you come up with words that no one else has on their lists. If your words match anyone else's words, no one scores points for that word. You have to be really imaginative to try and score the points—it's hard to see words that no one else will see:

High Score

When playing Anagrams, try to pick a word that has several vowels. This will make it easier for younger players to make words. Also, if you pick a word with an "s" in it, be clear on whether or not you will allow plurals.

➤ Each two-letter word equals one point.

➤ Each three-letter word equals two points.

➤ Each four-letter word equals three points.

➤ Each five-letter word equals four points.

➤ Each six-letter word equals five points.

Pick a point value to play up to, and whoever reaches the point value first is declared winner.

Word Bluff

I used to play Word Bluff as a kid in a classroom setting, but you can play it with any group of people—again, the more the merrier.

One person looks up a word in the dictionary and writes it on a piece of paper. It has to be a word you don't think anyone in the room has heard before. Everyone then writes down on a piece of paper what they think the word means and puts their name on the paper. All the definitions are then placed into a hat or sack of some kind. You can even just fold the pieces of paper and put them in the middle of the floor. The person who picked the word also puts a definition into the hat—the real definition that is!

All the definitions are read out loud by the person who picked the word and everyone gets to vote for the definition they think is correct.

Each person who guesses correctly scores a point. A point is also given to each person whose wrong definition was believed to be the correct one. If no one guesses the correct definition, the person who originally chose the word gets five points.

The best part about this game is all the crazy false definitions you'll hear. You can make them sound as real or as nutty as you want. But the reader knows the correct definition so he or she will have to read them all out loud with a poker-face.

Hangman

I used to play Hangman with my friend at the restaurants with the paper tablecloths—you know the places that supply a few crayons at the table so you can exercise your creative genius while your empty stomach growls. As everyone else drew cartoons, caricatures, and self-portraits, my friend and I played Hangman. He wasn't very good at it. I was only a tiny bit better. It's a fun way to pass the time.

You can play Hangman with more than two people. One player is the person who comes up with the word or phrase while the other players can take turns guessing the letters. It's up to you how you want to set up the game with more than two people.

It may sound kind of gruesome, but the first thing you do is draw the gallows—you've probably seen what they look like in the movies. From the platform going up, draw a straight line and another line perpendicular to the top of that straight line—that's the place your man will hang from when the game is underway.

The rules of the game can vary, but I'll tell you the way I always play.

Winning Plays

Word Bluff is also known as Dictionary in some circles.

High Score

Don't forget to put your name next to the definition so the points can be divvied up at the end of the game. The person who picks the word will also read out the definitions (but not the names of the players written on the paper).

249

Think of a word or phrase. You can tell the other player who will be guessing the letters if there's a theme or not—like famous quotes, animal noises, spring flowers, whatever you want. Or you can just pick one word and let the person figure it out. Next to the scaffolding, draw as many horizontal lines as there are letters in your word or phrase. Let's say you choose the word DAFFODIL—you would draw eight horizontal lines to represent the eight letters in the word. These lines are actually blanks—you will fill in the blanks as the guesser comes up with the right letters.

The play begins when your gallows is drawn and your blanks are set.

The person doing the guessing states a letter out loud. If the letter is part of the word or phrase, it is written in the corresponding blank space. If there is more than one of that letter in the phrase, they must all be written into their corresponding blanks.

If the letter is not there, a head is drawn onto the drawing of the gallows. You continue this way until the entire body is drawn. The last thing that should be drawn on the gallows is the noose. Once the noose is drawn, the game is over. The goal is for the guesser to figure out the word or phrase before the picture of the hanging man is completed.

High Score

To make Hangman more difficult, choose movie titles, book titles, clichés, or well-known phrases for your blanks. The game will go on much longer this way and will be more challenging. For instance, try "Don't count your chickens before they hatch," or "Monkey see, monkey do."

Some people say that you can only draw so many body parts on the diagram before drawing the noose. For example, you can draw the head, torso, arms, legs, and then the noose. If you draw two arms, two legs, the torso, the head, and the noose, you have seven chances of guessing it right. That's the hard way to play. I've never played with terribly strict rules. I've allowed eyes, nose, mouth, hands, feet, and even a hat before I drew the noose. I want the guesser to guess the answer—and I'd rather be the hangman drawer than the guesser. That's right—after the other player guesses the word or phrase the tables turn and you are on the guessing side. If the player doesn't get the word in time, you get another chance at controlling gallows.

Match Game

Match Game is based upon the old television game show of the same name. You can play it at least two different ways. My sisters and I used to play our own home version all the time. We just got pens and pieces of paper and made up our own questions.

You have to divide into two or more teams of an equal number of people. Each team has a captain. You'll also need one leader to ask the questions. This person will be a neutral party like a game show emcee. He or she is not part of either team.

Winning Plays

The television game show *Match Game* ran on NBC from 1962 to 1969, and was revived in 1973 as *Match Game PM*. It quickly became the number-one-rated daytime show for the next five years. Gene Rayburn, the host, was nominated for five Daytime Emmys during the game show's time on-air. Panelists often included Richard Dawson, Nipsy Russell, Charles Nelson Reilly, and Brett Sommers. Nowadays, reruns of the show are run on cable and satellite stations.

All the captains stand at the front of the room. Everyone should have a supply of pens and paper before the game begins. The leader asks the group a question and everyone writes down an answer—including the team captains. There is no speaking allowed. Your answer is secret and should not be shown to anyone else. All the pieces of paper are then handed up to the team captains. The team captains read aloud their own answers and then start reading out all the answers from their own teams. You add up how many matching answers you have and score a point per match.

Here are some sample questions:

If you could have the magical powers of any superhero, who would it be?

If you could live in any city in the world, what city would it be?

What is the greatest movie playing in the theatre right now?

What is the funniest sitcom on TV today?

Another way to play the game is closer to the television show method:

The team captain comes up with a sentence and all the players on his or her team has to fill in the blank. For example: "Harriet was at work one day. She looked up from her desk and said 'I am so hungry, I could eat my _____.'" Everyone must fill in the blank. If your answer matches that of your team captain, your team scores a point.

You can set a maximum on the points so that there is an end to the game—15 to 20 points are usually adequate.

Sentence by Sentence

The goal of Sentence by Sentence is to build a complete story by adding a sentence to a series of sentences—but only the preceding sentence is visible. The results are likely to be very silly and often even hilarious.

Take a piece of paper and have someone write down a sentence as though beginning a story. The sheet of paper is handed to the next person who adds a sentence on the line right below the first sentence. Before passing on the piece of paper this time, however, the player must fold the paper over the very first sentence so only the newly added sentence is showing.

The third player can only see player 2's sentence and must then add another sentence on the line below that sentence. Again, before passing the piece of paper on, player 3 must fold over player 2's sentence so that only his or her own sentence is visible. Only one sentence will be visible to the next player in line.

The outcome could be something like this:

> One day, a limousine pulled up to a house.
>
> The limousine was so long, it took up three parking spots.
>
> The police came to give the driver a ticket.
>
> The driver was so angry he screamed at them.
>
> "No more garbage pick-up for you dirty people."
>
> The streets were teaming with trash.
>
> Disease began to spread.
>
> "An epidemic," cried the local health officials.

No matter what word games you choose to play, your kids' brains will get a workout and the laughs will fly.

Quick on the Draw

While this game isn't really a word game, it is based on the game of Charades. But instead of having people guess a word (or phrase) with miming gestures, they have to guess a word by drawing it. This might sound easy, but it all depends on the word!

This game is a homemade version of the popular board game Pictionary. For this game, you'll need a lot of paper and a couple of pens or pencils. You may also want to use a stopwatch. If you don't have a stopwatch, someone with a second hand on his or her watch will work.

What you need to do is form two teams. Each team has to think of 12 things that they'd like the opposing team to draw. The things that they think of are written down on 12 separate pieces of paper. The "things" can be anything: objects, sayings, animals, and so on.

Each player on each team takes a turn at drawing one of the items on one of the pieces of paper. The other members of the same team must try and guess what is being drawn. While the players can call out what they think the item is as it is being drawn, the artist cannot say anything to help them along. The artist may also not use any hand gestures or use any numbers or letters in the drawing. Each team is only allowed one minute to draw the picture and figure out what it is.

If the team guesses what the item is before the minute is up, the team scores one point.

To really add to the tension, try an egg timer instead of a second hand. The players will get frantic with the ticking and buzzing as time runs out on their play.

Another team goes next and repeats the same techniques with the same rules.

You'll love to watch everyone's reactions during the game—from the frustrated guessers to the frantic artist. Sometimes crazy arguments break out in the heat of the moment. You'll hear things like "Oh come on … can't you figure it out?" Or "Oh come on—where'd you learn to draw?" It's very silly, fun, and action-packed. Even though the artist isn't supposed to speak, sometimes the stress is too much to bear. Each correct guess scores one point, and the team with the most points wins.

Three Strikes

Don't get caught without a pencil sharpener. Those fast and furious drawers will go through pencils in no time!

If you are the drawer, make sure you don't say anything. You can't help out the guessers by acting out, saying something, or gesturing to help people along. If you do so, you'll be disqualified.

The Least You Need to Know

➤ Word games stimulate kids' imagination and expand their vocabularies.

➤ An anagram is a word built from another word by rearranging letters.

➤ Word Bluff is a great game for imaginative kids. Inventing definitions for words will have them laughing out loud.

➤ To increase the difficulty rating of Hangman, use titles or phrases instead of just words.

➤ When playing Sentence by Sentence, you might end up with a funny story to tell!

Chapter 24

Let's Go Team!

In This Chapter

➤ Charades and Up Jenkins

➤ Hide and Seek

➤ Sardines

Team games are really important for kids to learn and play. They teach kids not only to have a great time with a group of people, but about strategy, teamwork, and camaraderie. Games like Charades and Up Jenkins teach kids to work together toward a common goal, to listen to their teammates to come up with good answers, and to use yet another aspect of their creative imaginations.

Learning to be part of a team is not only a social skill, but also an invaluable tool for school activities, adult work life, and successful relationships. In fact, it wouldn't hurt grown-ups to play more team games like the ones in this chapter!

Many of the games in this book have to do with taking sides, but the games in this chapter are classic team games, many of which have been played for centuries. Charades, for example, is believed to date back to eighteenth-century France. Hide and Seek is even older. There are several variants of these team games as a result of people adapting rules to suit their particular group or geographical location. You'll probably find yourself making up your own rules as you learn to play these games or teach them to your children. One way or another, these games will keep you and your kids busy for hours.

Charades

Charades isn't really considered a game for children. It's often played as an after-dinner entertainment at adult parties. While it started out as a riddle game where you guessed a word, it eventually evolved into the acting game we are familiar with today.

Winning Plays

Charades is believed to have originated in France in the eighteenth century as a riddle game. The goal of the game was to come up with a word or phrase by trying to figure out the riddle. The riddles were given either in prose or in rhyme.

Here is an example:

"My first is a Tartar,

My second a letter;

My all is a country,

No Christmas dish better."

(The answer is Turkey.)

The word version of the Charade game later evolved into an acted game where players had to guess the word or phrase by watching others act them out. That is the version of the game we are most familiar with today.

Charade Parade

Here is what you will need:

➤ A stopwatch or watch with a minute hand to time each charade

➤ A pen and paper to keep score

➤ Index cards to write words, sentences, phrases, names of people (your charade cards)

➤ A neutral player to keep the time and score

The point of the game is for players to act out a word, an idea, quotation, name of a person, name of a book, movie, or television show, in the shortest amount of time possible. Players should split up into two teams.

You should write-up the charades on index cards in one of two ways: You can write up the cards in advance—if you do this, you won't be able to play because you'll know the answers. If you choose to write them up before the game, then you should also be the neutral party that keeps the time and score. That way you have a part to play in the game but not in the guessing of the charades.

The other way you can write up charades is to have team 1 write up the charades for team 2 and vice versa. That way you ensure that team 1 and team 2 will not be acting charades that they already know. Each card can also have a theme written on it—something that will help the teams focus on a certain idea so the guessing doesn't take too long.

To start the game, each team designates a leader. It is the goal of the leader's team to guess the charade that he or she is acting out. The leader cannot use his or her voice in any way and cannot point to any inanimate object in the room as a means to aid the guessers. The secret word or phrase must be completely acted out. The guessing begins the second the acting begins. This is where things can get really rowdy. The closer the team gets to the answer, and the shorter the time left, you'll find people yelling and waving and laughing their heads off.

Team members can shout out randomly what they think the syllable, word, or sentence is. The other players should also try to listen to the guesses made by other players because every guess could stimulate other ideas—and you don't want to repeat the same guess over and over again. When a team member gets something right the actor can point to that team member and nod, then move onto the next syllable or word.

If the team successfully guesses the answer, the person who comes out with the final word or sentence gets to do the acting, and that team continues play. If the team doesn't guess the answer and time is up, the next team takes the stage with a new word or sentence.

Winning Plays

Acted Charades is believed to have originated in England. In fact, William Makepeace Thackeray makes reference to the game of acted Charades in his 1848 novel *Vanity Fair*. The game enjoyed a boost in popularity in the 1930s and then again after World War II. It was a party game then and remains a party game today.

Three Strikes

The opposing team is not allowed to shout out any guesses and may not do anything to derail the team doing the guessing. So tell them to butt out and follow the rules!

You can play charades in large or small groups. Most commonly it is played by a small group in a living room setting.

What's Your Sign?

It is important that all players involved know certain hand signals.

➤ **Movies:** Use one hand to shade your eyes and the other to pretend you're winding the film of a camera—squint one eye as though you're looking through a viewfinder.

➤ **Book:** Hold your palms together as though in prayer and open and close them as you would a book.

➤ **TV show:** With your finger in the air, draw an imaginary square in the air. Some people indicate that it's a TV show, by pretending to point a remote control.

➤ **Quote or phrase:** Make quotation marks in the air with your fingers.

➤ **One finger means first word:** Once everyone says "first word," you can start acting out the word. If no one is getting it, you can act out the first syllable.

➤ **Syllables:** First indicate how many syllables are in the word by laying the like number of fingers across your forearm—so if the word has two syllables, lay two fingers on your forearm. When everyone says "two syllables" indicate that you will act out the first syllable first by then laying one finger on your forearm.

➤ **Length of word:** Make a little or big sign using your two hands (like you're measuring a fish).

➤ **Sounds like:** Cup one hand behind an ear. This means that you will act out a word that rhymes with the original word.

High Score

Whether you have a neutral party or an egg timer, it's a good idea to establish how long you think each actor should get—usually three minutes is adequate. You don't want to give too much time because that takes the tension out of the play—and too little time might be frustrating for all players involved. You may find you need to play a couple of rounds before you figure out the right timing.

Some gestures you're just going to have to make up. There are only so many universal gestures you can establish in advance.

Act your heart out, as fast as you can, and hope your teammates figure out your waving, bending, hopping, skipping, and grimacing.

Ready, Set, Act!

Establish which team will go first by drawing a name from a hat: team 1 or team 2. The leader of the team that is going to go first pulls one of the index cards from the pile. The card will have a word, sentence, phrase, or person indicated on it (you will have to prepare these cards in advance of the game). The leader of team 1 then stands at the front of the room, or wherever your designated "stage" is located, and play begins.

Once the leader of team 1 has read the card and takes his or her place, the timekeeper clicks the stopwatch and the team 1 leader has to start to act—there's no time to waste.

The timekeeper can either be a neutral party (someone not involved in play) or a member of the opposite team who can concentrate on the time and not on the play. Make sure it's someone trustworthy! The timekeeper is responsible for saying "start" to begin play and "stop" when the clock runs out.

Score!

There are several different scoring methods you can use.

Each time your team wins a game you score a point. You can play as many rounds as you want. You can set a point limit also—let's say the first team to win 10 points is the winner.

Another way to score is to have the timekeeper record the amount of time it takes to guess the answer. For example, when a team guesses the answer, the time it took them to guess is recorded by the timekeeper (this is why you may need a neutral party). If the answer is not guessed before time is up, three minutes is marked down on the score sheet.

To determine the winner, you add up the times. The team with the lower score is the winner—because it took them the least amount of combined minutes to guess the answers.

Winning Plays

There are several versions of charades you can play; one of the funniest I've heard of is Hip Charades. Each team leader spells out a word in the air using ... you got it ... his or her hips. This game can have some really funny moments.

Up Jenkins

Up Jenkins is a very silly game that kids just love. It's great for kids' birthday parties or even small adult parties (that depends on what you and your friends are into). College kids have been known to play this game late on a Saturday night at the student union while some adults might have the best time playing the game at home with their kids and their kids' friends. However you play, or whomever you play with, the game is somewhat addictive and is good for an hour or two of good, rowdy fun.

If you decide to play with a group of kids, be prepared for some shrieking because kids really get into it, which makes it all the more fun for the grown-ups. You can play in small or large groups—but you have to sit around a table to play, so play with as many people as you have chairs.

Three Strikes

When playing Up Jenkins, the person who has the coin should not give the "stop" signal—that would be a dead giveaway.

High Score

To save time and chaos, you might want to pick team leaders before Up Jenkins begins. Team leaders can give the signal to stop the coin and start the hand banging and they can be the one to call "Up Jenkins."

All you need for the game is a coin, a table, and some chairs. Divide the players into two teams. The teams should sit across from each other at the table.

Play starts with everyone's hands under the table. Team 1 starts the play by passing a coin under the table from hand to hand, back and forth, amongst their own team. It is the goal of team 2 to figure out where the coin is at a given time. Because the coin is passed under the table, team 2 can't see where it is as it is passed along. The coin will finally rest with one person. Where it stops nobody knows (at least on team 2).

After about 15 seconds the coin passing should stop—it doesn't matter with whom it stops, but you should give it enough time to confuse the opposing team. On a given signal (which your team can agree to before play begins) the coin stops and everyone on team 1 starts to bang their hands, palms-down—on the table-top. One person will have the coin and the coin must stay in his or her hand—even as the banging is happening.

Now team 2 has to guess where the coin is. They do so by pointing to a player saying "Up Jenkins." Each time a player lifts an empty hand, team 2 scores a point. Why? Because the object of the game is to leave the palm containing the coin to the very end. If team 2 guesses the hand containing the coin before the very last hand is revealed, team 1 scores a point and gets to hide the coin again. If team 2 chooses all the empty hands and finds the coin in the very last palm, they get a chance to hide the coin.

You'll need to concentrate and keep a very straight face during this game. If you have the coin and you so much as smirk, you could give away the whole game! It's all about the art of the bluff.

Hide and Seek

Hide and Seek is believed to date back to the days of the caveman. Its premise is simple and it continues to be as much fun for kids today as it was thousands of years ago.

The object of the game is for several people to hide and at least one to seek.

To play the game, someone is chosen to be "It." To pick "It" check out some of the rhyming games mentioned in Chapter 21, "They Say It's Your Birthday!" The person who is chosen to be "It" closes his or her eyes and begins to count. Usually the counting occurs at "home base" and goes up to about 50 (or sometimes even 100). Make sure you agree on what "It" will be counting to before the game begins.

The game starts and ends at home base. It's an important spot because it's the place to where the hiders will run either once they are found or before they are found by "It." Home base is the safe zone.

Three Strikes

Kids should only pick safe places to hide. No one should put him- or herself in any kind of precarious situation. Kids are just going to try and find the best hiding place and will likely not be thinking about safety. Depending on the age of the kids involved, it's not a bad idea to supervise while they play the game. With really little kids, it's essential that you supervise—just in case a kid isn't clear on the rules and isn't sure when to come out of hiding. When I was a kid, one of the kids we played with fell asleep in the hiding place and we couldn't find him for quite some time. Don't let that happen in your house. You might have a really crazed parent on your hands.

While "It" is counting, everyone else is trying to find a hiding place. The hiding place should be clever enough so that "It" won't catch the players when he or she starts the search. "It" should be counting loud enough for everyone to hear. If you're doing the hiding, you'll have to listen to where "It" is in the countdown allowing yourself enough time to hide. When "It" reaches the count of 50, or 100, he or she shouts out the number and adds "ready or not … here I come."

By this point, all the players should be safely tucked away in their own unique hiding spots. The seeker has to go around looking for each player. There are a couple ways you can play this game:

➤ "It" goes around searching for each player. When he or she spots a hider, he calls out the person's name and the two of them race to home base. If the hider beats "It" to home base, the hider touches home base and says "one, two, three, home free" or "one, two, three for me." That player is considered "safe." If "It" beats the hider to home base, "It" touches home base saying, "one, two, three on Brittney" or "one, two, three on Vincent" (or whatever the name of the person is). The hider is considered "caught."

➤ The other way to play is to allow the hiders to race home before being found. While "It" is hunting around for hiders, if the hiders find a good moment, he or she is allowed to race home. If "It" sees the hider heading for home, he or she can try to tag that person. If the person is tagged, he or she is caught. If not, that hider is safe.

The first person to be caught in either of these versions of the game is the next "It."

The last person to make it home safely got to be the next "It."

Kids will make up all sorts of their own rules as they play the game. There's never just one way to play. But to keep the fights down to a minimum, tell your kids to establish the rules round by round.

High Score

To add a little more fun to Hide and Seek, you can play that all the people who are caught have to help "It" find the rest of the hiders—making the game a little more challenging for the hiders to get home.

Sardines

Sardines is Hide and Seek in reverse. All the kids close their eyes and count while one person hides. When the counting is completed (usually to about 25 is fine for this game) all the "Its" must begin the search. When one of the "Its" finds the hider, he or she doesn't say anything but quietly crawls into the hiding spot with the hider. The "It" who finds the player must wait until no one is nearby before crawling into the space with the hider because he or she doesn't want anyone else to find the spot.

Slowly the "Its" will start to disappear and the hiding place will become more and more cramped with hiders. Now you know why the game is called Sardines!

The game ends when the last of the "Its" finds the "sardines." By this point the last "It" will most likely just have to follow the sounds of giggles and squeals. It's not easy to keep quiet when you're all squished, uncomfortably, together.

The first "It" to find the hider gets to be the first hider in the next round.

The Least You Need to Know

➤ Team games teach kids about strategy, working with others, and camaraderie.

➤ The point of Charades is for players to act out a word, quotation, title, name, or an idea in the shortest amount of time possible.

➤ There are hand gestures you need to know in order to play Charades successfully. Otherwise your teammates will wonder what you're up to!

➤ You may want to have some adult supervision when little kids are playing Hide and Seek. You don't want any little ones getting lost or falling asleep in their hiding spot!

Part 6
Outdoor Games

Your kids will probably learn most of the games in this section in the schoolyard, but if your child is a television-watching, video game-playing kind of youngster, pull the plug and get them outside! You probably won't have to struggle too hard with this if you have a swimming pool. You'll find some great water games in this section that will have your kids splashing and laughing for hours. You'll really appreciate these games in the summer months.

Some of the games in here will require you to purchase a few things for backyard games—like a ball and net for Volleyball, badminton racquets, and a football—while the picnic games require just a few items that you already have in your home. And don't forget the sandwiches!

Chapter 25

Take Me Out to the Ballgame

In This Chapter

➤ Kickball

➤ Volleyball

➤ Touch Football

➤ Croquet

Many of the ballgames we play outside on a sunny summer day have their roots in ancient times. There are ancient Roman drawings that depict people playing what appears to be forms of Field Hockey, Soccer, and even Baseball. All these games that are so popular in modern times have been played for centuries. The games have evolved with new tools and modern rules, but basically we haven't changed them very much at all.

We still love to play ball! In this chapter, you'll learn how to play many of the games you probably played as a kid. If you've forgotten the rules, this chapter will certainly come in handy.

Kickball

I have very fond memories of Kickball. Where I grew up we called it Soccer Baseball—not a bad title for the game because you use your feet to kick the ball and the rules are basically the same as Baseball.

My friends and I discovered the game out of sheer boredom in our schoolyard one day. We were too old for clapping and Jump Rope games. We'd gotten very tired of hitting a tennis ball against the school wall, and the champ squares were always too crowded. As we sat upon the school wall complaining about the crowded schoolyard, I looked down and noticed the baseball diamond. Our schoolyard was made of concrete and there were hopscotch boards and champ squares painted on the ground. What we'd failed to notice were the two baseball diamonds at opposite ends of the schoolyard. I went inside and asked the gym teacher if we could borrow a large rubber ball and my friends and I started a schoolyard trend that became the most popular activity for years to come.

Winning Plays

There are people who take Kickball very seriously—there's even an official rulebook put out by the American Kickball Association!

In order to play the game for fun, you really just have to know some basic rules of Baseball.

You'll need enough yard space to play the game and a big solid rubber ball. It has to hold up to some hard kicking and should be tough and light enough to fly through the air.

Set up your playing area in the same way you'd set up a baseball diamond. You'll have a home plate, first, second, and third bases, and a pitcher's mound. In this game you don't want to pitch from a mound, but rather a flat surface. The best location to play the game is on a flat paved or gravel surface, but if you must play on grass you'll have just as much fun, but you might not be able to pitch as accurately because the grass will slow the ball's roll.

You divide into two teams—one team is the kickers while the other is the outfielders. The kickers line up behind home plate in order of who kicks first, second, third, and so on.

The outfielders can take their locations in the field. You'll need a pitcher, baseplayers, and a couple outfielders. If you only have a few people playing then the base players can double as outfielders, but they should be prepared to do a lot of running.

To pick the order of kickers you can go by alphabetical order of the last names. If your last name starts with a "W" and you get sick of having to go almost last every time (if you get a chance to kick at all), try going in reverse alphabetical order when you're up for the kick again.

The pitcher must pitch the ball toward home plate where a kicker will be ready to make that ball fly. The pitcher holds the ball in one hand and rolls it with a little bit of speed toward home plate. Like in Baseball, the pitcher can try to make the kicker strike out. If the ball rolls over home plate and the kicker misses or doesn't kick, that's a strike.

Three strikes equal an out. Three outs mean the next team is "at bat" (or up for the kick) and the kickers become the outfielders. You'll need a catcher to stand behind home plate and an umpire to call the shots.

If the kicker kicks the ball, he or she has to run to first base. If he or she sees that the ball is far enough out of the way, he or she can try to run to second base. It's the job of the base players and outfielders to try and tag the kicker before he or she can run all the way to home plate. If one of the outfielders catches the ball before it hits the ground, that's an out!

You can play as many innings as you want. There may not be enough time to play a full nine innings like in Baseball, but make sure you all agree in advance on the number of innings you have time to play. If you have all day, go for the full nine—if you only have recess period at school, play until the bell rings and pick up again where you left off the next day. One way or another, once you start playing, you'll be hooked!

Volleyball

Volleyball is a game that you will inevitably wind up playing in gym class, but it's even more fun to play outdoors. It's a great game for the beach and just as much fun in your backyard. All you need is a volleyball, a very high net, and at the most 12 players—you can play with less but the game is at its peak when you have six players on each side.

After you've set up your net (which you can purchase at a sporting goods store) divide the players into two teams—six players on each side. On both sides of the net there should be three people in a line in front of the net and three people standing in a line behind the front row.

A volleyball can also be purchased at any sporting goods store. The ball is lightweight (about 10 ounces) and is usually white with thick pads of white rubber-like material forming a sort of grid pattern around the outside. The material on the outside acts as a padding for your hands because they will take quite a beating during a few rounds of this game. The ball is no more than 26 inches in circumference.

The net should be pulled taught enough for the volleyball to bounce off. The net is usually set seven or eight feet high depending on who is playing the game. Since women are usually a little shorter, it is usually set at seven feet for women and eight feet for men. If you're playing with children, you can set the net even lower.

You will need several feet on either side of the net for your play area. The more space you have the longer your shots. The standard volleyball court is 30 feet wide by 60 feet long.

If you're playing on pavement, use chalk to draw the boundary and service lines. If you're playing in the sand, use a stick to draw the lines in the sand.

Jolly Volley

The object of the game is to volley the ball back and forth in an effort to try to make the ball hit the floor on your opponents' side of the net—within the play area. There are three ways to volley the ball—with the tips of your fingers, two cupped hands, or the flat of your hand when going for a slam.

The idea is to bounce the ball from one player to another until someone has a good enough angle to attempt to spike it over the net and make it hit the floor on your opponents' side. The other team can prevent this by hitting the ball back over the net or to another player on their same team. The ball can only be touched three times by the same team before it must be volleyed back over the net.

A *spike* is performed by a forward player (player closest to the net). A spike is a really hard shot for a team to return; you have to be very quick and strong to volley it back.

Join the Service

You can serve the ball in any form you want as long as you hit it with enough strength to get it over the net. The serve is made by the player in the back row on the far right of the court. That player must stand behind the service line and hit the ball over the net.

Try one of these service methods: Hold the ball in one hand and with the other hand turn your palm upward, close your fingers into your palm, tuck in your thumb, and use the bottom (or ball) of your palm to hit the ball. Toss the ball into the air and hit it underhand with the ball of your palm. After a couple tries, you'll find the ball soaring over the net.

You can also throw the ball into the air and hit it with your fist or arm to make it fly over the net—whichever way is most comfortable and doesn't make you turn black and blue.

The ball must go over the net on the first serve and cannot be touched by any member on the serving team. Like in Tennis, Ping-Pong, and Badminton, the team that serves is the team that scores.

The serving team scores when the opposing team does not successfully volley the ball back over the net. That means the serving team, serves again. The serving team continues to serve until they make an error or commit a foul. The service then switches to the opposing team. Before they serve however, the players must rotate in a clockwise direction so that there is a new server for each new play.

The Scoring

One point is awarded for each error and foul committed by the receiving team. Errors and fouls consist of hitting the ball out of legal bounds, failing to return the ball over the net, volleying the ball four times before it goes over the net, touching the ball more than once in a row, carrying the ball on your fingers—or in your hand—without volleying right away.

High Score

The correct way to hold your hands when making a cupped-hand shot is to place one hand palm-up on top of the palm of your other hand. Slightly cup your hands together so that your thumbs line up next to each other. It is the flat of your thumbs that will contact the ball when you use this method.

Winning Plays

Volleyball was invented in 1895 by William G. Morgan, a physical instructor at the YMCA in Holyoke, Massachusetts.

It was further designed by a group of businessmen as an indoor alternative to Basketball, which they found a little too rigorous. Morgan called the game "mintonette," which was later changed to "volleyball" by a professor at Springfield College in Massachusetts. The game escalated in popularity in the early twentieth century in schools and in the armed forces of the United States. There are now men's, women's, and youth divisions all over the world. Volleyball is also an Olympic sport.

You can never use your head or your feet to hit the ball—unless of course you're playing your own homegrown version and want to add some additional maneuvers for the purposes of fun.

The game is over when one team scores 15 points—but you must win by a two-point lead.

Touch Football

This is the game that families play after a hearty Thanksgiving meal. Not only is it a great way to hang out with your family but you'll work off some of that turkey and stuffing as well. If you have a big backyard, that's plenty of space to play the game—otherwise it might be best to head to a local park.

Before you play, make sure you have at least four players, a football, four chairs or markers of some kind, a flat grassy area, and some handkerchiefs or bandanas—some piece of cloth—that can dangle from a back pocket or in a waistband.

To start, use the chairs to set up the goal lines at either end of your play area. Divide the players into two teams and get ready for some fun. Each player should tuck the bandana or piece of fabric into their pocket or waistband—enough should be hanging out so that it's easy to grab.

Set a time limit for the game and flip a coin to determine which team will go first.

Each team lines up on its goal line. One player kicks the ball as far down the field as possible. The other team must try to catch it, or pick it up, and then run it back down the field toward the opponent's goal line in an attempt to score a touchdown.

The team without the ball must try to stop the team with the ball. They do so by chasing the person who is running with the ball and trying to grab that dangling bandana. If a player manages to pull the bandana out of a pocket or waistband that player is considered tackled and must stop running. That team has four tries (downs) to attempt to get the ball past their opponent's goal line. Before each run, the team with the ball may huddle to discuss their next play—like who will pass to whom and how to maneuver around the field so as to trick the tacklers.

Each down is played from where the game stopped. To begin the next play, the teams line up facing each other where the ball was stopped. You can use professional football methods by having one player pass the ball to a "quarterback" through his or her legs. Everyone runs wide and the "quarterback" may run with the ball or pass it to another player to start the run. If a team fails to score a touchdown after the fourth down, the ball is passed to the other team and play begins where the ball last stopped.

A team can also gain possession of the ball if it is dropped or intercepted during a pass.

A touchdown is worth six points. The team with the most points by the end of the time limit is the winner!

While some families get very competitive in their annual Touch Football match, you should always try to have fun with it. Have a game where everyone is required to run and pass backward. That's a great way to make the game silly. Little kids will love it.

Croquet

Croquet is a great game to have set up and ready to go for a backyard barbecue. It's a slow game of patience and precision and a great way to spend time chatting with your friends as you work your ball through the course. Croquet may be an ancestor of Billiards and Golf. The goal is to use a wooden mallet to hit a ball through a hole. Sound familiar?

The game is fine for kids to play—as long as they are big enough to hold the mallet; they are old enough to play.

You can buy a croquet set for under $100.

Winning Plays

Croquet has its origins in France and dates back as far as the thirteenth century. It migrated to England in about the sixteenth century and is still a popular game today.

You can play the game with two to six players. You can play in teams or as individuals (otherwise known as "Cutthroat Croquet.") Play usually takes about two hours.

To play the game, you will have to go to a sporting goods store and buy a croquet set. The set will consist of multicolored balls, long-handled mallets, about nine hoops (or wickets), and two wooden pegs.

The nine wire hoops are stuck into the ground in whatever pattern you choose, but the standard set-up is two diamond shapes—one on top of the other. Set your peg in the ground first with two hoops in front of it. Then a few feet ahead set two more hoops a few feet apart across from each other and another hoop aligned with the first two hoops you set in front of the peg. The shape should form a diamond. Repeat this pattern to create a second diamond on top of the first with the last point having two hoops and another peg behind the hoops.

The hoops should span over an area no more than 40 feet wide and 75 feet long. The wooden pegs mark the beginning and end of play. The balls must be struck through the hoops using the wooden mallets. The balls are also made of wood and are quite heavy. They are either solid in color or striped. You choose one ball and matching colored mallet and start the play at the wooden peg. You keep striking the ball through the hoops until you miss. Once you miss, you turn the play over to the next player. If someone's ball is in your way, you can knock it out with your own ball, but be careful not to knock your ball out in the process.

Croquet playing field.

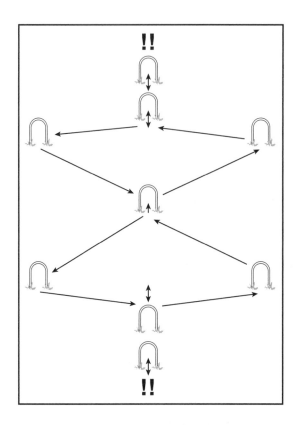

One point is scored for each hoop you hit your ball through as long as you make the hoops in the proper order. You also score a point when you hit a wooden peg.

Each ball in the game can score a total of 16 points. There are 14 wicket points and 2 points for hitting the pegs. When you reach the end of the pattern and hit the peg at the end, you have to go back through those last two hoops again to score two more points. You can play with more than one ball per team. If you are playing the four-ball game, you can score a total of 32 points; if you are playing the six-ball game you can score a total of 48 points.

The order of play is designated by the color of the balls.

➤ **Six-ball game:** Order of play is blue, red, black, yellow, green, and then orange. In teams one side plays blue, black, and green while the other side plays red, yellow, and orange.

➤ **Four-ball game:** Order of play is blue, red, black, and yellow. In teams one side plays blue and black while the other plays red and yellow.

➤ **Singles:** Use the four-ball version.

➤ **Doubles:** Two players per side—each playing one ball. Use the four-ball version.

➤ **Triples:** Three players per side—each playing one ball. Use the six-ball version.

➤ **Individual (Cutthroat):** Use the six-ball version.

Now let's play ball!

The Least You Need to Know

➤ Kickball is basically Soccer Baseball: Use the Baseball rules, but no bats and gloves—just a big ball to kick.

➤ To play Touch Football, all you need is four players, a football, a bandana or something else to stick in your pockets to distinguish team members, and something to mark the goal lines, such as some chairs.

➤ In order to play Croquet, you'll need a croquet set. You should be able to buy one for under $100.

Chapter 26

Fun in the Sun

In This Chapter

➤ Badminton

➤ Hopscotch

➤ Marbles

➤ Jump Rope

There is nothing like spending the afternoon playing a good game in the backyard or local park—and there are countless games that kids can play outdoors. The minute the weather gets warm, take the kids outside and show them how to play. I can't believe that kids don't play outside as much as they used to. I was lucky to have grown up in a couple of different neighborhoods where there were plenty of kids to play with.

The rule in our house was that as soon as the street lights came on, we had to go inside. We stuck to that rule—if we didn't, we'd hear our father's voice calling us from a window and he'd be none too pleased. The only time we disobeyed is if we were in the middle of a good game and couldn't stop right away—but that was still never a good excuse.

When we lived in the country, and there were no street lights, some kids' parents used to ring a bell and everyone would start to head home. Again my father would just use that voice of his. We could hear it at least half a mile away—and he knew it—so there was no pretending we didn't hear him. That voice! It sure could travel. If you don't have that kind of voice, try the bell—it's foolproof.

Some of the games you can play outside need special equipment, which you can purchase pretty inexpensively, while other games you won't need anything at all—just a group of kids and a lot of energy.

Fly Away Birdie: Badminton

I played Badminton for years before ever knowing a single rule. My mother bought us the racquets and the *birdies* (or "shuttlecocks"), and the net. We hooked up the net in

the backyard and played for hours. We were mostly just hitting the birdie back and forth—so proud that we could actually get enough power behind a swing to get the birdie back over the net. It wasn't until I took lessons that I actually learned the rules of the game. At least I knew how to hit the birdie at that point. That's half the battle.

The racquets are lightweight and have a small, round, netted surface that you use to hit the birdie. The handle is long and thin and has a rubber, padded grip. The birdie has a rubber tip and lightweight body. The weight is in the rubber tip, which propels the birdie back and forth. The body is usually made of serrated plastic designed to look like feathers. The holes in the plastic allow air to pass through, which slows the birdie down a bit, and make its movement slightly unpredictable. You have to learn to use the racquet in just the right way to make the birdie go where you want it to go.

> **Winning Plays**
>
> In the USA, most people pronounce "badminton" as "badmitten." It's funny to hear it that way when you were raised pronouncing it with the "n" and "t" sounds in the middle. But anyway you say the name it's a great game, and a good introduction to a really fun sport.

Courtside

The badminton court is divided into two rectangular sections—one on either side of the net—with several lines drawn to indicate where play takes place. When you look at a diagram of the court, it looks like a box within a box. The back line of the outer box indicates where play must take place. You cannot hit the birdie outside that back line. The inner box shows you where the service line is. You must stand behind the service line to serve the birdie. The service lines are about $15^1/_2$ feet from the back court lines, and the net is located 22 feet from the back court lines. The net should stand about five feet off the ground. If you buy a badminton set and you are playing in your

> **It's in the Cards**
>
> A **birdie** is the shuttlecock in Badminton: a lightweight, cone-shaped plastic object with a rounded, often rubber-tipped nose.

backyard, you will have to set the posts that hold the net into the ground. The net should be pulled taught enough so that it doesn't sag in the middle.

You can play with either *doubles* or *singles*.

To pick the team that goes first, you should toss a coin.

What Service!

The birdie must be served from behind the service line. The person to serve first should be standing in the box on the right, facing the net. To serve, hold the birdie by its "feathers" in one hand with the rubber tip facing downward. Hold the racquet underneath the tip of the birdie. Let go of the birdie and hit it with your racquet.

This will take several rounds of practice until you get it right. You will watch that birdie hit the deck repeatedly until you finally manage to strike it, let alone strike it over the net. The trick is to keep your eye on the birdie—not on the racquet.

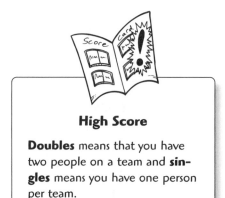

High Score

Doubles means that you have two people on a team and **singles** means you have one person per team.

Keep Score

The rules are not unlike tennis or Ping-Pong. The team that serves is the team that scores. You keep hitting the birdie back and forth over the net until a person on the opposite team misses. If it lands within the boundary lines, you score points. If you miss the birdie on your serve, the other team gets to serve and score. You can play to 15 or 21 points.

In a game of 15 points, if the score is 13 to 13 (or 13-all), the side that reached 13 first has the option to "set" the game. This means that you decide to play the game for five more points. If the game is set at 15-all, the game can be set to three points. Once the game is "set," the score is called "love all." The side that scores three or five first wins the game. You must set the game before the next service is made after 13-all or 14-all has been reached.

One Scoop or Two?

As in Tennis, you can play Badminton as doubles or singles. In doubles, the service must be made from the right court, facing the net, to the player diagonally across— on the other side of the net. If the person returns the birdie without it touching the ground, the birdie is in play, and must be hit back and forth until someone misses. Serves from this point on should be made from alternate service courts and always to diagonal receivers on the other side of the net. No player may make two serves consecutively in the same game. The side that wins the game gets to serve first in the next game.

In singles, the play is pretty much the same as it is in doubles except that the serve is made and received from each player's right-hand court when the score is zero or an even number. All other serves (odd number of points) are delivered and received from the left-hand side of the court.

When You're Out, You're Out!

A play is considered "out" when:

➤ The birdie falls into the wrong service court.

➤ The birdie falls short of the service line, beyond the long service line, or outside the boundary lines.

➤ If the players are not standing in their service or receiving courts.

➤ If the birdie passes through or under the net or touches a player's clothing.

➤ If the birdie is hit twice in a row by the same player or by a player on the same team.

The trick is to hit the birdie in such a way that it makes it hard for your opponent to lobby it back. But I have to say, it's also nice to play less aggressively and just lobby the birdie back and forth for a while. However you play or with whomever, you'll really enjoy Badminton on a pleasant summer day.

Winning Plays

It is believed that some of the earliest hopscotch boards may have resembled mazes—making hopping and skipping through them all the more difficult.

A Hop, Skip, and Jump: Hopscotch

Hopscotch was one of my favorite outdoor games growing up. There are many ways to play Hopscotch, and the versions are based on the way the board is drawn. Although Hopscotch is commonly played by little girls (maybe it has something to do with the skilled, controlled movements and the desire to skip and hop), it is not uncommon for young boys to indulge in the game as well. However, boys may prefer games that require more running and jumping—a little more action than Hopscotch allows.

All you need to play Hopscotch is a piece of chalk to draw the hopscotch board, a small rock, a button or piece of wood (a marker of some kind), and an empty stretch of sidewalk or pavement.

Sidewalk Turned Runway

One version of Hopscotch is called Airplane. This is the version that I used to play with my friends. The pattern is older than the invention of the airplane, but it has been coined "airplane" because of the way it looks. The board is a series of single and double boxes—the double boxes resemble wings.

To draw the board, start by drawing three single boxes—one on top of the other—and number them 1, 2, and 3. The next box should be a double box drawn on top of the number 3 box. Label the box on the left 4 and the box on the right 5. Then a single box is drawn on top of the double box for number 6, then another double box with 7 on the left and 8 on the right. Two more single boxes are stacked on top of the 7 and 8 double box. The single box directly above the double box is labeled 9 and the last box is 10. The top box should be drawn with a rounded top (so as to resemble the nose of an airplane).

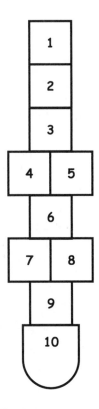

Diagram of Airplane Hopscotch.

Getting Your Footing

Now the fun begins. You have to hop your way through the pattern using your marker to keep your place. You start by standing outside the bottom of the board. Drop you marker into the square with the number 1. From outside the board, hop over number 1 and then hop into each square one at a time. You can only hop into the single boxes with one foot, but with both feet into the double boxes. After jumping over the box where your marker is, you must jump up the board and back down using the proper footing. When you get to 10, you have to do a spin and land on one foot in that box—so that you wind up facing the bottom of the board again.

High Score

Some kids play that the number 10 box is a rest space and you can hop into it with two feet. If you do use the number 10 box this way, you must hop again with two feet to face back to the number 1 box for your hopping trip home.

Three Strikes

Remember: You may never hop into the box where your marker rests!

The whole trick to Hopscotch lies in your footing. You can't do a double hop in a box, you can't put two feet down in a single box, and you can't miss a box. If you don't land cleanly and solidly on the proper foot, in the appropriate box, you're out—and the next player takes his or her turn. If you do go through the whole board without a misstep, you must stop with one foot in the number 2 box, bend down, pick up your marker from the number 1 box, stand up again, and hop outside the board. If you make it, you then throw your marker in the number 2 box. This time you have to hop into the number 1 box, over the number 2 box, and into the number 3 box.

Your marker must always land within the lines of the box. If it bounces out of the box or lands on a line, you must pick it up and let the next player take his or her turn.

When your marker is in a double box, you won't be able to use two feet—you'll have to hop into the box next to it on one foot.

You can end the game after you throw your marker into the number 9 box and hop all the way back home. Remember 10 can be a rest box, so you don't have to throw your marker up that high. Just establish what the number 10 box will be from game to game so that everyone is clear.

Each time you take a new turn, you don't have to start all over again. Just remember what number you last landed on and start your next turn with that same number.

Have You Lost Your Marbles?

My sister told me that when I was born her blissful days of Marble playing with my other sister and our father were abruptly ended. She loved playing Marbles so much that I don't think she ever forgave me for it! My parents, like all parents, had to put away small objects with a new baby in the house—those bright, glassy little objects are far too tempting for tiny minds (and mouths). The marbles never came out again—much to my sister's dismay—because there were two more babies welcomed into the family after my birth.

The game of Marbles as we know it today gets its name from the practice of making children's toys from chips of marble or stone.

Marrididdles, Cat's Eyes, and Taws!

That's right—different sizes and types of marbles have different names, and these names vary from country to country. Marrididdles are homemade marbles usually made of clay that's been left out to dry. Cat's Eyes, originally made in Japan, are made of clear glass with swirling colored glass injected inside of them. An Alley is your best marble and might even be your most expensive marble. A Taw is one of your shooters—simply put, it is your favorite marble—the one you use to shoot the most often and the one you don't want to lose to an opponent. If you are playing with an expensive Alley, you might want to have a stated rule in the beginning, that that marble is not up for grabs!

Winning Plays

Marble playing goes way back in history—possibly as far back as ancient Egypt. It is believed that Emperor Augustus of Rome played the game as a child using nuts and rounded pebbles. Carved "marbles" were dug up in the United States and are believed to be remnants of a Native American children's game similar to Marbles. Some say that the game goes back as far as the cave people. Children of early humans may have used rocks and pebbles to play.

Winning Plays

While Marbles has been played over the centuries with everything from rounded sea pebbles to fruit pits, today the game is played with small colorful balls of glass—but it took many different materials to reach this point. In the twentieth century, marbles were made of baked clay, agate, onyx, alabaster, plastic, wood, and steel. Antique marbles can be found at flea markets and auctions.

The different types of marbles are quite beautiful. You may want to collect them just for the way they look!

Because this game is so old, there are countless ways to play, countless games to make up, and countless names for marbles. You will definitely find yourself and your children making up rules to suit your own needs. Inventing new games is always good fun and a great way to stimulate your child's imagination.

Three Strikes

It is critical to keep marbles out of the hands and mouths of small children. You should only play the game with children over the age of five or six—and even then under strict supervision. Older kids should be okay.

Three Strikes

Tell your kids to be clear on the rules about taking marbles before they play. Some kids want to have their marbles back, while other kids feel the reward is to win other kids' marbles. This could be a big source of conflict if the kids don't state the rules in advance.

The Ring Game

This is the most famous version of Marbles, the one you see kids playing on TV and in the movies, and soon, hopefully in your own backyard.

Draw a ring on the ground either with a piece of chalk or with a stick in the dirt. Draw a starting line just outside the ring. Each player puts a few marbles into the ring and the goal is to shoot the marbles, from the starting line, out of the ring.

To choose the player who goes first, each player should shoot a marble from the starting line toward the ring; the player whose marble is closest to the edge of the ring gets to go first. The next closest is the second shooter, and so on. The players should pick up these marbles to shoot again when the game begins.

The first player knuckles down at the starting line and shoots his or her marble toward the ring in an effort to hit a marble out of the ring. If the player hits both his or her marble and the target marble out of the ring, he or she gets to keep the marble and shoot again—only this time he or she has to shoot from where his or her shooter rests. If a player shoots a target marble out, but his or her shooter stays in, he or she can get the shooter back by replacing it with another marble.

Kids get very attached to their favorite shooters, so you can bet they are going to want their "Taw" back! However, if his or her shooter stays in, the player is out and must put all the won marbles back in the ring. If a player doesn't hit any marbles out of the ring and his or her shooter stays in, the shooter can be replaced with another marble but the player is out altogether until the next game. If the player misses and the shooter goes outside the ring, the shooter stays where it is but the shooter loses his or her turn. On the next play, the player must shoot from where his or her shooter rested on the previous play.

Knuckles Down

There is an art to shooting a marble and it's done like this: Curl your fingers and rest the marble on the crook of your index finger. With your knuckles facing downward, place the knuckle of your index finger on the ground and use your thumb to flick the marble out of the crook—and watch the marble fly. You'll have to practice a few times until you get it right.

Jump Rope

What I wouldn't give to have the coordination to jump rope again the way I used to. Jumping rope for adults is a workout. Jumping rope for a kid is bliss. Again, little girls tend to be the jump ropers, while little boys seem to turn their noses up at such antics. Ironically, when the game of Jump Rope started, it was a boys' game. Boys used to do tricks like twisting or crossing the rope. When girls got into it, they added the rhyming games. To this day girls love to rhyme, jump, and skip—they love the art of rhythm, as evident in hand-clapping and Jump Rope games.

There are a couple ways to jump rope. You can buy your kids individual jump ropes and they can jump and rhyme alone, or you can get them a longer rope so they can play with their friends. When using the longer rope, you'll need *enders* to turn the rope for the skippers.

The enders turn the rope so that it makes a nice clean arch on every swing into the air. In most games, when the rope comes down, it should scrape the ground. The skippers, on the correct beat, must jump into the center as the rope is turned, and depending on the game, they either stay and jump or run in and out. Usually the rhymes dictate the game.

Winning Plays

It is believed that jumping rope started as a sort of superstition. People believed that if they jumped around the crops in springtime, the crops would grow. They believed the higher you jumped, the higher the crops.

It's in the Cards

The **enders** in jump rope lingo are the two people, one on each end of the rope, who turn the rope.

Jump Rope Lingo

Jumping rope has a whole language of its own:

➤ **Salt:** Turn the rope slowly.

➤ **Mustard and Vinegar:** Turn the rope at a moderate speed.

➤ **Pepper:** Turn the rope quickly.

➤ **Bluebells** or **Rocking the Cradle:** Rope swings back and forth but doesn't go over the skipper's head.

➤ **High Water:** The rope doesn't touch the ground when the skipper is skipping.

➤ **Chase the Fox:** All the skippers follow the fox—doing whatever he or she does as he or she skips rope.

➤ **Under the Moon:** Skippers run under the rope—no skipping allowed!

➤ **Over the Stars:** Skippers jump just once over the rope.

Here are some rhymes:

Ipsey, Pipsey,

Tell me true,

Who shall I be married to?

A, B, C, D ...

When the letters begin, the rope is turned faster and the letter that a player messes up on is the first letter in the name of the person they will marry. It's fun for kids to go through the names of the people they know whose name starts with that letter. When a skipper messes up, he or she must become an ender, freeing the current ender to participate as a skipper.

Bluebells, cockleshells,

Eevy, ivy, over.

My mother sent me to the store,

And this is what she sent me for:

Salt, mustard, vinegar, pepper!

When "pepper" is called, the enders turn the rope very fast, and whoever messes up becomes an ender.

All in together girls

It's fine weather girls

When is your birthday?

Please jump in.

January, February, March ...

The rope is turned very fast at this point, and the skippers must jump in and out when their birthday month is called.

Not last night but the night before,

24 robbers came knocking at my door.

I asked them what they wanted and this is what they said:

Spanish dancer do the splits, the twist, the turn-around and touch the ground and out the back door.

Spanish dancer please come back, back, sit on a tack, read a book and do not look.

One, two, three, four, five, six, seven ...

The rope is turned very quickly when the numbers are called out. The skipper must close his or her eyes. You keep going until you miss.

Teddy bear, Teddy bear, turn around,

Teddy bear, Teddy bear, touch the ground.

Teddy bear, Teddy bear, show your shoe,

Teddy bear, Teddy bear, that will do.

Teddy bear, Teddy bear, go upstairs,

Teddy bear, Teddy bear, say your prayers.

Teddy bear, Teddy bear, turn out the lights.

Teddy bear, Teddy bear, say goodnight!

The skippers must act out each action as it is stated in the rhyme. The kids will make up their own actions as they go along.

There are countless other rhymes you can teach your kids—many of which can be found on the Internet.

Double Dutch

Double Dutch is played with two ropes and several skippers. I never mastered the art of this Jump Rope game, but it is mesmerizing to watch kids who have. There are

Double Dutch contests held all over the country, and the kid-participants are almost acrobats.

For Double Dutch, you use two ropes and spin them intermittently. Much of the art is performed by the enders. While one rope is scraping the ground, the other is in the air.

It takes real hand-eye coordination and a good sense of rhythm to make these ropes turn just the way you need them to. The kids who do the skipping really have to keep time to hit the skips just right and not get all tangled in the ropes. Again, there are countless rhymes for Double Dutch games, and if your kids can master this game, perhaps you'll want to enroll them in dance class because this game really is an art form!

The Least You Need to Know

➤ For Badminton, you will need a net, racquets, and a birdie (or shuttlecock).

➤ To play Hopscotch, you will need a stretch of pavement you can write on, a piece of chalk, a rock, and a marker—like a button or coin.

➤ Marrididdles are homemade marbles usually made of clay; Cat's Eyes are made of glass and have swirling colored glass inside of them; and a Taw is simply your favorite marble.

➤ Jump Rope is an old-time favorite. There are so many rhymes that go with this game. Jumping rope takes practice and a good sense of rhythm.

Chapter 27

Going on a Picnic: Picnic Games

In This Chapter

➤ Tug of War and races

➤ Tag games and Capture the Flag

➤ Leap Frog, Frisbee, and Horseshoes

When the warm weather hits, families often pack up and head out for a picnic. Those lucky enough to live in the warmer climates of the world can party outside all year long if they want to. Picnics are a great idea for a family reunion. There are so many games you can play outside, and if you have a big enough family you can get into some really fun competitive activities. Even with a smaller family, these games will give you hours of giggles.

Many of these picnic games became popular in the pioneer days at country fairs and festivals, but some of the games date back even further than that. The games in this chapter are old picnic classics that if you've never played before, you'll surely want to play them now!

Tug of War

All you need for a good game of Tug of War is a long, heavy rope and two teams. This game goes way back to ancient times—it is so simple and so much fun. Draw a line on the ground or place a marker of some kind in the ground. The goal is for both sides to pull on their ends of the rope in order to make the other team cross the line or marker. Some people will use a big mudhole as the line. You know what that means—

whoever loses gets covered in mud. I wouldn't recommend that version unless you are by a lake where everyone can dive in when the game is over. You can try putting grease on the rope to make the game a little harder and worth even a few more giggles.

You can also play Two-Way Tug of War. Get two heavy ropes and tie them in the middle so that there are four pullable ends. Draw a wide circle on the ground. Divide players into four teams. Each team must stand on the outside of the circle and pull! The first team to be pulled into the circle is out and their end of the rope is left dangling. Now it is a three-way pull. The last team to remain outside the circle is the winner.

High Score

In all likelihood, you will be playing these picnic games with children. Children like to win prizes, so it might be a good idea to have some treats on hand. You can either award little prizes for each race or game, or give a bigger prize to the players or teams that win the most games and races. A pie is a nice prize or a couple jars of homemade jam—don't forget some candy, fruit, or little toys for the kids. The prize shouldn't be huge, just something fun for the team or players to take home.

Off to the Races

Who doesn't remember the fun of a good race? The screaming sideliners, the rush of adrenaline .... There's nothing like a good, close race to get the blood pumping and the appetite up.

Three-Legged Race

You'll need a start and goal line and several pieces of twine for this game. Form teams of partners. Each player must tie one of his or her legs to the other player's leg so that when they move, they move with three legs. The goal is to race from the start line to the goal line and back again. The first set of partners to reach the start line again is the winner. You can fall and get back up and continue the race, but you won't win unless you catch up to those who are still moving at a steady pace.

Kids will want to pair up with adults in this game, but be careful. You are likely to fall during this race, and kids take smaller steps than grown-ups. You don't want to fall and hurt a child, so if you do pair up with a kid, be sure to move slowly when the race is on.

Potato on a Spoon Race

For the Potato on a Spoon Race, you'll need some regular-sized stainless steel or plastic spoons and some small- to medium-sized potatoes. The potato should be slightly larger than the spoon to make balancing a little tricky. You will also need to establish a start line and a goal line. Everyone balances a potato on his or her spoon and when the whistle blows, you must make it to the goal line and back without dropping your potato. If you make it back first, you are the winner.

You can also play this game with an egg—but it might be a good idea to hard-boil the egg before the game begins!

High Score

For a Three-Legged Race, you'll want to have a little practice walking around for a while— before the race begins—until you and your partner figure out how to move that leg in unison. It's a lot harder than it looks!

Sack Races

For this game, you'll need to dig up some old pillowcases or burlap sacks. Kids really love this game. Each kid climbs into the sack and, holding the edges of the sack up around his or her hips or waist, must hop from the start line to the goal line and back again. Many kids will fall over and you'll laugh a lot during this crazy game. If adults grab a sack and start hopping with them, the kids will squeal with laughter—the adults will look even sillier than the kids!

Three Strikes

A word of warning! Because kids are jumping forward, chances are good that they will land on their faces when they fall. To prevent bloody noses and other injuries, make sure the race area is smooth, flat, and grassy. Also check that there are no sharp stones, sticks, or other kinds of debris hidden in the grass. You may also want to have your kids practice before they jump into a sack—practice falling, that is—so they don't land on their faces when they tumble.

Tag, You're It!

Tag is a game that goes way back to the days of cave people! It is perhaps the oldest known children's game in human existence. You don't need any special tools—just a bunch of kids and an idea. Its premise is simple and the variations exist in the hundreds. For a simple game of Tag, one child is picked as "It" (see Chapter 21, "They Say It's Your Birthday!" for choosing "It") and all the other children are runners. "It" must try to catch each runner by touching him and yelling "You're It!" In this case, "It" becomes a runner and the tagged runner becomes "It." Here are some of the Tag variations.

Shadow Tag

You have to play Shadow Tag on a sunny day. You can run and run and try to protect yourself from "It," but what you're protecting is not your body, but your shadow on the ground or on a wall. If "It" tags your shadow, you become the next "It."

There are several ways to deal with the people you tag. You can either switch roles so that player becomes "It" and you become a runner, or you can have the tagged player join you as another "It." Then the two of you have to keep tagging other players until everyone is an "It"—the first person tagged becomes the next lone "It" for the next game of Tag.

Freeze Tag

In Freeze Tag, when "It" tags a player that person must freeze where they are tagged—that means they freeze in the position in which they were standing when they were tagged. When "It" tags you, "It" yells "Freeze!" So if the person was tagged trying to crawl under a bench, that person must freeze under the bench. If that player was standing on one leg in mid-run, he or she must freeze on that same one leg. You can't move until another free player tags you—then you can "unfreeze" and run again. The game is over when "It" manages to freeze every player. The last person tagged becomes the next "It."

Try this variation: Rather than having to touch a frozen person to unfreeze them, you have to crawl between his or her legs. That can get really tricky—especially if "It" catches you in the act. You'll be frozen in a pretty awkward position.

Touch Tag

This is a great game of Tag for little kids—it's very silly. In Touch Tag, you have to hold the place you were tagged while you run. The person who is "It" in the beginning of the game tries to tag people on a spot on their body that will make it funny or hard for them when they become the next "It." For example: If "It" tags a player on the nose, that person becomes the new "It" and must hold his or her nose while he or she runs and tags other players. Once "It" tags someone else, he or she can let go of their nose and the next player has to be "It" while holding some funny body part.

British Bulldog

This was my favorite Tag game growing up, and we had so many kids in the neighborhood that it was always good fun. One person is "It" and all the other players line up against a wall or some other safe zone. We used to play in the schoolyard, so the school wall was the starting safe zone and the wall across the yard was the other safe zone. The goal was to reach the safe zone before being tagged by "It."

So, with all the players lined up against the school wall, "It" must stand midway between the two safe zones (one for each team). When "It" is ready, he or she calls "British Bulldog" and that's the cue for all the kids to start their run toward the opposite safe zone wall. "It" must tag as many players as possible. Whoever he or she tags becomes another "It." When players reach the other wall, they are safe. The kids who were tagged join the original "It" and the next time "British Bulldog" is called, all the "Its" must tag the other players before reaching the safe zone again.

Three Strikes

You can never run back to the safe zone from which you started! You must run to the safe zone directly across in order to remain safe. It is considered poor sportsmanship in any Tag game to hover around a safe zone. Tag games are about evading and capturing—not hiding!

This game gets really fun when there's just one runner left. If that runner somehow miraculously makes it to a safe zone without being caught, he or she is the champ! And there might be days of wild adulation and praise thrown his or her way—to maneuver your way through all those "Its" is a feat of brilliance in the eyes of children. The first person tagged can be the next "It" or you can let the champ be the next "It." Again, make sure everyone is clear on the rules by which you decide to play.

Capture the Flag

Capture the Flag is another very old game. Kids love it and it can be quite challenging.

The first thing you need to do is find a big, wide-open space—you can either use a large backyard or an open field at a local park. You should have some wooden marker that you can stick into the ground, and also a little flag on a marker that can be stuck in the ground. You can make the flag by tying an old rag to a wooden peg or you can buy little plastic flags from novelty stores.

Divide the field into two boxes. You can do this by bringing wooden pegs to push into the ground that mark out the playing area (tent stakes are great). At the back of each playing box in the far left corner is a "jail"—you can mark this out with more wooden pegs as well. One person on each team acts as a jailer and stands in front of the jail box. The flag should be located to the right of the jail right behind the place where the goalie will stand. The goalie should stand to the right of the jail and the flag (about 10 feet away). The rest of the teams stand behind the boundary line that divides the two territories. Once a team member steps into the opposing team's territory, he or she can be tagged.

High Score

It is not easy to capture the flag, especially with that goalie hovering around it. The trick to the game is to have a strategy worked out with your teammates before the game begins. You will have to find a way to distract the goalie so you can capture the flag and run it back into your own territory.

Obviously, the object of the game is to capture your opponents' flag by entering their territory. You must do so without getting tagged, tackled, or otherwise mangled! This game gets very rowdy, so you might want to wear a few layers of protective clothing!

When the game begins and players start running into the opposition's territory, it is the job of the other teammates to capture the opposing team's players. If you are tagged, you are sent to jail and must stand in the marked jail area at the back of the opposition's territory. You can only be freed from jail if one of your own teammates makes it that far into the territory and is able to tag you. If that happens, you don't have to dash about trying not to get caught—rather, you get a free walk back to your own territory without being tackled.

Capture the Flag is a great game for people of all ages.

Leap Frog

I've seen everyone from little kids to 30-year-olds play the game of Leap Frog. Adults look really silly playing the game and many of us with lower back pain should be careful about indulging in this popular activity too often. But if you're up for it, give it a whirl—especially with little kids. They'll laugh their heads off trying to climb over an adult's back.

Winning Plays

Leap Frog has been around for centuries. In fact, there is a reference to the game in a children's book dating back to 1744 called *Little Pretty Pocket Book*.

To play the game, everyone bends over in a line. The last child in the line jumps over all the bent-over backs, one after the other—by placing his or her hands on the flat of the back and lifting his body over. He or she keeps doing this until he or she reaches the front of the line and bends over for the next round. The last child again stands up and leaps over the other players ahead of him or her again—until he or she reaches the front of the line. This is a slow way to move forward, but you'll never have so much fun getting someplace.

For little kids, you can duck down all the way onto the ground by getting down on your knees and tucking your head under (called making a *low back)*. Little kids with little legs will have an easier time leaping over you that way.

You can play the game with as few as two people and as many as you can find to play. Two kids can play the game—leaping over each other on their way across the park. They're bound to be dizzy by the time they reach their destination, however.

It's in the Cards

A **low back** is a term used in Leap Frog for getting down on your knees, tucking your head under, and making yourself as small as possible—a good position to be in for little leapers.

A **high back** is bending over and holding your ankles or knees, making yourself higher than a low back, and making your position more challenging for the leaper in Leap Frog.

Frisbee Games

The history of the Frisbee is perhaps more interesting than the game itself. It's a true American product that came into popularity out of poverty and ingenuity. In the late nineteenth century and well into the twentieth century, children used to play with metal cookie tin and pie tin lids by tossing them to each other in a kind of game of catch. It is rumored that the most commonly tossed tin lid was that of an American company called the Frisbie Pie Company, which is how the Frisbee got its name. The Frisbie lids were especially popular on college campuses. The sport of tossing pie tin lids grew during the Depression years, and soldiers took the practice overseas during World War II.

The problem with the tin lid was that it didn't glide very easily and it made a horrible shrill noise when it flew threw the air. It also hurt to catch them. Sometimes the lids would crack or break and then the edges became sharp and dangerous.

So after the war, two veterans took it upon themselves to manufacture a kinder, gentler Frisbee—they were Walter Morrison and Warren Franscioni. They manufactured a better flying disc, but it still had some major flaws due mainly to primitive plastic materials. Morrison later developed a better flying disc and called it the Pluto Platter—named after the planet Pluto—which looked like a flying saucer. When two small toy company owners met up with Morrison, they offered to perfect and mass manufacture his product. They struck up a deal and took the product to college campuses. Students at Harvard were thrilled by the invention because, as they admitted, they'd been playing with the tin lids from the Frisbie Pie Company for ages. So the small toy company called "Wham-O" named the flying disc "Frisbee"—changing just one letter in the spelling—and the life of the Frisbee came full circle.

Most picnic goers will bring along a Frisbee and use it just for fun—tossing it back and forth and catching it—with no heavy-duty competition involved. You need a wide-open space, and make sure you're not too close to other picnic goers. Frisbees have a tendency to fly a little erratically on a windy day and you don't want anyone to get hurt. There are loads of different games you can play if you get tired of tossing the flying disc back and forth aimlessly. Try a couple of these.

Ultimate Frisbee

Frisbee has become a very popular game in many countries of the world. Ultimate Frisbee is probably the most popular and most competitive version of Frisbee out there today.

To play the game, you need seven players on each side and a large field at least half the size of a football field. You also need markers to mark the end zones at either end of the field. You will find that this game is similar to football, only it is played with a Frisbee. The major difference is that a player can never run with the Frisbee—it must always be in motion.

The regulation field is 70 yards by 40 yards with end zones 25 yards deep.

Both teams line up in front of their own end zone lines. You can flip a coin to determine who tosses the Frisbee first. The team that tosses is the defense and the receiving team is the offense. To start play, the defense throws the Frisbee to the offense. It is now the job of the offense to throw the Frisbee past the end zone of the defense. The defense must intercept the toss. Each time the offense is successful, they score a point. If the offense is intercepted, the play transfers to the defense and the roles are reversed: The defense becomes the offense and the offense becomes the defense.

The disc can be tossed to a teammate before an attempt to toss it across the end zone is made. The teammates can run and toss to try to get closer to the opponent's end zone. The Frisbee must always be in motion; a player cannot hold it for longer than 10 seconds and can never run with it in hand.

You can assign each player to be a "marker" when you are on the defensive team. Each marker is assigned to a thrower. As a marker you should attempt to block the thrower from making a successful toss without touching him or her—touching constitutes a foul. The marker is also responsible for counting, to make sure the thrower doesn't hold the Frisbee for more than 10 seconds. If a toss is not completed, the teams switch offensive and defensive roles.

Horseshoes

Horseshoe pitching is another very old game—dating back to pioneer times and beyond. It is believed that the game was started by blacksmiths, because they are the ones who would have had several extra horseshoes lying around.

There are some people who play the game very seriously, and there are official rules—but if you're playing at home, just divvy out the horseshoes and start tossing them at the stake. You'll find the challenge of getting the horseshoe around the stake competition enough when you first get started. Those horseshoes are pretty heavy and you'll be surprised how hard it is to predict where they will land after being tossed.

Three Strikes

The horseshoes used in these games are very heavy—heavier than the actual shoes put on the horses—so be careful if little children are around. They shouldn't be too close to the playing area because they could get hurt when the shoes start flying. You can buy plastic sets for children to use. They are very inexpensive and can be picked up at almost any toy store. The adult kits can also be purchased at sporting goods stores and can range quite a bit in price.

If you want to make the game a little more competitive, try these rules, which are loosely based on the NHPA official rules (National Horseshoe Pitchers Association of America).

You should have several feet of playing area—at least 50 feet. Two stakes should be placed at either end of the field—at least 40 feet apart. You can play on any surface: grass, gravel, or pavement. Just remember: the harder the pavement, the louder the game. Those horseshoes can really clatter when they strike the ground. You should mark a foul line about three feet in front of each stake. This means you have to throw past the foul line in order for the pitch to be good. This will make your throwing distance 37 feet—you should throw all the way from the opposite stake on the other side of the field.

Winning Plays

An average horseshoe weighs about 2 pounds, 10 ounces. That may not sound like a lot, but it feels pretty heavy when you have to toss it.

Each player or team gets two horseshoes. The teams stand at opposite sides of the field and take turns pitching their shoes. The teams alternate throwing the two shoes. Player 1 throws his or her two shoes then player 2 throws his or her two shoes. You throw from behind your own foul line toward the stake at the other end of the field.

A shoe must fall within one horseshoe width to be considered for points. A horseshoe width is the distance between the two sides on the open end of the shoe. The closest shoe to the stake scores 1 point. If two of your shoes are closer to the stake than any of your opponent's shoes, you score 2 points. Horseshoes that completely encircle the stake ("ringers") score 3 points. If you have the closest shoe and it's a ringer, you score 4 points. If your opponent throws a ringer on top of yours, neither one of you scores any points. If your shoe rests leaning on the stake ("leaner"), you score a point and it is considered the closest shoe next to a ringer.

You keep playing the game until someone scores 40 points.

Now you're ready for that picnic. Don't forget the ants!

The Least You Need to Know

➤ Have some prizes on hand for children when playing picnic games. Everyone loves to win something!

➤ Races are great picnic games for getting the action going and the appetites up! Try Three-Legged Races, Sack Races, or Egg and Spoon Races.

➤ It is poor sportsmanship in any Tag game to hover near a safe zone. So keep moving!

➤ Frisbee is a great game for wide-open spaces. A particularly popular version of Frisbee is the growing game of Ultimate Frisbee.

➤ Horseshoes is always a crowd pleaser but may not be appropriate for small children. Those horseshoes weigh over two and a half pounds!

Chapter 28

Water World

In This Chapter

➤ Water tag games

➤ Wet and wild games

➤ Water team games

➤ Poolside water games

Cooling off in the pool on a hot summer day—that's what summer is all about! Of course, if you live anywhere near a lake or pond you can have just as much fun in the water. If you don't have your own pool or nearby body of water, try these games at a friend's house or when you're on vacation. Your kids will be water-logged and all pruned-up by the time you manage to get them out of the pool.

I spent many long hours swimming in a lake in the country when I was a kid and we managed to play quite a few of these games even as our feet got all twisted in the tall green, squishy reeds. I think most of the games in this chapter are best played in the controlled environment of the swimming pool.

Water Tag

We've already seen all the fun Tag games we can play in Chapter 27, "Going on a Picnic: Picnic Games." Now let's up the ante and take "It" into the pool!

Marco Polo

Marco Polo is the classic Water Tag game that almost every kid has played at some point in his or her life. Marco Polo is best played in a swimming pool—it's not really a good idea to play in a lake or pond unless you have flat, level ground and good footing.

The person who is "It" is "Marco" and must tag the other players in the pool. You can play with as many people as can fit safely in the pool.

Marco goes to one end of the pool and closes his or her eyes. Marco counts to 10 and then shouts "Marco." Everyone else in the pool then shouts "Polo." Marco, with his or her eyes shut, must go around the pool and try to tag anyone who shouts "Polo." Every time Marco shouts "Marco," the other players must shout "Polo" to give Marco an idea as to where people are located in the pool. When Marco catches someone, that player becomes "It."

If Marco notices that someone did not respond with a "Polo," he or she may state that person's name. If the other players concur that someone did not respond, that rule-violator automatically becomes "It." The only exception to the rule is if that player was underwater at the time everyone said "Polo."

Another variation on the game is to let anyone, except Marco, get out of the pool as long as he or she keeps at least one body part in the water. The body part can be a hand, or foot, or leg—whatever you want. You still have to shout "Polo" in response to every "Marco." If you play this version, be very careful getting in and out of the pool—you don't want to slip and fall.

And yet another variation is to let players get out of the pool, but if Marco catches one of them when that person shouts "Polo" he or she can shout "Fish Out of Water." If the person is caught out of the pool, he or she automatically becomes "It."

Winning Plays

Marco Polo was an Italian explorer who lived in the thirteenth century. He was the first European to cross the continent of Asia. He left a record of all the great things he saw and is credited with bringing ice cream, eyeglasses, pasta, and the riches of Asia to the Western world. Thanks, Marco Polo!

Octopus Tag

This game is bound to be a favorite with your kids. It's good for hours of fun. Set up an area within the pool that can be the "ocean." It's best just to play in the shallow end because the kids will need to have footing. If you play in a lake or pond, make sure the kids play in a shallow area and use floating dividers to designate the "ocean" area. If your pool is small enough, the whole shallow end can be the "ocean."

One player is designated the Octopus, while the other players are the Fish. The Fish line up against one side of the pool (ocean), and the Octopus stands in the middle. The Octopus chants aloud, "I am the Octopus, Queen (or King) of all motion. Let's see if you can cross my ocean."

The Fish must try to sneak past the Octopus as he or she tries to tag them. Once tagged, the players become "Seaweed" and must keep one foot on the bottom as they try to help tag the other passing Fish. Any Fish tagged by Seaweed become Seaweed, too.

If some Fish manage to get to the other side, the Octopus and the Seaweed say the chant together and the Fish must try to get across the ocean again. The last Fish tagged gets to be the new Octopus for the next round of the game.

Team H$_2$O

As we learned earlier, team sports are great for teaching kids about strategy, teamwork, and social interaction. Add some water and see how quickly they learn how much fun summer can be!

Water Basketball—Splashketball!

To play Water Basketball (or as some like to call it, "Splashketball"), you may have to invest a little money in the equipment. Head to your local pool supply store and see if they have any inexpensive water basketball equipment. You'll need a basketball hoop suitable for the poolside and an aquatic basketball. I've seen the sets priced anywhere from $200 to $600, but shop around and you might be able to find something a little cheaper.

If your family is really into it and you think they'll play, then invest in a good set—it'll be hours of outdoor fun. The good sets are made of heavy-duty plastic and can be filled with water to keep them from tipping over.

If you have enough players, form two teams. The goal is to shoot the ball into the hoop. For every shot, the team scores 1 point. If you make a clean shot without passing to another player first, you score 2 points. You can either give the game a time

High Score

To include little kids in the game, have them team up with the big kids. For example, a big kid and a little kid will make a great two-person Octopus!

High Score

You can also try to construct your own water basketball hoop—all you need is a piece of plywood that can be anchored down with sand bags, and a hoop and some netting. It might not be pretty, but it'll do the trick. For the ball, try using any kind of large aquatic ball—they'll have plenty at the local pool supply.

limit or play to a certain number of points. You can use just one basketball hoop if you don't want to buy or make another. If you're up for it and want to spend the money, get two nets and place them at opposite ends of the pool for a more realistic game.

For a real challenge, put the hoop in the deep end; you'll laugh forever as you watch players try to shoot a hoop as they disappear underwater.

You can also play Water Basketball with two people. Just shoot hoops the way you would in your own driveway or at a local gym. Each player takes a turn making a clean shot a certain distance away from the net. If you get the ball in without hitting the sides of the hoop, you score 2 points; if the ball goes through on a rebound, you score 1 point. The first player to reach 21 points wins. You should play to a 2-point lead. So if the score is 20-20, you will have to score 22 points to win.

Water Volleyball

You can buy the gear for Water Volleyball for very little money. If you shop on the Internet, you'll find the net and ball for as low as about $40. If you go to a local pool supply or toy store, you may find it for even less. What you should have is a net that sits about 5 feet above the water. It will come with poles that can be anchored down with sandbags.

You'll also need an aquatic ball that can bounce off your fingertips the same way a regular volleyball would. You can use any ball that will float on the water as long as it is waterproof and not too hard on the hands. If you don't want to invest in the net, you can play without one, but you'll still have to go out and buy the ball! You can use a pool divider to mark the teams' sides or a piece of rope that you can run across the pool. Just make sure that the players hit the ball high enough—as though they were playing a regular Volleyball game.

Use the same rules as Volleyball, which you will find in Chapter 25, "Take Me Out to the Ball Game."

Here's the game in a nutshell: Have both teams form two lines on each side of the pool—try not to put one side in the deep end! You'll need enough shallow end for both teams. If you don't have that many people, just stagger the players on their respective sides, so that the team is covering enough pool space to hit the ball. The person in the back row on the right serves the ball. It must go over the rope and onto the opposition's side of the pool. The ball should be volleyed back and forth until one team misses. Only the serving team can score. You cannot volley the ball within your own team more than three times, and no player may hit the ball more than once consecutively. Give the game a time limit or play to a certain number of points.

For a twist, play the whole game in the deep end ... you'll never get a better workout than keeping your head above water while trying to hit that ball.

Wet and Wild!

As you can see, there is plenty of fun to be had in the water. Now get really wet and create some waves as you kick, dive, and scavenge for some wild water fun.

Biggest Splash Contest

This game is exactly as the title suggests. The goal is to make the biggest splash! You can play several different ways: Everyone stands in a circle facing each other in the pool. On the count of three, you start to splash. Of course, you'll need a dry person outside the pool to be the judge because you won't be able to open your eyes to figure out who the winner is.

Another way to play is to line up, facing a wall of the pool—grip the edge of the pool and start kicking. Again, you'll need an objective, dry person to judge this game because you won't be able to see what you're doing.

And finally … my favorite way to have the biggest splash contest: Each kid lines up at the diving board, or edge of the pool, and takes turns doing cannonballs. A *cannonball* is the best way to make the biggest splash.

You can also try to the reverse the game by seeing who can make the "smallest splash." The best way to make the smallest splash is to dive in head first—a good way to teach older kids how to dive.

My father used to make the most incredible cannonballs—we used to giggle and giggle when the water in the middle became a huge plume and splashed over the sides of the pool. He could beat anyone in a splash contest!

High Score

Biggest Splash is a great way to teach younger kids how to kick. They'll need to know how to kick in order to become good swimmers.

It's in the Cards

What's a **cannonball?** Jump high into the air off the diving board, and when you're in the air pull your knees up and hold them with your arms. Your body will form a ball and you'll make a tremendous splash when you hit the water.

In the Pool Scavenger Hunt

Buy a bunch of toys that will sink to the bottom of the pool, and toss them into the pool. Do not use anything with sharp or pointy edges. Buy two of each toy in case you want to play the game in teams. Give each team a list and tell them they must retrieve the toys on the list from the bottom of the pool.

High Score

Be sure to buy your kids goggles, and nose- and earplugs if they are going to do a lot of underwater swimming and diving. Goggles will protect their eyes from harsh chemicals like chlorine, the noseplug will give them the freedom to move their hands underwater without having to plug their noses, and earplugs will protect against trapped water. Water in the ear can be uncomfortable and even painful. Kids are prone to ear infections, and water trapped in their ears can cause a lot of grief later on.

Give each team a certain amount of time in which to retrieve the toys. The team that pulls up the most toys in the allotted time is the winner!

Use the shallow end for younger kids and the deep end for adults and older kids.

Everybody, Out of the Pool!

The pool ain't the only place for wet summer magic. Put on your suits and stay poolside. More fun to come!

Water Limbo

This game can be played on the back lawn. What you'll need is a hose with a nozzle that will allow for a straight, steady stream of water. You can either play the game as a limbo game or a hurdle game. Use the steady stream of water as the limbo stick. Kids must maneuver their bodies under the stream of water without getting soaked. The lower the stream is, the harder it is to go under it. The stream will be lowered when every kid makes it under the previous stream.

You cannot crawl on the ground to get past the stream—you have to walk—arching your back as you go! If the ground is too slippery for kids to arch their backs while walking under the stream, let them hunch forward instead—we don't want anyone to get hurt!

If you decide to play the game as a hurdle, you might want to put some padding on the ground because kids could slip when they land on the ground. Try some rubber matting—something that might have a little traction for wet, slippery feet.

Water Gun Wars

Here's a good way to enjoy a hot summer day without a swimming pool. For this game, you might want to invest in some of those supersoaker water guns. They don't have to be the super-powered supersoakers because, again, the idea of water play is safety. But some of the super capacity but low-powered supersoakers are perfect. If you can't get a supersoaker, a regular water pistol will do. To play the game, you can just fire at each other, or you can include a game of Tag in all the squirting!

The player who is "It" gets the water gun and must tag the other players by squirting them with the gun. The person who is tagged first gets to take over the gun and do the squirting.

Try playing this game as Freeze Tag. You must freeze in place when you are squirted by the water pistol. You can be unfrozen by having another player crawl (or swim) between your legs. If "It" manages to freeze everyone, he or she gets to squirt again.

Three Strikes

Please only use the water pistols inside your yard and always make sure they are brightly colored. There are too many horror stories in the news these days about kids and realistic-looking toy guns. Be careful!

You can also play that "It" has the pistol, but only until he or she is tagged by another player. If "It" cannot squirt the player before being tagged, he or she must relinquish the power of the pistol to the person who tagged him or her.

You can also play this game in the pool. It just makes it harder to get out of the way when you're waist-deep in water.

Freeze-Up

Try this game on a really hot summer day in your backyard kiddie pool. Kids will love it, but believe me—if it's hot enough adults will play, too.

Fill the kiddie pool with water and add ice cubes! Have each person try to remove the ice cubes with their feet. You'll be cool before you know it! For a real challenge, have each person remove the ice cubes using only one foot. The person to remove the most ice cubes is the winner. With adults, don't worry about who wins—just think ... "cold!"

The Least You Need to Know

➤ Water games require adult supervision. Remember—safety first!

➤ Don't limit team games to the green. Take them in the pool with Water Basketball and Water Volleyball.

➤ Biggest Splash is a good game for teaching very small children how to kick in the water.

➤ When playing with water guns, be careful to limit the play to your backyard for safety's sake.

Glossary

anagram   A word or phrase created by transposing the letters in another word or phrase. For example, anagrams of *tea* are *eat* and *ate*.

ante   A Poker stake usually put up before the deal to build the pot. Before the cards are dealt, players toss in a minimum amount of change or chips to start the pot. In home games, a nickel is recommended. In the casinos, the ante will be a low-valued chip.

available   Cards are said to be available when they can be moved. In other words, there's nothing blocking them from being moved from one place to another.

Billiards   From the French "billart" referring to the wooden stick used to strike the ball. "Billiard" may also derive from another French word, "bille," meaning "ball." Today, it is any of several games played on a rectangular table where you hit balls against one another into pockets with a stick called a cue.

birdie   The shuttlecock in Badminton; a lightweight, cone-shaped plastic object with a rounded, often rubber-tipped, nose.

board games   Games of strategy—such as Chess, Checkers, Backgammon, or Monopoly—that you play by moving pieces around on a board.

boneyard   The draw pile in a game of Dominoes.

book   Four of a Kind (four cards of matching rank); also the number of tricks a player must win before any trick can have scoring value.

bull's-eye   The center of the dartboard.

call shot   A shot in a Pool game such as Eight Ball that you must call before you take. First, you would pick your shot, then say it aloud so your opponent can hear you: "Five ball in the corner pocket," or whatever the shot is that you're about to make. Bank shots, combination shots, and 8-ball shots are generally call shots.

caller   The main dealer in Baccarat.

cannonball   A way of jumping into a pool. Jump high into the air off the diving board, and when you're in the air pull your knees up and hold them with your arms. Your body will form a ball and you'll make a tremendous splash when you hit the water.

capture   A move made in Checkers where you "jump" your opponent's piece and remove it from the game board, thereby "capturing" the other side's checkers piece by piece.

contract   The required combination of cards a player must obtain before laying down his cards.

crawling   A term used in Pinochle. It means to play a card higher in rank than the highest card played at that point.

croupier   A person in a casino who assists the players at the gaming tables and collects and pays bets.

deck of cards   A set of anywhere from 24 to 78 thin, rectangular, plastic or paper pieces marked on one side to show a suit or placement in the rank of cards, and used to play numerous games. A typical deck contains 52 cards, 13 cards per suit, the suits made up of Clubs, Hearts, Spades, and Diamonds.

dix   The 10 in Pinochle. Dix ("deece") is French for the number 10.

domino effect   A cumulative effect whereby one action can cause a whole series of actions.

doubles   Two people on a team.

doublet   Two thrown dice with the same number of spots on the upper face of the dice.

doubling-down   When you double your bet.

doubter (or **caller**)   The person in a game of chance, such as Liar Dice, who calls the bluff of another player.

enders   In Jump Rope, the two people—one on each end of the rope—who turn the rope.

equipment   The physical resources you need to play your game. For example, you can't play Kickball without the ball and the bases.

fan   A pile of cards fanned out and facing up. Only the top card of the fan will be fully visible—the rest will be partially covered. Fans may be spread out in any direction.

Foosball   This table game originated in Germany. The word "foosball" is actually a derivation of the German word "Fussball" (meaning "football").

footspot   The little white dot on the green cloth of a pool table where you put the apex of the rack.

foundation piles   The piles in Solitaire on which you are building. The goal of most Solitaire games is to move the cards from the tableau to these foundation piles. Often, the foundation piles are empty at the start—you build to them as the play continues.

game   Any activity used for diversion, amusement, and enjoyment.

Grandmaster   An expert Chess player who has consistently scored high in international competition.

group (or **set**)   Three cards of the same rank (such as three 3s).

headstring   The line on the head end of the pool table between the second diamonds of the long rails, passing through the head spot.

high back   A term used in Leap Frog for bending over and holding your ankles and making your position more challenging for the leaper.

hit   When you request a hit in Blackjack, you are asking the dealer to give you another card.

hole card   In Blackjack, the dealer's face-down card.

low back   A term used in Leap Frog for getting down on your knees, tucking your head under, and making yourself as small as possible—a good position to be in for little leapers.

meld   A card or combination of cards in a card game laid face-up on the table and claimed for score.

overtrick (or **sandbagging**)   The difference between what you bid and the tricks you actually take. So if you bid four and you win six tricks, you have two overtricks (or sandbags) and would therefore score 42 points.

palming   Using your hand to stop the puck in Air Hockey. Palming will result in forfeiture of the puck.

parlor game   A game that is meant to be played indoors.

pips   The official word for the "spots" on the dice.

poker face   Refers to keeping a straight face no matter what cards you hold in your hand. You don't want to tip off your opponents to either a good hand or a bad hand.

referee   Someone chosen as the official having final authority in administering a game. The ref makes the call when an action is questioned.

rules   A prescribed guide for conduct, telling you how to proceed with your next course of action.

sequence (or **run**)   Three cards of the same suit in sequence (such as Ace, 2, 3 of Spades).

set   To be set means to fail to make your bid on the meld (in Pinochle). Your entire bid is subtracted from your total score and you score none of your points in that hand.

singles   One person per team.

sisal   A strong and durable white fiber, often used to make professional dartboards.

snooker   A word that refers to the position of the cue ball in an "impossible" shot. For example, if it's your turn and you need to pocket the pink ball, but your cue ball is in a position on the table that makes that shot virtually impossible—you are said to be "snookered."

Solitaire   Any of a number of card games that are played by one person, alone.

spike   To hit the ball sharply downward with your fist or palm with a very hard blow so it goes over the volleyball net and into your opponent's court.

split   A strategy in Blackjack where you turn your two cards face-up side-by-side and play two hands. The dealer will deal to the hand on your right first—until you stand or bust—and then the dealer will play to your other hand.

spread   Another word for melding cards.

squidger   A piece in Tiddlywinks used to press down on smaller pieces in an attempt to propel the smaller pieces forward.

stake   A prize you can win in a contest.

stock pile   The pile of cards from which you deal. Sometimes you draw three cards from the stock pile, sometimes two cards, and in yet other games, you draw one card. It all depends on what rules you decide to set for a particular game.

tableau   Your working cards in Solitaire. You build and maneuver cards on your tableau in order to eventually move them to your foundation piles.

topping   Placing your mallet on top of the puck in Air Hockey. Topping is considered an offense resulting in forfeiture of the puck.

trick   In card games, a trick is the group of cards collected in a round of a game that are used as a scoring method. In games such as Hearts and Spades you take tricks by playing a card that beats all other cards in a particular hand, thereby "winning" that hand.

trump   A card of a suit that will beat any card of another suit that is not a trump suit, regardless of hierarchy.

visit   A visit to the pool table consists of a shot, or a series of shots, that comprise a player's turn at the table. The visit lasts until a player fails to pot a ball—or until he or she fouls or the frame ends (all the balls, except the cue ball, are potted).

war A term used in the children's card game of War, which means to break a tie. When two cards of the same rank are played, you break the tie by playing new cards. The player with the highest-ranking new card wins the tie-breaker and all the played cards.

waste pile The pile of cards that you cannot draw from to build either on your foundation or on your tableau in Solitaire.

Resources

Books

Bayone, Jeff and Amanda Beesley. *It's Bridge, Baby: How to Be a Player in Ten Easy Lessons*. New York: Riverhead Books, 1998.

Bell, R.C. *The Boardgame Book*. London: Marshal Cavendish Ltd., 1979.

Brown, Douglas. *The Key to Solitaire*. Brooklyn, NY: New Imperial Book, 1966.

Frey, Richard L. *According to Hoyle*. New York: Fawcett-Columbine, 1956.

Kantar, Edwin B. *Introduction to Declarer's Play*. Wilshire Book Co., 1990.

Kelly, Bill. *Gamblers of the Old West*. Canyon Lake, CA: B & F Enterprises, Inc., 1996.

Klutz Press, ed. *The Book of Classic Board Games*. Palo Alto, CA: Klutz Press, 1990.

Lagoon Books, ed. *After Dinner Games*. UK: Lagoon Books, 1996.

Medley, H. Anthony. *The Complete Idiot's Guide to Bridge*. New York: Alpha Books, 1997.

Morehead, Albert and Geoffrey Mott-Smith. *The Complete Book of Patience*. Faber & Faber, 1950.

Parlett, David. *Solitaire: "Aces Up" and 399 Other Card Games*. New York: Pantheon, 1979.

Petricic, Dusan and Camilla Gryski. *Let's Play: Traditional Games of Childhood*. Toronto: Kid's Can Press, Ltd., 1995.

Rice, Wayne and Mike Yaconelli. *Play It! Great Games for Groups*. Grand Rapids, MI: Zondervan Publishing House, 1986.

Root, William S. and Patricia L. Magnus. *The ABCs of Bridge*. Three Rivers Press, 1998.

Truscott, Alan. *Basic Bridge in Three Weeks: The Beginner's 21-Day Guide to Bridge Mastery.* New York: Perigee Books, 1997.

Wall, Jeanette Ryan. *More Games and Giggles.* Middleton, WI: Pleasant Co. Publishing, 1998.

Web Sites of Note

Good site for Bridge information:

    downtown.ala.net/~beckyy/books.html

Spades information:

    members.nbci.com/_XMCM/niferbee/frames/Cards/spades.htm

Information on casino games:

    casino-gaming.com/games-blackjack-rules-strategy.htm)

About.com is a good source for almost any game: Check out the sites for kids' games, especially. Go to About.com and look under the Games heading for all types of games:

    kidsportsrec.about.com

Backgammon, Dominoes, Billiards, Chess, Cribbage—a good source for traditional games:

    web.ukonline.co.uk/james.masters/TraditionalGames/html

You can find anything here! Britannica has extensive information on the history of games and some good rule guidelines. Just type in the name of the game in the search area and a lot of great information will come up:

    www.britannica.com

Another about.com site:

    www.casinogambling.about.com

The Chess Archives at http://chess.liveonthenet.com/chess/ is a resource for players of all skill levels. Beginners can browse a variety of information designed to rapidly improve playing skills. The site offers plain talk and simple explanations of key concepts. Coaches, parents, and tutors can find basic information about starting the new player in the right direction with links to other valuable resources. The beginning chess player is well advised to start at the Chess Archives. The Chess Archives supports advanced players with an endgame server, opening database, diagram creator, best-game analysis, history pages, graphics library, and tactics exercises. The Chess Archives rounds out its content with humorous Chess Pie and correspondence card pages:

chess.liveonthenet.com/chess/

Tiddlywinks! Need we say more?

www.cpcug.org/user/rwtucker/tiddlywinks.html

Good information on all things Frisbee:

www.cs.rochester.edu/u/ferguson/ultimate/ultimate-simple.html

All you need to know about darts:

dartgames.homepage.com

Horseshoe fun:

www.ece.neu.edu/personal/stricker/horseshoes/horseshoe_rules.html

Like the Britannica site, this is a good site for general information on games:

www.encarta.msn.com

Generic game site:

www.familygamenight.com

Generic game site:

www.familyplay.com

Check out the Game Play:

www.fortunecity.com

For Pinochle information:

www.geocities.com/TimesSquare/2767/pinochle.html

Gambling and casino games:

www.gamblingtimes.com

General information on kids' games:

www.gameskidsplay.net

For your favorite old game show!

www.matchgamepm.com

Card game rules:

www.pagat.com/alpha.html

Card games and more. Spades, especially:

www.playsite.com/games/card/spades/history.html

Poker fun:

www.pokerpages.com

Courtside! Badminton stuff:

www.sportcraft.com/badmintoncourt.html

For information on the history of Sack Races:

www.tetbury.com/info/history.htm

Backgammon madness:

www.ukonline.co.uk/james.masters/Traditional Games/Backgammon

Bridge history and facts:

wl.iglou.com/baronbarclay/HISTORY.html

Of course, your best resource is always your own imagination. Be creative and have some family fun!

Index

A

Aces Around, Pinochle, 209
acting, Charades, 259
Air Hockey, 36, 102-106
  drifting, 106
  footing, 104
  goals, 105
  palming, 103
  playing surface, 105
  pucks, 104
  rules, 102-103
  shots, 106
  topping, 104
Alleys, Marbles, 283
Alphabetical Camping Trip, 227
Anagrams, 247-248
Annie's Room, Darts, 76
antes, Poker, 200
Anthony and Cleopatra, reference to Billiards, 90
arrows, Darts, 76
availability, Solitaire, 144

B

baby ton, Darts, 76
Baccarat, 168-170
  callers, 169
  card combinations, 170
  hand values, 170
  payouts, 170
  rules, 169-170
  word derivative, 169
Backgammon, 55-60
  bearing off, 58-60
  blots, 58-59
closed boards, 58-59
crooked dice, 58
doublets, 57
doubling, 58, 60
equipment, 56-57
gammon, 58
history of, 56
objective, 56
points, 58
primes, 58-59
rules, 58-60
scoring, 59
setting up, 57-58
terms, 58-60
Badminton, 278-280
  birdies, 278
  courts, 278-279
  doubles, 279
  equipment, 278
  out of bounds, 280
  pronunciation, 278
  scoring, 279
  serving, 279
  singles, 279
bag o' nuts, Darts, 76
Baker, Elwood, Rummy, 176
ball-jumping, Billiards, 94
ballgames, 267
  Croquet, 273-275
  Kickball, 267-269
  Touch Football, 272-273
  Volleyball, 269-272
    equipment, 269
    rules, 270
    scoring, 271-272
    serving, 270-271
    spikes, 270
barrels, Darts, 76
basements, Darts, 76
bearing off, Backgammon, 58-60
betting, Poker, 199-201
bidding
  Bridge, 188-190
  Double-Deck Pinochle, 214
  Spades, 119-120
Biggest Splash contests, 303
Billiards, 36, 87. *See also* Pool
  ball-jumping, 94
  breaking, 91-92
  call shots, 93
  current state, 89
  fouls, 94
  games
    Eight Ball, 92-95
    Nine Ball, 95-97
    Snooker, 97-99
  headstrings, 91
  history of, 87-88
  illegal pocketing, 95
  lagging for the break, 92
  plays, 92
  Pocket Billiards, 91
  pool tables, 90
  racking, 91-92
  rules, 90-91
  scratches, 92
  shooting, 94
  visits, 92
birdies, Badminton, 278
birthday party games, 229-230, 241-246
  equipment, 231-232
  indoor/outdoor games, 236-238

little children, 238-239
outdoor games, 233-235
  Red Light/Green
    Light, 235
  Red Rover, 233-235
  What's the Time,
    Mr. Wolf?, 235
rhyming games, 230-232
  Eenie, Meenie,
    Meinie, Moe, 233
  Engine Engine, 232
  Icka Bicka, 233
  One Potato, 232
Bishops, Chess, 46
black ball (Snooker), 97
Blackjack, 163-168
  dealer's hand, 166
  doubling-down, 167-168
  history of, 164
  hits, requesting, 165
  hitting, 166
  hole cards, 165
  insurance, 166-167
  rules, 164-165
  scoring, 166
  splitting, 167-168
  standing, 166
  strategy, 168
blanks, Dominoes, 69
Blind Nil bids, Spades, 120
block games, Dominoes,
  70, 72
blots, Backgammon, 58-59
blue ball (Snooker), 97
Bluebells, Jump Rope, 286
board games, 34
boards, Checkers, 52
boneyards, Dominoes, 68
books, suggested reading.
  313-314
books (cards)
  Bridge, 189
  Go Fish, 160
breakfast, Darts, 76
Bridge, 185-193
  bidding, 188-190
  doubles, 190

history of, 186-187
popularity, 188
redoubles, 190
rubber, 192
rules, 187-188
scoring, 191-192
strategy, 190
tricks, 188-189
British Bulldog Tag, 293
brown balls (Snooker), 97
buckets of nails, Darts, 76
buckshot, Darts, 76
bull's-eyes, Darts, 80
busting, Darts, 76

C

"C," Darts, 76
Calculation, 147
call shots, billiards, 93
callers
  Baccarat, 169
  Liar Dice, 68
calling, Poker, 200
Camping Trip, 226-227
cannonballs, 303
Capture the Flag, 293-294
capturing, Checkers, 52
card combinations,
  Baccarat, 170
card games, 37-38
  Bridge, 185-193
    bidding, 188-190
    books, 189
    doubles, 190
    history of, 187
    popularity, 188
    redoubles, 190
    rubber, 192
    rules, 187-188
    scoring, 191-192
    strategy, 190
    tricks, 188-189
  casino games
    Baccarat, 168-170
    Blackjack, 163-168

children
  Concentration,
    155-156
  Go Fish, 160-161
  Old Maid, 154-155
  Spit, 156-160
  War, 152-153
Crazy Eights, 123-124
  changing suits, 124
  drawing cards, 124
  reversing, 124
  rules, 123
  scoring, 123-124
  skipping, 124
Cribbage, 127-132
  cribbage board, 128
  revealing cards,
    131-132
  rules, 128-129
  scoring, 129-130
fans, 142
Hearts, 115-119
  bonus points, 119
  Hearts (suits), 118
  passing cards, 116
  rules, 116
  scoring, 116
  tricks, 116-118
Knockout Whist, 121
  dealing, 121-122
  knockouts, 122
Pinochle, 207
  Basic Pinochle, 208
  Double-Deck
    Pinochle, 213-214
  popularity, 208
  Three-Handed
    Pinochle, 213
  Two-Handed
    Pinochle, 208-213
Poker, 195-205
  betting, 199-201
  card rankings,
    198-199
  Draw Poker, 202-204
  history of, 195-197
  Straight Poker,
    197-201
  Stud Poker, 204-205

Rook, 132-135
  rules, 133-135
  scoring, 132-133, 135
Rummy, 175-176
  Basic Rummy,
    176-178
  Contract Rummy,
    182-184
  Gin Rummy, 178-180
  Knock Rummy,
    180-181
  melds, 176
  Rummy 500, 181-182
Skip-Bo, 135-137
  draw piles, 136
  rules, 136
  scoring, 137
Solitaire, 141-143
  Calculation, 147
  Clocks, 143-144
  Double Solitaire,
    141-142, 149-150
  Forty Thieves, 145
  Golf, 144
  Pyramid, 145-147
  Russian, 147-149
Spades, 119-121
  bidding, 119-120
  dealing, 119
  scoring, 121
  tricks, 120
Tripoley, 137-140
trump card games, 116
UNO, 123
cards, decks, 6, 37
casino games
  Baccarat, 168-170
    card combinations,
      170
    hand values, 170
    payouts, 170
    rules, 169-170
  Blackjack, 163-168
    dealer's hand, 166
    doubling-down,
      167-168
    hitting, 166
    insurance, 166-167

    rules, 164-165
    scoring, 166
    splitting, 167-168
    standing, 166
    strategy, 168
  Poker, 195-205
    betting, 199-201
    card rankings,
      198-199
    Draw Poker, 202-204
    history of, 195-197
    Straight Poker,
      197-201
    Stud Poker, 204-205
Castling, Chess, 48
Cat's Eyes, Marbles, 283
Chamberlain, Neville,
  Snooker, 36
Champ, 16
Champions, Chess, 44-45
Charades, 256
  acting, 259
  equipment, 256-257
  hand signals, 258
  history of, 257
  rules, 257-258
  scoring, 259
  versions, 259
Chase the Fox, Jump Rope,
  286
Chaturanga, 5, 44
cheat seats, rules, 18-19
check, Chess, 49
Checkers, 51-54
  boards, 52
  capturing, 52
  crowning, 53
  history of, 51
  huff or blow, 53
  moves, 52
  pieces, 52
  rules, 54
  setting up, 52
  winning, 54
checking, Poker, 202
checkmate, Chess, 49
Chess, 5, 44-51
  antique sets, 47
  Bishops, 46

Castling, 48
champions, 44-45
Chaturanga, 44
check, 49
checkmate, 49
computer games, 47
Deep Blue (IBM com-
  puter chip), 44
education, 45
en passant, 48
Fischer, Bobby, 45
Grandmasters, 44
history of, 5, 44
Kasparov, Garry, 44
King, 45
Knights, 46
moves, 48-50
notation, 50-51
Pawns, 46
pieces, 45-46
Queen, 46
Rooks, 46
rules, 48-50
sets, 47
setting up, 46-47
Spassky, Boris, 45
stalemates, 49
Staunton, Howard, 44
tournament rules, 48-50
children
  age group considera-
    tions, 25-26
  ballgames, 267
    Croquet, 273-275
    Kickball, 267-269
    Touch Football,
      272-273
    Volleyball, 269-272
  card games
    Concentration,
      155-156
    Go Fish, 160-161
    Old Maid, 154-155
    Spit, 156-160
    War, 152-153
  elementary school chil-
    dren
      games, 13-14

319

engaging, 25
outdoor games, 277-278
    Badminton, 278-280
    Hopscotch, 280-282
    Jump Rope, 285-288
    Marbles, 282-285
    picnic games, 289-298
    swimming pool
        games, 299-305
party games, 229-230,
    241-246
    equipment, 231-232
    indoor/outdoor
        games, 236-238
    little children,
        238-239
    outdoor games,
        233-235
    rhyming games,
        230-232
preschool children,
    games, 11
spending time with,
    23-24
teaching, 24-25
team games, 255
    Charades, 256
    Hide and Seek,
        261-262
    Sardines, 262-263
    Up Jenkins, 260-261
teams, picking, 233
teenagers, games, 14
travel games, 221-223
    Camping Trip,
        226-227
    equipment, 221-222
    I Spy, 223-224
    License Plate Bingo,
        224-225
    purse game, 228
    thumb wrestling,
        227-228
    What If, 225-226
    Who Am I?, 227
word games, 247
    Anagrams, 247-248
    Hangman, 249-250

Match Game, 250-251
Quick on the Draw,
    252-253
Sentence by Sentence,
    252
Word Bluff, 248-249
chuckers, Darts, 76
circle it, Darts, 76
cleaning up, 29-30
Clocks, 143-144
clocks, Darts, 76
coloring books, storing,
    223
closed boards,
    Backgammon, 58-59
combination shots, Eight
    Ball, 95
computer games, 24
    Chess, 47
Concentration, 155-156
Contract Rummy, 182-184
contracts, Contract
    Rummy, 182
corks, Darts, 76
courts, Badminton,
    278-279
crawling, Pinochle, 215
crayons, storing, 223
Crazy Eights, 123-124
    changing suits, 124
    drawing cards, 124
    reversing, 124
    rules, 123
    scoring, 123-124
    skipping, 124
Cribbage, 127-132
    cribbage board, 128
    flushes, 131
    history of, 128
    One for His Nob, 132
    revealing cards, 131-132
    rules, 128-129
    runs, 130-131
    scoring, 129-130
    start cards, 132
cribbage boards, 128
Cricket (Darts), 84-85
crooked dice, Backgam-
    mon, 58

Croquet, 273-275
crowning, Checkers, 53
dartboards, 78, 80
    bull's-eyes, 80
    hanging, 80
    playing area, 79
    proper surroundings, 79
    scoreboards, 79
    throw lines, 80

D

Darts, 35
    Annie's Room, 76
    arrows, 76
    baby ton, 76
    bag o' nuts, 76
    barrels, 76
    basements, 76
    breakfast, 76
    bucket of nails, 76
    buckshot, 76
    bull's-eyes, 80
    busting, 76
    "C," 76
    chuckers, 76
    circle it, 76
    clocks, 76
    corks, 76
    Cricket, 84-85
    dartboards, 78, 80
        hanging, 80
        playing area, 79
        proper surroundings,
            79
    diddle for middle, 77
    double in, 77
    double out, 77
    double top, 77
    double trouble, 77
    doubles, 77
    downstairs, 77
    easy in, 77
    environment, 79
    feathers, 77
    half-a-crown, 77
    hat trick, 77

history of, 75
Huff and Blow version, 85
islands, 77
legs, 77
mad houses, 77
mongers, 77
mugs away, 77
Murphys, 77
popcorn, 78
right church, wrong pew, 78
Robin Hood, 78
rules, 80-81
scoreboards, 79
shafts, 78
Shanghai, 78
shut out, 78
skunks, 78
slop, 78
spiders, 78
splashes, 78
straight in, 78
terminology, 76-78
three in a bed, 78
throw lines, 77, 80
tons, 78
triples, 78
upstairs, 78
wires, 78
x01, 81-84
X's, 78
Dawson, Richard, *Match Game*, 251
dealer's hand, Blackjack, 166
dealing
    Knockout Whist, 121-122
    Spades, 119
    Two-Handed Pinochle, 208-209
decks of playing cards, 6
declaring out, Two-Handed Pinochle, 213
Deep Blue (IBM computer chip), Chess, 44

Dice games, 34-35
    history of, 66
    Horses, 68
    Liar Dice, 68
    Poker Dice, 67-68
    Yahtzee, 66-67
Dictionary. *See* Word Bluff
diddle for middle, Darts, 77
disputes, rules, settling, 20
Dix, Pinochle, 209
domino effect, 73-74
Dominoes, 35, 68-74
    blanks, 69
    block games, 70, 72
    boneyards, 68
    building, 73-74
    domino effect, 73-74
    double nines, 70
    double sixes, 70
    double twelves, 70
    doubles, 69
    draw games, 70
    draw piles, 70
    drawing, 70
    heavier, 70
    history of, 69
    lighter, 70
    match games, 70
    plays, 71
    point games, 70
    rules, 71-72
    setting up, 71-72
    shuffling, 70
    tiles, 69
Double Dutch, Jump Rope, 287-288
double in, Darts, 77
double nines, Dominoes, 70
double out, Darts, 77
Double Pinochle, 209
double sixes, Dominoes, 70
Double Solitaire, 141-142, 149-150
double top, Darts, 77
double trouble, Darts, 77

double twelves, Dominoes, 70
Double-Deck Pinochle, 213-215
    bidding, 214
    melding, 214
    scoring, 215-217
    trumps, 214
doubles
    Badminton, 279
    Bridge, 190
    Darts, 77
doubles, Dominoes, 69
doublets, Backgammon, 57
doubling, Backgammon, 58, 60
doubling-down, Blackjack, 167-168
doubters, Liar Dice, 68
downstairs, Darts, 77
draw games, Dominoes, 70
draw piles, Dominoes, 70
draw piles, Skip-Bo, 136
Draw Poker, 202-204
drawing, Dominoes, 70
drawing cards, Crazy Eights, 124
drifting, Air Hockey, 106
Duck Duck Goose, 238
easy in, Darts, 77

E

Eenie, Meenie, Meinie, Moe, 233
Eight Ball (Billiards), 92-95
    ball-jumping, 94
    call shots, 93
    combination shots, 95
    fouls, 94
    illegal pocketing, 95
    losing, 95
    rules, 93-94
    scoring, 95
    shooting, 94
    solids, 94
    stripes, 94

Eisenhower, Dwight D., Bridge, 186
elementary school children, games, 13-14
en passant, Chess, 48
enders, Jump Rope, 285
Engine Engine (rhyming game), 232
English deck of cards, 37
English Tiddlywinks Association, 62
equipment
  Backgammon, 56-57
  Badminton, 278
  Charades, 256-257
  children's party games, 231-232
  outdoor games, 38
  Ping-Pong, 109
  travel games, 221-222
everywhere games, 39-40

F

family time, finding time for, 7-8
fans, cards, 142
feathers, Darts, 77
Fischer, Bobby, 45
Five-Card Stud Poker, 204-205
Flushes
  Cribbage, 131
  Poker, 199
folding, Poker, 201
Follow the Leader, 243
Foosball, 36, 106-108
  history of, 106
  rod spinning, 108
  rules, 107-108
  tables, 107
footing, Air Hockey, 104
footspots, pool tables, 90
Forty Thieves, 145
fouls, Billiards, 94
foundation piles, Solitaire, 143

Four of a Kind, Poker, 198
Franscioni, Warren, Frisbee, 295
Freeze Tag, 292
Frisbee
  history of, 295
  Ultimate Frisbee, 296-297
Full House, Poker, 198
gambling games
  Baccarat, 168-170
    card combinations, 170
    hand values, 170
    payouts, 170
    rules, 169-170
  Blackjack, 163-168
    dealer's hand, 166
    doubling-down, 167-168
    hitting, 166
    insurance, 166-167
    rules, 164-165
    scoring, 166
    splitting, 167-168
    standing, 166
    strategy, 168
  Poker, 195-205
    betting, 199-201
    card rankings, 198-199
    Draw Poker, 202-204
    history of, 195-197
    Straight Poker, 197-201
    Stud Poker, 204-205

G

games, 4
  appeal, 9
  board games, 34
  card games, 37-38
  categorizing, 12-13
  choosing, 8-9, 28-29
  cleaning up, assignments, 29-30

  elementary school children, 13-14
  equipment, 10
  everywhere games, 39-40
  finding time for, 7-8
  history of, 4-5, 7
  manufactured games, 5
  outdoor games, 10, 26-27, 38-39
  parlor games, 33-34
    Billiards, 36
    Board games, 34
    Darts, 35
    Dice games, 34-35
    Dominoes, 35
    table games, 36-37
  playing, starting, 7
  preschool children, 11
  quiet time, 30-31
  reasons to play, 4
  rules, 15
    cheat seats, 18-19
    discussing, 20-21
    disputes, 20
    enforcing, 17-18
    fairness, 18
    setting, 16-17
  setting up, 30
  table games, 43
  team play, 11
  teams, 27-28
  teenagers, 14
  travel games, 39-40
  winning, proper behavior, 19
gammon, Backgammon, 58
geographic games, 5
Gibb, James, Ping-Pong, 108
giggle games, children, 241-246
Gin Rummy, 178-180
  drawing cards, 179
  knocking, 179-180
  rules, 179
  scoring, 180
  strategy, 180

Go Fish, 160-161
goals, Air Hockey, 105
Golf (Solitaire), 144
Grandmasters, Chess, 44
Grapevine (children's game), 239
green balls (Snooker), 97
Green, Jonathan H., Poker, 19
groups, Rummy, 177

H

half-a-crown, Darts, 77
hand signals, Charades, 258
hand values, Baccarat, 170
hanging dartboards, 80
Hangman, 249-250
hat trick, Darts, 77
headstrings, Billiards, 91
Hearts, 115-119
    bonus points, 119
    Hearts (suit), 118
    passing cards, 116
    Queen of Spades, 118
    rules, 116
    scoring, 116
    tricks, 116-118
    trumps, 116
heavier, Dominoes, 70
Hickok, Bill, deadman's hand, 196
Hide and Seek, 261-262
high back, Leap Frog, 295
High Bid, 26
High Card, Poker, 199
High Water, Jump Rope, 286
hitting, Blackjack, 166
hole cards, Blackjack, 165
Holliday, Doc, 21
Honey, Do You Love Me?, 243-244
Hopscotch, 280-282
Horses, 68

Horseshoes, 297-298
Hot Potato, 237
Huff and Blow, Darts, 85
huff or blow, Checkers, 53

I–J

I Spy, 223-224
Icka Bicka (rhyming game), 233
illegal pocketing, Eight Ball, 95
insurance, Blackjack, 166-167
islands, Darts, 77

Jacks Around, Pinochle, 209
Jump Rope, 285-288
    enders, 285

K

Kasparov, Garry, 44
Kickball, 267-269
King, Chess, 45
King of the Castle, 4
Kings Around, Pinochle, 209
Knights, Chess, 46
Knock Rummy, 180-181
Knocking, Gin Rummy, 179-180
Knockout Whist, 121
    dealing, 121-122
    knockouts, 122
knockouts, Knockout Whist, 122

L

lagging for the break, 92
Leap Frog, 294-295
legs, Darts, 77
Liar Dice, 68

License Plate Bingo, 224-225
lighter, Dominoes, 70
Limbo (Water), 304
losing Eight Ball, 95
low back, Leap Frog, 295

M

mad houses, Darts, 77
manufactured games, 5
    Concentration, 155
    Go Fish, 161
    Old Maid, 161
    Rook, 132-135
    sales of, 29
    Skip-Bo, 135-137
    Tripoley, 137-140
    UNO, 123
Marbles, 282-285
    Alleys, 283
    Cat's Eyes, 283
    history of, 12, 283
    Marrididdles, 283
    Ring Game, 284-285
    safety considerations, 284
    shooting, 284-285
    Taws, 283
Marco Polo, 300
Marriages, Pinochle, 209
Marrididdles, Marbles, 283
Masterpiece, 26
Match Game, 250-251
Match Game, 251
match games, Dominoes, 70
mats, Tiddlywinks, 62
Maugham, Somerset, Bridge, 185
Melding, Double-Deck Pinochle, 214
melds
    Rummy, 176
    Two-Handed Pinochle, 209

Mennonites, Rook, poular-
ity of, 133
mongers, Darts, 77
Morgan, William G.,
Volleyball, 271
Morrison, Walter, Frisbee,
295
Mother May I?, 236
moves
Checkers, 52
Chess, 48-50
mugs away, Darts, 77
Murphys, Darts, 77
Musical Chairs, 236
Mustard and Vinegar,
Jump Rope, 286

N–O

Names of … (children's
game), 241
Never Ending Words, 244
NHPA (National Horseshoe
Pitchers Association of
America), 297
nil bids, Spades, 120
Nine Ball (Billiards), 95-97
Notation, Chess, 50-51

Octopus Tag, 300-301
off-goal shots, Air Hockey,
106
Old Maid, 154-155
One for His Nob, Cribbage,
132
One Potato, 232
out of bounds, Badminton,
280
outdoor games, 10, 26-27,
38-39, 277-278
Badminton, 278-280
birdies, 278
courts, 278-279
doubles, 279
equipment, 278
out of bounds, 280

scoring, 279
serving, 279
singles, 279
ballgames, 267
Croquet, 273-275
Kickball, 267-269
Touch Football,
272-273
Volleyball, 269-272
children
Hopscotch, 280-282
Jump Rope, 285-288
Marbles, 282-285
picnic games
Tag games, 292-293
swimming pool
games, 299-305
equipment, 38
party games
children, 233-238
little children,
238-239
picnic games, 289-298
Capture the Flag,
293-294
Frisbee games,
295-297
Horseshoes, 297-298
Leap Frog, 294-295
races, 290-291
Tug of War, 289-290
swimming pool games,
39, 299-305
Biggest Splash con-
tests, 303
scavenger hunts,
303-304
team games, 301-302
water gun wars, 305
Water Limbo, 304
Water Tag, 299-301
Over the Stars, Jump Rope,
286
overtricking, Spades, 121

P

Pairs, Poker, 199
Palming, Air Hockey, 103
ParentCenter.com, thumb
wrestling, 227
parlor games, 33-34
Billiards, 36, 87
board games, 34
Darts, 35, 75
Dice games, 34-35
Dominoes, 35
table games, 36-37
party games, children's,
229-230, 241-246
equipment, 231-232
indoor/outdoor games,
236-238
little children, 238-239
outdoor games, 233-235
rhyming games, 230-232
passing cards, Hearts, 116
Pawns, Chess, 46
payouts, Baccarat, 170
Pepper, Jump Rope, 286
Pick-Up Sticks, 60-61
picnic games, 289-298
Capture the Flag,
293-294
Frisbee games, 295-297
Horseshoes, 297-298
Leap Frog, 294-295
races, 290-291
Tag games, 292-293
Tug of War, 289-290
pieces
Backgammon, 56-57
Checkers, 52
Chess, 45-46
Tiddlywinks, 62
Ping-Pong, 108-111
equipment, 109
history of, 108
points, 110
returns, 110
serves, 109

pink balls (Snooker), 97
Pinochle, 207-217
    Aces Around, 209
    Basic Pinochle, 208
    crawling, 215
    Dix, 209
    Double-Deck Pinochle,
       213-215
        bidding, 214
        melding, 214
        scoring, 215-217
        trumps, 214
    Jacks Around, 209
    Kings Around, 209
    Marriages, 209
    Pinochle, 209
    popularity, 208
    Queens Around, 209
    Royal Marriages, 209
    runs, 209
    sets, 215
    Three-Handed Pinochle,
       213
    Two-Handed Pinochle,
       208-213
        card values, 212
        dealing, 208-209
        declaring out, 213
        melds, 209
        rules, 210-212
        scoring, 209
        tricks, 209-212
Pinochle, Double Pinochle,
   209
playing area, dartboards,
   79
playing cards. *See* cards,
   decks
playing surface, Air
   Hockey, 105
plays
    Billiards, 92
    Dominoes, 71
Pocket Billiards, 91
point games, Dominoes, 70
points
    Backgammon, 58
    Ping-Pong, 110

Poker, 195-205
    antes, 200
    betting, 199-201
    Blackjack, 163-168
        dealer's hand, 166
        doubling-down,
           167-168
        hitting, 166
        insurance, 166-167
        rules, 164-165
        scoring, 166
        splitting, 167-168
        standing, 166
        strategy, 168
    calling, 200
    card rankings, 198-199
    checking, 202
    Draw Poker, 202-204
    folding, 201
    Green, Jonathan H., 19
    history of, 195-197
    Holliday, Doc, 21
    raising, 200
    Straight Poker, 197-201
    Stud Poker, 204-205
Poker Dice, 67-68
Poker face, 197
Polo, Marco, 300
pool. *See also* Billiards
    ball-jumping, 94
    breaking, 91-92
    call shots, 93
    footspots, 90
    fouls, 94
    games
        Eight Ball, 92-95
        Nine Ball, 95-97
        Snooker, 97-99
    headstrings, 91
    illegal pocketing, 95
    lagging for the break, 92
    plays, 92
    Pocket Pool, 91
    pool tables, 90, 92
    racking, 91-92
    rules, 90-91
    scratches, 92
    shooting, 94

pool tables, 90
    footspots, 90
    visits, 92
popcorn, Darts, 78
popularity
    Bridge, 188
    manufactured games, 29
Potato on a Spoon races,
   291
pots, Tiddlywinks, 62
preparation, games, 30
preschool children, games,
   11
primes, Backgammon,
   58-59
pucks, Air Hockey, 104
Purse Game, 228
Pyramid Solitaire, 145-147

Q–R

Queen, Chess, 46
Queen of Spades, in
   Hearts, 118
Queens Around, Pinochle,
   209
Quick on the Draw,
   252-253
quiet time, 30-31

races, 290-291
racking, Pool, 91-92
raising, Poker, 200
rankings, card combina-
   tions, Poker, 198-199
Rayburn, Gene, *Match
   Game*, 251
red balls (Snooker), 97
Red Light/Green Light, 235
Red Rover, 233-235
redoubles, Bridge, 190
referees, 17
Reilly, Charles Nelson,
   Match Game, 251
resources
    books, 313-314
    Web sites, 314-316

returns, Ping-Pong, 110
rhyming games, 230-232
    Eenie, Meenie, Meinie,
        Moe, 233
    Engine Engine, 232
    Icka Bicka, 233
    One Potato, 232
right church, wrong pew
    (Darts), 78
Ring Game, Marbles,
    284-285
road trip games, 221-223
    Camping Trip, 226-227
    equipment, 221-222
    I Spy, 223-224
    License Plate Bingo,
        224-225
    Purse Game, 228
    thumb wrestling,
        227-228
    What If, 225-226
    Who Am I?, 227
Robin Hood, Darts, 78
Rocking the Cradle, Jump
    Rope, 286
rod spinning, Foosball, 108
Rook, 132-135
    history of, 132
    Mennonites, popularity
        of, 133
    rules, 133-135
    scoring, 132-133, 135
Rooks, Chess, 46
Royal Marriages, Pinochle,
    209
rubber
    Bridge, 192
    invention of, 8
rules, 15
    Air Hockey, 102-103
    Baccarat, 169-170
    Backgammon, 58-60
    Billiards, 90-91
    Bridge, 187-188
    Charades, 257-258
    cheat sheets, 18-19
    Checkers, 54
    Chess, 48-50

Crazy Eights, 123
Cribbage, 128-129
Darts, 80-81
discussing, 20-21
disputes, settling, 20
Dominoes, 71-72
Eight Ball (Billiards),
    93-94
enforcing, 17-18
fairness, 18
Foosball, 107-108
Gin Rummy, 179
Hearts, 116
Rook, 133-135
Rummy, 177-178
setting, 16-17
Skip-Bo, 136
Tiddlywinks, 63-64
Two-Handed Pinochle,
    210-212
Volleyball, 270
Yahtzee, 66-67
Rummy, 175-176
    Baker, Elwood, 176
    Basic Rummy, 176-178
        rules, 177-178
        scoring, 178
    Contract Rummy,
        182-184
    Gin Rummy, 178-180
        drawing cards, 179
        knocking, 179-180
        rules, 179
        scoring, 180
        strategy, 180
    groups, 177
    Knock Rummy, 180-181
    melds, 176
    Rummy 500, 181-182
    sequences, 177
Rummy 500, 181-182
runs
    Cribbage, 131
    Pinochle, 209
Russell, Nipsy, *Match
    Game*, 251
Russian Solitaire, 147-149

S

sack races, 291
sales, manufactured games,
    29
Salt, Jump Rope, 286
sandbagging, Spades, 121
Sardines, 262-263
Sausage (children's game),
    244
scavenger hunts (water),
    303-304
schools, Chess, 45
scoreboards, Darts, 79
scorecards, Yahtzee, 67
scoring
    Air Hockey, 105
    Backgammon, 59
    Badminton, 279
    Blackjack, 166
    Bridge, 191-192
    Charades, 259
    Crazy Eights, 123-124
    Cribbage, 129-130
    Double-Deck Pinochle,
        215-217
    Eight Ball, 95
    Gin Rummy, 180
    Hearts, 116
    Knock Rummy, 181
    Rook, 132-135
    Rummy, 178
    Skip-Bo, 137
    Spades, 121
    Two-Handed Pinochle,
        209, 212
    Volleyball, 271-272
scratches, Billiards, 92
Sentence by Sentence, 252
sequences, Rummy, 177
serving
    Badminton, 279
    Ping-Pong, 109
    Volleyball, 270-271
sets, Pinochle, 215
setting up
    Backgammon, 57-58
    Checkers, 52

Dominoes, 71-72
games, 30
Seven-Card Stud Poker,
204-205
Shadow Tag, 292
shafts, Darts, 78
Shakespeare, William,
Billiards, 90
Shanghai, Darts, 78
Sharif, Omar, Bridge, 185
shooting
Billiards, 94
Marbles, 284-285
shots, Air Hockey, 106
shuffling dominoes, 70
shut outs, Darts, 78
shuttlecocks, Badminton,
278
Simon Says, 238
singles, Badminton, 279
Skip-Bo, 135-137
draw piles, 136
rules, 136
scoring, 137
skipping, Crazy Eights, 124
skunks, Darts, 78
slop, Darts, 78
Snooker, 97-99
Chamberlain, Neville,
36
solids, Eight Ball, 94
Solitaire, 38, 141-143
availability, 144
Calculation, 147
Clocks, 143-144
Double Solitaire,
141-142, 149-150
English equivalent, 146
fans, 142
Forty Thieves, 145
foundation piles, 143
Golf, 144
Pyramid, 145-147
Russian, 147-149
stock piles, 144
tableaus, 143
waste piles, 145

Sommers, Brett, *Match
Game*, 251
sore losers, 19-20
Soubeyrand, Catherine, 7
Spades, 119-121
bidding, 119-120
dealing, 119
history of, 119
scoring, 121
tricks, 120
Spassky, Boris, 45
Spiders, Darts, 78
spikes, Volleyball, 270
Spit, 156-160
splash contests, 303
splashes, Darts, 78
Splashketball, 301-302
splitting, Blackjack,
167-168
squidgers, Tiddlywinks, 62
squirt gun wars, 305
stakes, 9
stakes board, Tripoley, 138
stalemates, Chess, 49
standing, Blackjack, 166
start cards, Cribbage, 132
Staunton, Howard, Chess,
44
stock piles, Solitaire, 144
Story Line, 245
straight in, Darts, 78
Straight Poker, 197-201
betting, 199-201
card rankings, 198-199
Straights, Poker, 199
strategy
Blackjack, 168
Bridge, 190
Contract Rummy, 183
Gin Rummy, 180
Stripes, Eight Ball, 94
Stud Poker, 204-205
Studebaker, Henry and
Clement, 225
suggested reading, 313-314

swimming pool games, 39,
299-305
Biggest Splash contests,
303
scavenger hunts,
303-304
team games, 301
Water Basketball,
301-302
Water Volleyball, 302
Water Tag, 299
Marco Polo, 300
Octopus Tag, 300-301

T

table games, 36-37, 43
Air Hockey, 102-106
Backgammon, 55-60
Checkers, 51-54
Chess, 44-51
Dice games, 66-68
Dominoes, 68-74
Foosball, 106-108
Pick-Up Sticks, 60-61
Ping-Pong, 108-111
Tic-Tac-Toe, 61
Tiddlywinks, 62
Table Tennis. *See* Ping-Pong
tableaus, 141-143
tables, Foosball tables, 107
Tag, 4
Tag games, 292-293
Water Tag, 299-301
Taws, Marrbles, 283
team games, 11, 27-28
Charades, 256
acting, 259
equipment, 256-257
hand signals, 258
rules, 257-258
scoring, 259
versions, 259
children, 255
Hide and Seek,
261-262
Sardines, 262-263
Up Jenkins, 260-261

327

choosing, 27, 233
water games, 301
   Water Basketball,
    301-302
   Water Volleyball, 302
teenagers, games, 14
Telephone (children's
  game), 239
terminology, Darts, 76-78
Thackeray, William
  Makepeace, Charades,
  257
three in a bed, Darts, 78
Three of a Kind, Poker, 199
Three-Handed Pinochle,
  213
Three-Legged Races, 290
throw lines, Darts, 77, 80
thumb wrestling, 227-228
Tic-Tac-Toe, 61
Tiddlywinks, 62
  English Tiddlywinks
    Association, 62
  pieces, 62
  pots, 62
  rules, 63-64
  squidgers, 62
  winks, 62
tiles, Dominoes, 69
tons, Darts, 78
topping, Air Hockey, 104
Touch Football, 272-273
Touch Tag, 292
Tournament Directors
  (TDs), Chess, 49
tournament rules, Chess,
  48-50
travel games, 39-40,
  221-223
  Camping Trip, 226-227
  equipment, 221-222
  I Spy, 223-224
  License Plate Bingo,
    224-225
  Purse Game, 228
  thumb wrestling,
    227-228

What If, 225-226
Who Am I?, 227
tricks
  Bridge, 188-189
  Hearts, 117-118
  Spades, 120
  trump card games, 116
  Two-Handed Pinochle,
    209-212
triples, Darts, 78
Tripoley, 137-140
  history of, 137
  stakes board, 138
trump card games, 116
  Bridge, 185-193
    bidding, 188-190
    books, 189
    doubles, 190
    history of, 187
    popularity, 188
    redoubles, 190
    rubber, 192
    rules, 187-188
    scoring, 191-192
    strategy, 190
    tricks, 188-189
  Crazy Eights, 123-124
    changing suits, 124
    drawing cards, 124
    reversing, 124
    rules, 123
    scoring, 123-124
    skipping, 124
  Hearts, 115-119
    bonus points, 119
    Hearts (suits), 118
    passing cards, 116
    rules, 116
    scoring, 116
    tricks, 116-118
  Knockout Whist, 121
    dealing, 121-122
    knockouts, 122
  Pinochle, 207-217
  Rook, 132-135
    rules, 133-135
    scoring, 132-135

Spades, 119-121
  bidding, 119-120
  dealing, 119
  scoring, 121
  tricks, 120
tricks, 116
Tripoley, 137-140
trumps
  card games, 116
  Double-Deck Pinochle,
    214
Tug of War, 289-290
Two Pair, Poker, 199
Two-Handed Pinochle,
  208-213
  card values, 212
  dealing, 208-209
  declaring out, 213
  melds, 209
  rules, 210-212
  scoring, 209
  tricks, 209-212

U-V

Ultimate Frisbee, 296-297
Under the Moon, Jump
  Rope, 286
UNO, 123
Up Jenkins, 260-261
Upstairs, Darts, 78

Vanderbilt, Harold S.,
  Bridge, 187
versions, Charades, 259
video games, 24
  Chess, 47
visits, pool tables, 92
Volleyball, 269-272
  equipment, 269
  history of, 271
  rules, 270
  scoring, 271-272
  serving, 270-271
  spikes, 270

W

War, 152-153
Washington, George, Pool, 88
waste piles, Solitaire, 145
Water Basketball, 301-302
water games, 299-305
    Biggest Splash contests, 303
    scavenger hunts, 303-304
    team games, 301
        Water Basketball, 301-302
        Water Volleyball, 302
    water gun wars, 305
    Water Limbo, 304
    Water Tag, 299
        Marco Polo, 300
        Octopus Tag, 300-301
water gun wars, 305
Water Limbo, 304
water scavenger hunts, 303-304
Water Tag, 299
    Marco Polo, 300
    Octopus Tag, 300-301
Water Volleyball, 302
Web sites, suggested resources, 314-316
What If, 225-226
What's the Time, Mr. Wolf?, 235
Whist, 121
    dealing, 121-122
    knockouts, 122
Who Am I?, 227
winks, Tiddlywinks, 62
winning, proper behavior, 19
wires, Darts, 78
Word Bluff, 248-249
word games, 247
    Anagrams, 247-248
    Hangman, 249-250
    Match Game, 250-251

Quick on the Draw, 252-253
Sentence by Sentence, 252
Word Bluff, 248-249

X–Y–Z

X's, Darts, 78
x01, Darts, 81-84

Yahtzee, 66-67
    history of, 66
    rules, 66-67
    scorecards, 67
yellow balls (Snooker), 97